GALWAY

AND

THE GREAT WAR

GALWAY

AND

THE GREAT WAR

WILLIAM HENRY

MERCIER PRESS

WHAT YOU NEED TO READ

In Memory of all the Casualties of the Great War

Irishmen!

YOU cannot permit your Regiments to be kept up to strength by other than Ireland's sons! It would be a deep disgrace to Ireland, if all her regiments were not Irish, to a man

A Call to 50,000 Irishmen

Excluding Munition Workers

TO JOIN THEIR BRAVE COMRADES IN IRISH REGIMENTS

Lord Kitchener has told you—his fellow-countrymen—that Ireland has done magnificently; and all the world knows of the splendid valour of the Irish Regiments, horse and foot. So glorious is the record that it must be maintained by the men of our race—by Irishmen alone.

It is your proud duty to support your gallant Countrymen who have fought so well. Ireland must stand by them!

You are asked to SERVE FOR THE PERIOD OF THE WAR ONLY.

Your relatives, whom you have looked after, will be looked after while you are away—your wife, your parents, your children.

You will be fed, clothed and boarded, and your pay will be 1/- per day. Married men will receive the same, subject to a deduction of 6d. per day, which goes to their wives entitling them to receive 12/6 per week and 5/- for one child; 3/6 for the second child, and 2/- each for others. The dependents of unmarried soldiers will receive substantial allowances.

You will be equipped and receive your preliminary training in Ireland, completing your training in different parts of the World, and serving with Irishmen wherever you go.

Pensions may be given to disabled Soldiers discharged in consequence of disablement by wounds or disease due to War Services. If wholly disabled, weekly rates, according to rank, 25/- for Privates, 40/- for Warrant Officers. If partially disabled, Pensions may be granted to bring the wages of Soldiers capable of earning to the rate referred to above. Extra Allowances for Children.

Every famous Irishman urges this duty very earnestly on you. Every Irishman should answer the Call—farmers' sons, merchants, men in shops and offices, all must act a man's—an Irishman's part.

JOIN AT ONCE-TO-DAY

FILL IN AND POST THIS FORM: NO STAMP NEEDED
To the Dept. of Recruiting: c/o the G.P.O., Dublin, Belfast, or Cork.

Mark with a ✗ the Irish Regiment you wish to join:
ROYAL IRISH REGIMENT
ROYAL INNISKILLINGS
ROYAL IRISH RIFLES
ROYAL IRISH FUSILIERS
CONNAUGHT RANGERS
LEINSTER REGIMENT
1st to 7th Battalions.
8th or Farmers Batt. for Farmers Sons
ROYAL MUNSTER FUSILIERS,
ROYAL DUBLIN FUSILIERS
1st to 9th Battalions.
10th or Scholars' Battalion for Professional Men & Clerked Workers.

I undertake to enlist when called upon for the **PERIOD OF THE WAR ONLY** in the Irish Regiment mentioned.

Age_____ Height_____

Occupation_____

NAME_____

ADDRESS_____

Mercier Press
Douglas Village, Cork

Trade enquiries to CMD Distribution
55A Spruce Avenue, Stillorgan Industrial Park, Blackrock County Dublin

© William Henry 2006

ISBN: 978 1 85635 5247

10 9 8 7 6 5 4 3 2

A CIP record for this title is available from the British Library

Mercier Press receives financial assistance from the Arts Council/
An Chomhairle Ealaíon

Printed and bound in Ireland by ColourBooks Ltd.

CONTENTS

ACKNOWLEDGEMENTS

Thanks to my wife Noreen, sons, Patrick and David and my little daughter Lisa, for bearing with me, through all the long hours. I wish to thank the following people for their generous support, providing very important information and photographs without which, this book would have proven extremely difficult. Brian Walsh, Niall McNelis, Michael Connelly, Michael Lynskey, Francis Keaney, Helen Spelman, Gerry Carthy, Eamon McNally, Stephen & Heather Smyth, Frank Lynott, Joe Loughnane, Michael John Crowe, Padraic McCormack, Gerald Comber, John Jordan, Jonnie Fallon, Elizabeth Hackett, Mary Walsh, Patsy O'Connor, Linda Finnerty, Brod Long, Brian Long, Tom May, Maureen Annetts. Tom Small, Brendan O'Donnell, Maurice Henderson, Frank Lally, Billy Lally, Tony & Margaret Carolan, Sales Langan, Edel Langan, Thomas Lynch, Oliver Henry, Cathriona Conneely, Fr Michael O'Flaherty, Mary O'Shea, Nuala Nolan, John Lawless, P. J. O'Reilly, Tom McDonagh, Oliver Maloney, Michael Joseph Gardiner, Donal Silke, Bernard McLoughlin, Reggie Darling, Anne Everiss, Mike Everiss, Michael Coughlan, Mike Clancy, Frank Carney, Brian Fahy, Geraldine Raftery, Mary Lambe, Mike Flynn, Colm Walsh, P. J. Summerly, Christopher O'Byrne, Seán Malone, Vincent Griffin, Richard Connolly, Patrick Heaney, Collett Heaney, Valera Raftery, Martin Flaherty, Chris Costello, Mary Raftery, Edward Caulfield, Douglas Rafter, Gabriel Fogerty, Paddy Monaghan, Pádraig Mannion, Dennis Kearney, Mary O'Connor, Paul O'Holloran, Jimmy Gillespie, P. J. Fallon, Brian Ruffley, Maurice Lahlen, Pat O'Farrell, Joe Burgess, Seán McSweeney, Donal Quinn, Christy Craughwell, Mary Smyth, Ferdy Wheelen, Maureen Parslow, Margaret 'Dillie' Thornton, Anne Campbell, John Connolly, Ultan Macken, Michael Diskin Paul Nobel, Bunny Devlin, Martin Devlin, Colman Shaughnessy, Anna Cronin, Pat Barrett, Bernie Higgins, Frank Costello, Threasa King,

Martin Lynskey, Michael Gannon, Paddy Curran, Anne Curran, Stephen Curran, Tom Riddle, Simon McKiernan, Mary Deely, Michael Deely, Peadar Houlighan, Gerard Kennedy, Heather Gardiner, Michael Fahy, Eugene Duggan, Jimmy McElroy, Marcella Jordan, Danny Tiernan, Seán Stafford, Kathleen Berry, Gerry Aagent, Paddy 'Moore' Flaherty, Anne Walsh, Margaret Stewart, Tom O'Donnell, Olive Organ, Peadar O'Dowd, Raymond Scully, Noel Carney, Patsy Dood, Brenda Murphy, Liam Nolan, Mary Molloy, Bridget O'Breen, Seán Ashe, Jimmy McElroy, Vivienne O'Connor, Leo Larkin, Pat Sweeney, Edward 'Chick' Sweeney, Anna Cronin, Thomas Feeney, Frank Feeney, Brian Smyth, Dominick Kearney, Lieut Col R. J. S. Bullock-Webster, Dominick Henry, Bill & Alice Scanlan, Colm & Valerie Noonan, Paddy & Anne O'Flaherty, Sonny & Mary McHugh.

A special thanks to all of the following; the staff of the following libraries: James Hardiman Library, NUIG; Galway County Library, Island House; The National Library of Ireland, Dublin. Michael Faherty, Marie Boran, Michael O'Connor, Geraldine Curtain, Liam Frehan, Anne Mitchell, Maureen Moran. To all in the media who gave excellent publicity to this project: Brendan Carroll, Dave Hickey, Stan Shields, Joe O'Shaughnessy, Margaret Blaze, Ronnie O'Gorman, Dickie Byrne, Tom Kenny, Keith Finnigan, Tom Gilmore, Jim Carney, Mary Conroy, Peadar O'Dowd, Eamonn Howley, Bob Flynn, Brian O'Connell, Mary Conroy, Jim Higgins, Ray Dukes and Des Kelly. Special thanks also to Kieran Hoare, Noreen Henry, Ger Power, John Morrissey, James Casserly, Tony Finnerty, Oliver Fallon, Liam Curley, Marita Silke, Anne Maria Furey, Tim Collins, Laura Walsh, for proofreading my work and making many valuable suggestions. Bob Waller for his excellent work in reproducing some of the photographs. I am deeply indebted to a very special friend, Jacqueline O'Brien, for her expert advice, encouragement and support throughout this project, and for giving so generously of her time, researching and proofreading.

FOREWORD

Anniversaries and commemorations of major historical events invariably generate debate and, very often, controversy. This is not surprising, nor is it a peculiarly Irish phenomenon. The bicentenaries of both the American and the French revolutions were, at an academic and at a popular level, provocative events. In Ireland, the bicentenary of the 1798 rebellion generated a healthy debate on the origins of Irish republicanism and of religious division in late eighteenth century Ireland. The sesquicentenary of the Great Famine prompted an important public debate on issues as diverse as 'memory and trauma in Irish history', and the urgent issues of justice and food entitlement in our contemporary world.

We do not have to search very far to find the reasons why such anniversaries and historical commemorations are potentially provocative. It is generally acknowledged that the past casts its shadow on the present. But it is equally the case that our understanding of the past is strongly influenced by our present preoccupations and concerns. Try as they may to achieve some 'distance' between themselves and the historical events which they seek to explain and to assess, historians cannot altogether escape the preoccupations and concerns which dominate the world they inhabit: all history is, to some degree or other, 'present-centred' history. Thus, anniversaries and commemorations reflect the concerns of our own time as much as they recall events in the past. This pertains to the historical events which we – as a society – choose to commemorate, as well as to the manner in which our commemorations are conducted. An 'official' commemoration undertaken by a state, for example, confers a particular and affirmative seal on the event being commemorated: its importance for the history of the nation is not in question. The significance of other commemorative events, however – ceremonies of remembrance conducted by various groups from one end of the year to the other – is very often questioned and contested.

These reflections on the general issue of historical 'memory' and commemoration have a certain topicality in Ireland in this first decade of the twenty first century. The end of a protracted and violent episode of conflict in Northern Ireland has created a space within which a calmer consideration of the history of British-Irish relations, and of the complex roots of conflict within Ireland, has become possible. The public, as well as professional historians, has demonstrated a lively interest in this historical reflection. Inevitably, however, anniversaries have provided a particular focus for debate. Major centenaries loom on the horizon. Already in early 2006, the decision of the Irish government to resume (after an interval of more than thirty years of) the state commemoration of the 1916 Easter Rising, with full military participation declaring the origins of state and army alike in the Rising, has prompted debate. This debate, on the significance and the legacy of the 1916 Rising, seems likely to continue in the years leading to the centenary in 2016.

However, the centenary of the outbreak of the Great War in 1914 is also beckoning. The first of the great calamities of the twentieth century known to history as the 'two world wars', saw large stretches of the continent of Europe, in particular, become a charnel house for the flower of European manhood for more than four horrific years. The Irish presence on the battlefields of Europe in these years of slaughter was considerable; the records of bravery in battle and the roll call of the fallen are both well adorned with Irish names. These names were never forgotten by those who mourned and loved them, or who cared for them when they returned home at the war's end. Voluntary associations and the British Legion continued to take an interest in the welfare of war veterans, and to commemorate the sacrifices of that terrible slaughter. But the independent Irish state to which the Irish war veterans returned found it difficult to acknowledge their sacrifice, and many of those who grew up in an independent Ireland avoided for many years, in uneasy silence, any discussion of the involvement of thousands of Irishmen and Irishwomen in the Great War.

There were reasons for this silence. The convulsive events of 1916–

1920, the Rising and the popular revulsion at the British response to it, produced a seismic shift in sentiment in nationalist Ireland. Redmond's Home Rule banner, under which so many thousands of young Irishmen enlisted in the Irish regiments of the British Army and went 'to fight in Flanders' for the rights of small nations, gave way to the flag of the Republic proclaimed in 1916 and carried after 1917 by a resurgent Sinn Féin. By 1918, the Home Rule party was succeeded by Sinn Féin as the voice of nationalist Ireland. The request that Britain concede Home Rule was replaced by the demand that she, and the world, acknowledge the Irish Republic. Well might Yeats declare that all had changed, utterly. The heady rhetoric, which had accompanied the call to arms in 1914, was now almost an embarrassment, drowned in the blood and suffering of the trenches and soured beyond redemption by the repressive strategy of the crown's agents in Ireland after 1916. The political landscape had been transformed.

The creation of two states in Ireland by the partition settlement of 1920 further compounded the polarised view of the recent past as well as of the political present; its implications for popular attitudes towards Irish participation in the 1914–18 war were enormous. Stated simply, the legacy, the commemoration, the historical 'ownership' of Irish sacrifices in the Great War became part of the foundation myth of the Unionist state in Northern Ireland – it cemented the 'Britishness' of Northern Ireland. But, despite the thousands of Irish Home Rulers who had seen service in the war years, the great war was an episode virtually omitted from the heroic foundation myth of the Irish Free State, where the struggle for independence from 1916 through to the war of independence was the dominant story. This omission was complete by the early 1930s; 'poppy day' was identified with residual pro-British sentiment (and seen as, in a certain sense, un-Irish), and the commemoration of Armistice Day became largely a discreet event for ex-soldiers and their families and friends.

Times change, however, and the pendulum of historical interest swings back across its arc. The changing political and ideological climate generates its own perspectives and questions. The role of the Irish in the Great

War has re-emerged in recent years as a subject for historical research and publications, for special documentaries on radio and television, and, indeed, as a subject for exploration in works of historical fiction. It is only very recently, however, that research into the impact of the Great War at a local or regional level has begun to yield results. Local case studies are likely to prove invaluable in providing the level of intimate detail by which we can explore the many ways in which the Great War affected local communities throughout Ireland: recruitment, economic impact, security considerations, the 'home front', changing attitudes over time, the threat of conscription, propaganda, the challenges of demobilisation, the legacy and legends of the Great War at a local level.

This volume, on *Galway and the Great War*, addresses a wide range of issues. The industry of the author, William Henry, in examining a fascinating range of source material, is commendable. His intimate knowledge of the geography, and the social ranks, of early twentieth century Galway, give an assuring immediacy to his lively account of the many ways in which Galway responded to the Great War and of the shifting attitudes and responses of the people of Galway to the conduct and cost of the war, as well as to the changing political climate in Ireland. Professional historians as well as the general public with an interest in the past will find much to engage their interest in William Henry's latest book.

Gearóid Ó Tuathaigh
2006

INTRODUCTION

In 1995, Patsy O'Connor, a local man, drew my attention to the fact that a number of Galwaymen had fought at the battle of the Somme. He suggested that I write a short account of them sometime. Having raised the subject a number of times, he finally said to me: 'If you don't write about them, then nobody else will, because no one really cares about the men of the Great War.' This conversation took place in the new cemetery, in Galway, as he pointed to the grave of an old soldier, Jack King from Bohermore. Jack had joined the British Army at sixteen years of age and within three months, found himself on the Somme. He was only one of some 250,000 under-age soldiers who fought in the Great War, some were as young as fourteen years of age. Given that it was such a terrible war, people often ask, why did they go?

When war was declared, a surge of euphoria swept across the country engulfing all in its path. In England, many young men joined to fight for 'King and Country', while in Ireland the reasons were many and varied. All of these reasons are explored in the recruiting chapter, which because of its nature is the longest in the book. Its length was dictated by the extensive methods and tactics used during the intense recruiting campaigns, which for over four years, literally combed every part of the country to ensure the military secured their numbers for the western front. It gives a clear understanding of why these men went to war.

One example came from the memories of Jack King, who attended a recruiting meeting at Eyre Square, Galway. During the meeting, two 'nuns' were brought on stage by the military, and both looked heavily pregnant. According to the recruiting officer, both nuns had been raped by German soldiers a number of months earlier. The audience was stunned with this announcement and became more troubled when they were told that many Irishwomen would suffer the same fate if the Germans were not stopped. It had the desired effect, Jack and a number of his friends enlisted immediately.

Many years later, a wiser, older, Jack, remembered how easily they had been fooled by two 'bogus pregnant nuns.'

Initially, this book was to include photographic profiles of the men who fought and died, as well as a list of the dead. However, because of the sheer amount of information and photographs that became available, it was decided to produce two books. The second book, *Forgotten Heroes of the Great War 1914 – 1918*, will contain the photographic profiles and the list of the dead. It will also briefly explain the history of the First World War. This first book, *Galway and the Great War* is written in two sections, the first deals with the outbreak of the conflict, and Galway's involvement.

The chapters in this section explore the various effects that the war had on Galway under the following categories: Mobilisation, Recruiting, Conscription & Home Rule, Opposition, Rumours & Suspicion, Sea War, War Industry, Support and Aftermath. Each chapter covers its particular topic from 1914 until 1918. This story could reflect any town or village in Ireland. The effect that the war had on Galway, is in a sense a forgotten, or even a hidden, history. Very little has been written on the subject from a Galway perspective and while there are accounts of the Easter Rebellion and indeed other events that took place during this period, the war is, for one reason or another, ignored. Because of this, I have had to rely mainly on contemporary newspaper accounts.

The second section contains a brief account of the main battles and campaigns in which Galwaymen fought. The battle chapters are in chronological order. However, where more than one battle of the same name occurs, such as Ypres, where four battles were fought, all these battles are included in the same chapter. Obviously all of the battles and campaigns of the Great War are not included, as this book was primarily to represent the effects that the war had on Galway. At the end of each battle, there are contemporary letters and interviews with Galwaymen who fought in that particular battle, or sector. While some letters are from private family archives, others are taken directly from newspaper sources, and therefore would necessitate a more detailed analysis. Only particular letters and interviews would have been published, as the authorities were careful about information being released to the public. Positive, not negative was the 'rule of thumb' and reporters were known to embellish stories. However, the author has used these sources, without completing a critical analysis, as the initial purpose of this book is to show the effects that the war had on Galway, and these letters, in their 'raw state', contributed to some of the thinking of the day. The one noticeable factor that emerged during research was the sharp drop in letters and interviews being published as the war progressed. While the recruiting and support for the troops on active service continued, the euphoria had certainly diminished. The book concludes with an appendix of monuments, memorials and mementoes associated with the Great War.

The Great War is symbolised by the horrors of trench warfare, shrapnel, gas and appalling casualties. Many of the wounded died in no-man's land awaiting medical attention. The war cemeteries bear testament to the shocking death toll, but thousands of others were literally 'blown to pieces,' thus no remains could be found for burial. These men are remembered on the various war memorials spread across the western front. The battlefields of the First World War have become infamous, and names such as the Somme, Ypres and Gallipoli can still strike terror in those with knowledge of the conflict. Europe was no stranger to war in 1914, as it has a bloody history stretching back centuries, but the slaughter of the Great War had never been witnessed before, or indeed since. The horrendous casualties, and age of some soldiers, leaves one numb with shock and disbelief. Most sources indicate that between 112,000 and 150,000 Irishmen fought in the war. However, this is a conservative estimate, the true figure may never be known, but it is likely that it could have been as high as 300,000. The larger numbers would seem more realistic given that some 49,400 Irishmen never returned, may God have mercy on their souls.

William Henry

CHAPTER I

THE GREAT WAR BEGINS

Shortly before noon on Sunday 28 June 1914, crowds gathered in Sarajevo, which was at that time the capital of the Austrian province of Bosnia. The people had come to see Archduke Franz Ferdinand, heir to the throne of Austro-Hungary, and his wife Sophie. As their car passed a section of the crowd a man jumped onto the running board of the vehicle and fired a number of pistol shots with two bullets hitting the Archduke and one hitting his wife, killing them both. The assassin, a young Bosnian student living in Sarajevo, Gavrilo Princip, had succeeded where an earlier attempt that day had failed, and so plunged Europe into the colossal conflict which over four years later had left over 8,300,000 servicemen dead. Yet the origins of the Great War, though sparked by this assassination, have their roots in an arms race which engulfed Europe in the preceding twenty years or so.

The prevailing wisdom of the time was that a war would be too disruptive to the economic well-being of a liberal Europe which dominated the world stage. However, the military and diplomatic expansion among European powers posed a worrying development. The empires of Austria, Germany and Russia for example, faced a serious threat from the growth of minority nationalities within their provinces. This was particularly true for Austro-Hungary, dominated by Germans and Magyars, but populated mainly by Slavic populations. The quest for full democratic rights, or in Russia's case any democracy at all, was a further issue. The other European empires, Britain and France, faced a burden of a different sort. Although relatively untroubled by nationalist separatism, the pressure of running vast overseas colonies, and the jealousies of other empires, presented their own problems. As direct consequence of this, we find very expensive fleet building operations in both England and Germany in the early years of the twentieth century.[1]

Coupled with this, were the small but significant wars fought in the years preceding the Great War. Of primary importance was the Franco-Prussian conflict of 1871 which saw Alsace-Lorraine acquired by the Germans, and which was to remain a source of constant enmity between the two powers over the following years. This enmity was deepened by the first (1905) and second (1911) Moroccan crises, which saw German resentment rise over the extension of French influence in North Africa. There was also the first (1912) and second (1913) Balkan Wars which saw Austria, Germany's ally, placed at a disadvantage. It was the Second Balkan War in particular which we must look to, as one of the prime factors in the slide towards a more far-reaching conflict, bringing as it did Germany, Austria and Russia into the war. Russian support for Serbia was a major area of resentment for the central power. Indeed the response of European powers to these diverse problems was not to seek some sort of mechanism to avert conflict, but instead to achieve security through military superiority. At the heart of all land forces was the core fighting organisation, the division, comprising twelve battalions of infantry and twelve batteries of artillery. Overall, two hundred of these divisions and their immense fire-power were available for immediate deployment. The army that could mobilise most quickly and bring firepower to bear on the opposition would carry the day.[2]

Military commanders prepared for the Great War by drawing up detailed mobilisation plans designed to give them the upper hand in any conflict which might develop, this approach has since been characterised by A. J. P. Taylor as 'war by timetable'. In Germany, the great general staff had formulated the 'Schlieffen Plan' in 1905. This plan saw seven-eighths of the German army committed to the western front to defeat France in six weeks, and then move to defeat Russia at their leisure. For France, Plan XVII, the brainchild of Joseph Joffre was essentially a defensive line along France's border with Germany. The French did not expect the Anglo-French-Prussian treaty of 1839, guaranteeing Belgian neutrality, to be broken, but if it was, there was an understanding that the British would send an expeditionary force to northern France. In Russia, Variants A (an offensive against Austria) and G (one against Germany) were formulated in 1913 in close association with the French. It would see 800,000 Russians on the German border on the fifteenth day of the war with France, should it break out. Austrian plans saw ten divisions committed to the Balkan theatre, thirty divisions to the Polish theatre with twelve 'swing divisions' in reserve. These secret war plans should only come into play and commence the Great War, if what was termed 'sensible diplomacy' failed. Sensible diplomacy had settled the Moroccan and Balkan crises, but these were matters of national interest, rather than matters of national honour and prestige. So when an assassin identified with aggressive Serb nationalism murdered the heir to the Austro-Hungarian throne in June 1914, the fragile empire was shaken to its core and a military response was required.

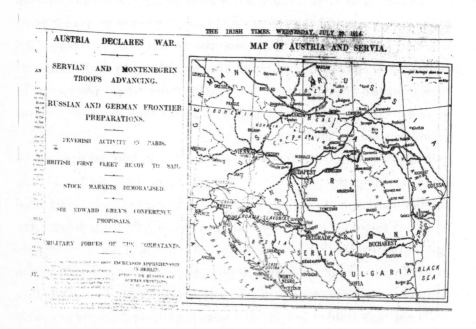

Declaration of War by Austria, dated 29 July August 1914. (*The Irish Times*)

Had Austria acted unilaterally against Serbia, without seeking German endorsement for military action, it is tempting to think that what would have been a serious, but essentially local conflict would not have evolved into general warfare. The Austrians feared that a local war with Serbia would weaken their ability to fight Russia

THE IRISH

GERMANY DECLARES WAR ON RUSSIA.

ULTIMATUM TO FRANCE.

RUSSIA GERMANY AND FRANCE MOBILISING.

ITALY REMAINS NEUTRAL AT PRESENT.

GERMAN TROOPS CROSS FRENCH FRONTIER.

GERMANY DECLARES WAR ON RUSSIA.

Declaration of War by Germany, dated 3 August 1914

(*The Irish Times*)

and hence the ability of the central powers to protect themselves against the triple alliance. The fact remains that the Austrians sought and received the endorsement of Germany in early July 1914 to issue an ultimatum to Serbia on 25 July. Serbia rejected the ultimatum on 27 July and Austria declared war on 28 July. Russia's reaction was to order general mobilisation, an unnecessary step and one which precipitated general mobilisation by other European powers. The tragedy is that if 'sensible diplomacy' had prevailed it is probable that with time the crisis of July 1914 could have been resolved. Time was the one thing that the European powers did not have once the various mobilisation plans swung into action. The invasion of Belgium by Germany on 4 August signalled what Lloyd George later described as: 'All the powers [of Europe] slithered over the brink into the cauldron of War'.[4]

In his speech to the House of Commons the previous day, John Redmond, leader of the Irish Nationalist Party suggested that Britain could safely withdraw her forces from Ireland and leave the defence of the country to the Irish Volunteers. However, this declaration was misinterpreted as a total pledge of Irish support for England's war

THE IRISH TIMES, WEDNESDAY,

ENGLAND DECLARES WAR ON GERMANY.

BRITISH ULTIMATUM ON BELGIAN NEUTRALITY.

MR. ASQUITH'S GRAVE STATEMENT.

MOBILISING THE ARMY.

ENGLAND'S DECLARATION OF WAR.

The following is the text of an official statement issued by the Government last night :—

"Owing to the summary rejection by the German Government of the request made by His Majesty's Government, that the neutrality of Belgium will be respected. His Majesty's Ambassador at Berlin has received his passport, and His Majesty's Government has declared to the German Government that a state of war exists between Great Britain and Germany, as from eleven p.m. on August 4."

A Council, which the King had arranged to hold at midnight, was held in consequence at an earlier hour, and certain Proclamations, which follow a state of war, were disposed of.

In the House of Commons yesterday,

Mr. Asquith, in reply to Mr. Bonar Law, said—In conformity with the statement of policy which was made by Sir E. Grey, a telegram was sent early yesterday morning by him to our Ambassador in Berlin. It was to this effect :—The King of the Belgians has made an appeal to His Majesty the King for diplomatic intervention on behalf of Belgium. His Majesty's Government are also informed that the German Government has delivered to the Belgian Government a Note proposing friendly neutrality, pending a free passage through Belgian territory, and promising to maintain the independence and integrity of the kingdom on the conclusion of peace, and threatening in case of refusal, to treat Belgium as an enemy. An answer was requested within twelve hours. We also understand that Belgium has categorically refused this flagrant violation of the laws of nations. (Cheers.) His Majesty's Government are bound to protest against this violation of a treaty to which Germany was a party in common with ourselves, and must request an assurance that the demand made upon Belgium will not be proceeded with, and that her neutrality will be respected by Germany. (Cheers.) We asked for an immediate reply. (Loud cheers.)

M. Asquith then read the telegrams from Belgium, announcing that the Germans had crossed the frontier, and

KING'S MESSAGE TO THE NAVY.

We are officially informed that the following message has been addressed by His Majesty the King to Admiral Sir John Jellicoe :—

"At this grave moment in our national history. I send to you, and through you to the officers and men of the fleets of which you assume command, the assurance of my confidence that, under your direction, they will revive and renew the old glories of the Royal Navy, and prove once again the sure shield of Britain and of her Empire in the hour of trial.

Declaration of War by England, dated 5 August 1914. (*The Irish Times*)

effort and was met with great enthusiasm by an emotionally charged House of Commons. It was a period when Home Rule for Ireland was a major political issue. The outbreak of war changed priorities for the government and the implementation of Home Rule was suspended, at least until the war ended. Redmond also agreed with the suspension and encouraged the Irish Volunteers to support England by enlisting for service. Fearing that the leadership of the Irish Volunteers would not support his stance, Redmond wrote to Eóin MacNeill, commander-in-chief of the Volunteers, explaining the situation and requesting his support. He ended the letter by writing: 'Do not let us by our folly or temper destroy the situation.' However, there was growing concern and suspicion among the Volunteers over the Home Rule question and many of them feared that it might never be implemented because of strong opposition by Ulster unionists. The promise of support by Redmond and the suspension of Home Rule eventually caused a split in the Irish camp. An estimated 170,000 men followed Redmond and became known as the National Volunteers, leaving Eóin MacNeill with some 10,000 Irish Volunteers.[5]

At the outbreak of war, Germany had the largest and best-equipped army in Western Europe and its troops were somewhat better trained. Their artillery, especially the heavy calibre weapons were also superior. In Europe, the central power formed a solid land block and could move men and equipment quickly to any of its fronts. Although the allies had far greater manpower, it took them longer to mobilise. The allies were also split by geography with their biggest army, Russia, cut off from Britain and France. The Russian Army was poorly equipped and with the central powers cutting off all land supply routes, the Royal Navy had to supply Russia by sea. Almost immediately the German armies swept across Belgium and into France nearly reaching Paris. A gap opened up between the German forces which the British Expeditionary Force exploited, forcing the Germans to retreat. The German retreat eventually halted north of the River Aisne and the British formed new lines of defence, with the result that both sides settled down to trench warfare.

Probable Theatre of War, dated 1 August 1914. (*The Irish Times*)

THE GALWAY EXPRESS, Saturday Morning, August 8, 1914.

EUROPEAN POWERS AT WAR.

ON LAND AND SEA.

Ultimatums and Declarations of War

England Declares War on Germany.

British Naval and Army Reserves Called Up.

Empire's Enthusiastic and Determined Resistance to German Aggression.

Ireland's Armed Sons to Defend Irish Shores.

FRENCH NAVAL VICTORY.

One German Cruiser Sunk and Two Captured.

Belgium's Struggle Against Germans.

Relative Strength of Great Powers.

	Men.	Ships.		Men.	Ships.
Russia	8,000,000	173	Austria-Hungary	1,400,000	105
France	4,000,000	388	Italy (neutral)	1,500,000	161
England	600,000	454	Germany	5,000,000	296

7s and the quotation for eggs drawn. In Glasgow sugar rose to 6½d per lb.

Earl Kitchener has been Secretary of State for War.

The Home and China Fleets loyal replies to King George

On Wednesday afternoon Council met at 10 Downing street from 4 o'clock until 5.15. Earl Kitchener, Sir John French, John Grierson were the men who attended. The Cabinet sealed by the Prime Minister, ill; the Lord Chancellor, and Grey.

It is officially announced that phion and the third to rise half sunk the German mine laye Louise.

A large number of German vessels have been seized in Irish ports.

Confused reports are coming from various parts of Belgium the German advance through try. One fact lends some importance to the operations which are going that is the departure of King the front. The statements as strength of the German force vancing towards the northern of France through the valley are obviously exaggerated, gathered from the reports, however the Belgians are putting up a resistance, and they claim a victory the Germans at Fleron, a small front of one of the outlying positions around Liege. They are stated to have suffered heavily.

There is nothing reported of Irish Fleet, from the Franco-German tier, or from Austria or Russia to any important degree on the these areas of war.

Anti-German riots in St. Petersburg minated in an attack on the which was sacked by the mob man Eagle was torn down, damage was done to the fine ornaments.

Mr. Asquith, in the House on Tuesday, announced that he a war credit of £100,000,000

Mr. Lloyd George, in explaining Government's proposals for dealing the financial crisis, said it only due to the stoppage of from abroad. There had been failure of British credit.

The suspension of the Bank Act was meant to secure a supply of notes, but it was not to suspend specie payments.

He warned the public that no necessity for hoarding foodstuffs. Such action was as it tended to increase difficulties. In order to relieve the stringency, the Government, issue £1 and 10s notes, which used as legal tender.

Postal orders would also be

Announcement of War, dated 8 August 1914. (*The Irish Times*)

The opposing sides built second and third line trenches, and also communication trenches so troops and supplies could be moved to the front in relative safety. Large underground caverns were constructed to house troops and also serve as first-aid centres. Life in the trenches was miserable for the men. Rain often filled the dug-outs with water and mud, and rats swarmed through the vermin-infested trenches adding to the problems. Most of the fighting took place across the western, eastern and southern battlefronts. The western front ran for about 600 miles at its greatest length, from the English Channel to the border of Switzerland. Along this front soldiers dug in and faced each other across barbed wire barriers and 'no-man's-land'. The eastern front stretched approximately 1,100 miles from Riga on the Baltic Sea to the shores of the Black Sea, while the southern front extended about 320 miles from Switzerland along the Italian frontier to Trieste. Another battlefront extended across the southern Balkans. Other areas of conflict included Mesopotamia, Egypt, Palestine, Africa and the German colonies in Asia. Some fighting also took place in the Pacific Ocean.[6]

Once war was declared, the British Expeditionary Force was ordered to sail for France. On 12 August 1914, these troops began embarking for mainland Europe. They sailed from Southampton and Dublin. Supplies were also sent from other ports. The troops of the British Expeditionary Force were placed under the command of Field Marshal Sir John French. Although born in Ripple Vale, Kent in 1852, Sir John French was directly descended from the French family of French Park, County Roscommon. This family was a branch of the well-known Tribes of Galway.

His military career began in 1866 when he joined the Royal Navy. In 1874, he entered the army where he proved himself an excellent cavalry commander. Sir John French served through much of the action in the second South African War 1899-1902. He was the commander at the battle of Elandslaagte and was in charge of the cavalry at Reitfontein and Lombard's Kop, resulting in the capture of Bloemfontein and Pretoria. In 1913, he was created Field Marshal and when the First World War broke out, he was given command of the British Expeditionary Force.

The following letter was sent to Sir John French informing him of his command:

War Office, August 1914

To Field Marshal Sir John French, G.C.B., G.C.V.O., K.C.V.O.

Owing to the infringement of the neutrality of Belgium by Germany ... His Majesty's Government has decided, at the request of the French Government, to send an expeditionary force to France and to entrust the command of the troops to yourself ... It must be recognised from the outset that the numerical strength of the British Force and its contingent reinforcements is strictly limited and with this consideration kept steadily in view, it will be obvious that the greatest care must be exercised towards a minimum of loss or wastage.

Therefore, while every effort must be made to coincide with the plans and wishes of our Ally, the gravest consideration will devolve on you as to participation in forward movements where large bodies of French troops are not engaged and where your Force may be unduly exposed to attack. Should a contingency of this sort be contemplated, I look to you to inform me fully and give me time to communicate to you any decision which His Majesty's Government may come to in the matter. In this connection I wish you distinctly to understand that your command is an entirely independent one, and that you will not in any case come under the orders of any Allied General ... The high courage and discipline of your troops should, and certainly will, have fair and full opportunity of display during the campaign, but officers may well be reminded that in this their first experience of European warfare, a greater measure of caution must be employed than under former conditions of hostilities against an untrained adversary ...

Kitchener, Secretary of State.[7]

On 14 August 1914, Sir John French left his temporary headquarters in the Metropole Hotel, Northumberland Avenue, to join up with his forces. Mobilisation orders had been sent out across the United Kingdom and thousands of troops were being sent to France. By 20 August, the entire force, consisting of 100,000 men and 40,000 horses assembled around Maubeuge, with the headquarters being set up at Le Cateau. The force was divided into five infantry divisions and one cavalry, with a sixth infantry division joining them in September. Bases were set up at selected seaports to accommodate the troops, large supplies of food, military stores and animals being assembled for war.

From these depots all the requirements for the war began their journey by rail to stations closest to the front lines. Motor lorry supply columns were also used, with each convoy supporting its own division. Many commanders on both sides believed that it would be a short war, or were at least indicating this to the troops. Some on the British side were saying that they would be home for Christmas, while the Kaiser's assurance that his troops would be home before the 'leaves had fallen', was even more optimistic. However, both sides were on a collision course to a bloodbath, the like of which had never been witnessed before. So the stage was set for a mammoth challenge between the central power, consisting of Austria–Hungary, Germany, allied with Turkey and later Bulgaria and the allied countries including Belgium, France, Great Britain, Russia and Serbia, with other countries joining later.[8]

CHAPTER II

CALL TO ARMS
GALWAY MOBILISATION

It was reported in *The Galway Express* on 1 August 1914, that: 'The first shot has been fired in a conflict which may set Europe in a blaze.' It occurred when Serbian troops travelling on a Danube steamer fired on Austro-Hungarian forces, who promptly retaliated. News of the impending war officially reached Galway on 4 August 1914 at 6.53 p.m. when a telegram arrived at Renmore Barracks. It was addressed to Lieut Col Henry Francis Jourdain, commander of the Connaught Rangers and a Boer War veteran. He had gone walking towards Cromwell's Fort at the rear of Renmore Barracks with his wife and two officers. It was a warm, calm evening and as they were returning he was commenting on how one word, 'mobilise,' could change everything given the recent developments in Europe. As he spoke, he noticed an orderly running towards him clutching a telegram, and instinctively said 'and here it is'. He immediately opened the telegram which stated: 'Commanding Depot, Galway General mobilisation ordered'. He immediately had other telegrams sent around the province calling up all reservists. Many of them arrived that same evening and others continued to arrive throughout the week. Urgent dispatches for recruits were sent throughout Galway and there was an immediate response from Renmore Barracks with 621 men being sent on 7 August to reinforce the Second Connaught Rangers in Aldershot. Following these departures, a strong appeal for additional recruits was issued. Hundreds of copies of the following advertisement were printed and sent out to various locations around the province:

GRAVE DANGER OF EUROPEAN WAR.

GLOOMY VIEWS IN THE CAPITALS.

PREPARATIONS ON RUSSO-GERMAN FRONTIERS.

PARTIAL MOBILISATIONS IN BOTH COUNTRIES.

FRANCE ALSO MAKING READY.

CONFERENCES IN PARIS AND BERLIN.

AUSTRIANS BOMBARD BELGRADE.

It is semi officially announced that the Austrians yesterday bombarded Belgrade, the Servians having blown up a bridge on the Danube, between Semlin and the Servian capital. The Servians withdrew after a short engagement.

n most Continental capitals the outlook is gloomy, an European war being regarded as most probable.

Russia and Germany are hastily mobilising forces on their respective frontiers.

n St. Petersburg it is declared that Russia is determined to stop Austria's advance in Servia, and that only a political miracle can avert war.

urried Ministerial Councils took place yesterday in Paris and Berlin.

he *communiqué* published in St. Petersburg regarding Russia's pacific intentions is received with considerable reserve in Vienna, and is not viewed as offering any tangible assurance that the Conference will be localised.

r. Asquith, in the House of Commons yesterday, described the situation as grave, but said that Great Britain would still strive to exert pacific influence.

e effect of the outbreak of hostilities on the Stock and Grain Markets was most marked yesterday; but late in the afternoon, on receiving statements by great

RUSSIA AND GERMANY.

FRONTIER ACTIVITY.
SIGNIFICANT RUMOUR FROM FRANCE.

(FROM OUR SPECIAL CORRESPONDENT.)

(COPYRIGHT.)

BERLIN. July 29.

News received this evening through London of the mobilisation of South and South-West Russia would appear to be accepted in official circles as intensely serious.

As yet no statement has been made by the Foreign Office, but the measures to be taken by Germany in reply would appear at this moment to be under discussion.

This new report of mobilisation in Russia was published in the *Frankfurter Zeitung*, and in Berlin, at eight o'clock this evening.

As yet the public, surfeited with earlier false rumours, attaches little importance to it.

Should the report be true

Mobilisation begins, dated 30 July 1914

MEN OF CONNAUGHT ... A CALL TO ARMS ... AN ADDITION OF 100,000 MEN TO HIS MAJESTY'S REGULAR ARMY IS IMMEDIATELY NECESSARY IN THE PRESENT GRAVE EMERGENCY ... COME AND JOIN YOUR OWN REGIMENT THE CONNAUGHT RANGERS.[1]

Under the headline 'Seven Nations At War', The Connacht Tribune of 8 August 1914 recorded that the bloodiest conflict in history had begun. It also stated that a special 'War-Sheet' containing the latest news from the front would be issued every day between four and five o'clock. There was an excellent response to the call to arms, which included a number of under-age recruits who gave incorrect dates of birth in order to take part in the 'great adventure' unfolding in Europe. Large numbers of Galway men who enlisted at Renmore Barracks were transferred to the Curragh Military Camp, County Kildare, where they underwent training including trench digging, which was to be a major part of front line technology.

Lieut Col Jourdain went into action himself, was later mentioned in the honours list for gallant services in the field, and was appointed to the distinguished Order of St. Michael and St. George. Although many young men walked out along the old Railway Line to enlist at Renmore Barracks,

Russian Mobilisation, dated 1 August 1914

(*The Irish Times*)

there were a number of other temporary enlistment offices set up in the town. According to one source, a pub located in Williamsgate Street was used as a recruiting office. It seems that a British army officer was almost in permanent residence there and encouraged young men to enlist by offering them a half-crown. A number of resourceful young men signed up under assumed names and addresses, and then mysteriously disappeared. Men could also enlist at the Royal Hotel in Eyre Square when the Irish Guards were in town, as this became their recruiting premises. Two young men who decided to sign up were out on a lunch break from their jobs in McDonoghs when they saw the recruiting banner displayed across the hotel. One of them, Michael Crane, survived the war, but his friend was killed. He later recalled that of the 1,000 men who were with him going to war, only 120 answered the roll call in 1918.[2]

By the end of October 1914, due to the high casualty rates at the

Increased Separation Allowances

for soldiers' wives and children.

FROM MARCH 1ST the Separation Allowances paid by the Government to the wives and children of soldiers have been increased, so that the total weekly payment to the family, if the soldier makes the usual allotment from his pay, is now as follows:—

	Corporal or Private.	Sergeant.
Wife - - - - per week	12/6	15/-
Wife and 1 child - per week	17/6	20/-
Wife and 2 children, per week	21/-	23/6
Wife and 3 children, per week	23/-	25/6

and so on with an addition of 2/- for each additional child.

Each Motherless child - - - 5/-

From February 1st, 1915, Separation Allowance is payable for all children up to the age of 16 years. This includes adopted children.

Allowances for other Dependants.

If an unmarried soldier has supported a dependant for a reasonable period, and wishes the support he gave to be continued, the Government will help, during the war, by making a grant of Separation Allowance, provided he will contribute part of his pay.

Full particulars can be obtained at any Post Office.

God Save the King.

Separation Allowance Advertisement, dated 18 March 1915 (*The Connacht Tribune*) front, Renmore Barracks struggled to supply the troops required for the First and Second Battalions of Connaught Rangers. In January 1915 the local papers were reporting that the Germans could not continue the war beyond another six months. These reports of a short war had also helped young men make up their minds and join the initial mobilisation. Large numbers of the Royal Irish Constabulary were also joining the military ranks. Although 1,623 recruits had passed through Renmore Barracks between 10 August and 11 October 1914, they still required additional men. A steady stream of recruits continued to arrive, and although not all were from Galway City, many of them were indeed local men. Considering that the population of the city at the time was merely 13,000, the male population of the town was diminishing at an alarming rate. In fact by January 1915, the official figures for Galway City men serving stood at over 500, with an additional 200 from the Claddagh. These figures were very high when one considers the average that could be expected from a population of this size would be about 300 men of military age. The high enlistment rate possibly reflected the economic conditions existing in Galway at that time. In February 1915, large huts had to be erected at Renmore Barracks to accommodate the number of troops going through the depot. One must also remember this was well in advance of the major recruiting campaigns which were to follow in the summer of 1915.[3]

In the Claddagh, men responded immediately with the vast majority joining the navy, as many of them were experienced seamen. Practically none of the male population, except the middle-aged were left in the community by Christmas 1914, and within three months most of these had volunteered for service. By April 1915, the total enlistment figures for the Claddagh had risen to over 250 and the newspapers proudly proclaimed it as the 'Claddagh's Magnificent Response'.

The report stated that the numbers of young men in this historic little community, which: '… possessed a population of some of the finest and hardiest men in the Kingdom', had, within a few months, been decimated. By May the manpower in the Claddagh was reduced to the very old and very young. These figures were later confirmed in an autobiography, *The*

Claddagh Boy written by Michael Flaherty and published in 1963. In his book, Flaherty states that in the Claddagh: 'Every mother's son who was old enough was called on or volunteered for service', and that: 'Every family in the village had one, two or more men in the service.' He also stated that there were twenty sailors for every soldier who joined from the village. He recalled vividly the day when war was declared and how his father went to enlist, but was refused because of his age.

Another episode that caused great excitement in the Claddagh and indeed the town was the capture of a German submarine. He stated that every youngster in the village made their way down to the harbour to investigate the enemy vessel. At the time his brother, Larry, was in the navy and a few weeks before the submarine affair, Michael remembered that his mother had received a letter stating that Larry was 'missing in action'. His mother found it difficult to cope with the news and the house was plunged into mourning for some time. On the day that the German submarine was escorted into Galway Bay by British ships, Michael ran home to inform his mother of the excitement. She was sitting close to the open fire turning the turf and made no comment as he eagerly told her about the submarine. He suddenly felt a presence behind him in the doorway and turning he saw Larry standing there, putting his finger to his lips in a gesture to 'be quiet'. His mother then turned towards the door, began blessing herself, and fainted. Larry had been wounded during a gun battle at sea and it was some time before he was identified.

Another very clear memory that Michael recorded was coming out of his house one morning to find a hole dug in the road. People wondered for some time how this was happening, but soon discovered that it was an unfortunate soldier, who was home on leave. It seems the war had seriously affected him, and he had spent so much time on burial detail that he was getting up at night to dig what he believed were graves. His neighbours did not confront him, but simply repaired the road during the day. These accounts give some idea of the Claddagh's contribution to the war. The women of the Claddagh were also commended for the support and loyalty they gave to their men at the front.

Many of their friends and relatives from Long Walk and Quay Street also followed their example and enlisted. It became a familiar sight to see large crowds gathering at Galway railway station to bid family members and friends farewell as they left for war. Many commented that when the history of the Great War was being recorded, Galway would be to the fore for its contribution to the war effort. This trend certainly continued, because in June 1918 it was reported that the two small areas of the Claddagh and Munster Lane alone, supplied 600 men to the army and the navy.[4]

The enlistment in Galway continued as it did in many other areas, with the vast majority of southern recruits being Roman Catholic. Given the sheer amount of Irish Catholics serving at the front, it is difficult to believe that Ulster Unionists were accusing them of 'apathy and indifference'. In December 1914, a reporter from *The Tuam Herald* challenged these allegations and pointed out some interesting facts, regarding Galway City and county. He stated that in the first two months of the war, 1,200 Galwaymen had gone to the front, and many of them, both officers and men of all ranks had already distinguished themselves on the field of battle. Many had already lost their lives, while many more had been wounded.

His report continued, stating that members of every family 'of position' in the county were in training for war. In conclusion, he said that he was not aware of any other county in the United Kingdom that had contributed as many recruits per head of population as Galway. Having quoted a number of other facts, he wrote that such 'strange' accusations on the part of the unionists were 'certainly not calculated to encourage a people to fight for the Kingdom, particularly when they find their efforts in this matter so grossly misrepresented'.

The reporter's argument was supported in December when thousands of people from all over Connacht converged on Tuam for a meeting on the war situation. John Redmond was the principal speaker and he addressed the large gathering after letters were read from Dr Healy (Catholic archbishop) and Dr Plunkett (Protestant archbishop) both of Tuam. In response to the numbers of Irishmen being mobilised, Redmond stated that the official government figures on 30 November 1914, stood at 89,000 Irishmen joining the colours, 52,000 of which were Catholic. He went on to say that when these figures were added to the thousands of Irishmen who were enlisting in England, Canada, Australia and New Zealand, the numbers would be closer to 130,000 or 140,000.

As soon as he mentioned Sir Edward Carson and the Ulster Volunteers, there were groans and jeers from the crowd, but he immediately pointed out that this was the 'wrong spirit', saying that nationalists and unionists were fighting shoulder to shoulder in the trenches, and that they should continue to do so for the greater good of the country. The official figures released in 1916, for Irish recruits alone, stood at 130,241. *The Tuam Herald* was obviously keeping a close eye on the numbers of Irishmen enlisting, because in January 1916, it again emphasised this fact. This report stated that not only were the native Irishmen being mobilised, but also 'tens of thousands' of exiles, and children of Irish parents in England and Scotland were volunteering. People were reminded of the men overseas who were joining the London Irish, Manchester Irish, Liverpool Irish, Tyneside Irish and Irish Guards while many others were joining Scottish regiments, such as the Black Watch and the Seaforth Highlanders.[5]

Even as far away as Africa, Irishmen were being mobilised with the formation of the South African Irish Regiment. As the war progressed, many more Irishmen and indeed Galwaymen who were living in the United States were mobilised when America entered the war. It is commonly accepted that it was the sinking of the *Lusitania*, with the loss of so many American lives that eventually brought America into the war, however, this was not the case.

Two events in the spring of 1917 changed America's outlook on the war. The first was Germany's decision to resume an unrestricted U-boat campaign of sinking merchant ships in international waters without warning. The other reason was the 'Zimmermann Telegram', which was intercepted and transmitted to the American government by British naval intelligence. The telegram was an attempt by Germany to draw Mexico into the war by promising them the states of Texas, Arizona and New

Mexico as part of their territory in return for their support against the allies.

The letter was published in the newspapers on 1 March 1917 and caused outrage in the United States. Germany was possibly encouraged to make such proposals based on reports published in 1916 in which American and Mexican troops had clashed after America launched a punitive expedition into Mexico. America entered the war on 6 April 1917 and their expeditionary force was immediately mobilised. By July 1918, it was estimated that over half a million Irish and Irish-Americans had enlisted in the American forces.[6]

CHAPTER III

KING AND COUNTRY

RECRUITING IN GALWAY
CITY & COUNTY

Call for Irishmen to enlist, 6 November 1915 (*The Connacht Tribune*)

People sometimes ask why so many Irishmen went to war, considering there was no conscription in Ireland? Although it is often said these men went out to fight for 'King and Country', the evidence indicates this was well down on the priority list. While enlistment in the army was not compulsory in Ireland, a number of diversionary tactics were used to ensure the military secured the required manpower. It is evident from many recruiting speeches that young men were being coerced into joining the army.

The newspapers were full of advertisements giving an assortment of reasons why men should join. Letters glorifying the war, condemnation of German atrocities, and heroic deeds of soldiers at the front were also published. Girlfriends and wives were requested to use their influence and encourage their men to join the war effort. The threat of losing their homes, land, finance and their loved ones being killed 'when' the Germans arrived on Irish shores was used at many recruiting meetings.

Some men were also subjected to the threat of being called a coward if they did not enlist. The promise of Home Rule for Ireland encouraged many to join. Employment was also a major issue at the time and a regular army income with additional allowances for married men and their families gave significant security to recruits. The dependents of unmarried soldiers were also promised substantial allowances.

Military personnel and bands turned many a young man's head as they paraded through the towns and villages. It was described as a war for the 'defence of freedom and civilisation' and for the safety of Irish women and children. Poems and songs were composed to frighten, and influence the public. War heroes such as Lieut Michael O'Leary, the famous Victoria Cross winner from Cork spoke at a number of Galway rallies. The authorities also welcomed visits by Sir John French and Gen. Bryan Mahon, who commanded the army in the Balkans. The methods and tactics used in Galway were by no means unique and were typical of what was occurring throughout the country.

On 24 April 1915, members of the Irish Guards accompanied by their own military band arrived in Galway by train. They had been invited by Galway Urban Council and for almost an hour before their arrival, crowds gathered at Galway railway station to welcome them. A company of Connaught Rangers and National Volunteers were also present. St. Patrick's Brass and Reed Band and the Industrial School Band attended to entertain the locals and visitors alike.

Upon arrival they were greeted with tremendous applause and were heartily welcomed by senior political figures. They were then escorted in military formation to their accommodation at the Royal Hotel. A public meeting was arranged at Eyre Square for the afternoon, and following introductions by the chairman of the urban council a number of speakers

Irishmen!

What will you Do?

YOUR political leaders, your famous countrymen and particularly your brave Irish soldiers have asked you to do your duty to your country.

The need for more men is urgent. We must not merely win, but win handsomely. Half hearted measures will not suffice. Anything less than a supreme effort invites defeat. Germany is putting forth her full strength.

Every possible step has been taken to meet the wishes of Irishmen. They are trained together, and will serve together.

They are invited to select the regiments and divisions to which they would like to be posted.

To do nothing is to say "No." There are few considerations which justify a man of military age in refusing to come forward when his country is fighting for its very existence.

Full particulars of pay, of allowances to those who are dependent on you, and of pensions, may be obtained from any Post Office or Recruiting Office.

The response already received is an earnest of what Irishmen can do, but more and more men are wanted. If you are willing freely and voluntarily to respond,

SIGN THE FORM

You are invited to fill in and post this form to the Department of Recruiting, c/o The G.P.O., Dublin, Belfast, or Cork, without delay. No stamp is required.

I voluntarily undertake to enlist, when called upon, FOR THE PERIOD OF THE WAR, in the Division, Regiment or Battalion I mention.

Name

Address

Occupation

Age   Height

If you have any preference, write below, the name of the Regiment you desire to join, specifying the Battalion or Division to which you would like to be posted.

Call for Irish men to enlist, dated 6 November 1915.

(*The Connacht Tribune*)

addressed the gathering, among them Bryan O'Donnell of the Army Recruiting Staff.

O'Donnell told the crowd that the First Battalion Irish Guards had suffered greatly since the war began. They had sustained up to 1,500 casualties, and it was the need to replace those 'fallen heroes' that triggered this recruiting campaign. Quoting John Redmond, he said that it was the duty of all Irishmen to fight against the common foe. Having spoken about atrocities committed against the people of Belgium, he made a direct appeal to the women of Ireland to send their men to save the women of Belgium, who were still suffering unspeakable crimes under the Germans.

On a lighter note, he said that married men should have no worries about joining, as they were already trained in the hard school of discipline and should have no fear of any drill sergeant. In conclusion, he appealed in the name of Ireland, faith, justice and humanity, for them to join the 'gallant Irish Guards' so that when the flags were flying, and the victory drums beating, Galway would be well represented.

The following morning the Connaught Rangers, Irish Guards and their regimental bands marched to St Nicholas' pro-Cathedral, Middle Street to attend 11.00 a.m. mass. The National Volunteers were also present and following the mass, all military sections lined up, and led by the band of the Irish Guards, marched to Eyre Square. The band attracted a large crowd and another recruiting meeting was then held. Galwegians were told that although they had done more than their part since the war began, there was still much to do. After a number of people had spoken, recruiting officer, Capt. Stephen Gwynn, told the crowd that the army and navy had been enriched with the best blood of the town, but more was required. There was an excellent response from those present and forty city men presented themselves for enlistment immediately.[2]

At the time, Capt. Wyndham Waithman of Merlin Park was one of the senior recruiting officers in Galway. He was one of the organisers of the big recruiting campaign in May 1915, when arrangements were made to hold an 'Irish Recruiting Week'. A band and thirty other performers were organised to entertain the crowds. They travelled throughout the county along with military personnel, and representatives from the various district councils and county councils were always available to support the campaign.

The main objective of this campaign was to attract young men from the farming community, as they felt that the town had done its part for the moment. In Tuam, recruiting officer Capt. N. J. Balfe reminded the crowd of German atrocities committed against Catholics and the need to protect their homes and families against such savagery.

Among the many issues addressed, was the escalating cost of the war and the increased taxation which would result from a prolonged war. They condemned all those opposed to recruiting, stating that these people had no regard for the slaughtered innocents. Capt Balfe said that those who pose as patriots and cry out against England do so because they have not risen high enough above the 'clay' to realize the cultured civilisation in which they live. They might be forgiven or pitied for their misguided opinions, but could not, because even the cry of a murdered child could not pierce their cold hearts. 'They are outcasts, let them, if there is any ray of valour in their "clayey carcases", have the courage of their convictions and go to their "fellow brutes", for they are not wanted in this country, whose money these hypocrites gobble up. 'Sons and daughters of discord – let them reap what they sow'. Such comments almost certainly added fuel to the fires of recruiting, while at the same time, discouraged the anti-war people from voicing their opinions.[3]

By June 1915, it was felt that an organised local recruiting committee needed to be formed. Joseph Young, a businessman and member of Galway Urban Council proposed the setting up of the Galway Recruiting Committee, observing that such committees had already been successfully established throughout Ireland. Young said that a great number of city men had already gone to fight, and did not think that the town could spare many more. A recruiting committee could travel about the county and encourage men from urban areas to join the army.

Adding a bit of humour to the meeting, Councillor Bailey asked if any of the councillors could be spared to go to war, which raised much laughter

God save Ireland !

"God save Ireland————"

When you sing these words you think you really __mean__ them.

But since the War began, what have you __done__ to help make them a reality ?

If __you__ are an Irishman between 19 and 40, physically fit and not already serving your Country as a sailor or a soldier, or in the munition factory, there is but one way for __you__ to help to save Ireland from the Germans——

__you__ __must join an Irish__ __Regiment and learn to sing__ __"God save Ireland" with__ __a gun in your hands.__

Join To-day

GOD SAVE THE KING !
GOD SAVE IRELAND !

Recruiting poster, dated 19 June 1915. (*The Connacht Tribune*) among all those present. After a few moments, Young continued, saying that the Connaught Rangers and their band should also be involved in any organised recruiting campaign. Councillor Cunningham asked why Galway had been ignored as a training depot, when over 30,000 troops were being trained in the south of Ireland. Cunningham also stated that although three million pounds a day was being extended towards the war effort, Galway was no 'better off'. After a commitment that all concerns would be addressed in due course, it was agreed that the urban council would act provisionally as the Galway Recruiting Committee.[4]

By late June 1915, the Galway Recruiting Committee had begun concentrating its efforts throughout the county as agreed. They were accompanied by the Connaught Rangers band, who played military tunes as they paraded through the streets of the various towns and villages targeted. This had the desired effect, attracting huge crowds to attend the meetings.

On 27 June 1915, the recruiting party arrived in Tuam. The chairman of Galway County Council, James McDonnell, presided over the meeting. Having explained the purpose of the visit, he made a direct appeal to the young men of the 'farming class', to enlist. The next speaker, Mr H. Concanon, explained that members of his extended family were at the front, helping to drive back the Germans from Irish shores. He mentioned that one of them, a nephew, had already given his life and that his brothers had gone out to 'redress the wrong'. He said that both ecclesiastical and political leaders had agreed that this was a just and holy war. He had recently attended a most interesting and instructive lecture in the Convent Hall, during which the audience were shown slide images of a prosperous little town in Belgium before the Germans created havoc there. In a bid to encourage empathy for the people of Belgium, Concanon said that the town reminded him of 'dear old' Tuam. His reply to those who still question the validity of the war, was simple, if England are defeated then the Irish people will be left with little or no land.

Concanan reminded them of a recent scare when people were warned to be ready to leave for Athlone in the event of the Germans landing in Galway. At the time, many of the older people said they would rather die in their homes than run from the Germans. This comment was met with great roars of approval to the delight of Concanon, who continued by asking the young men if they were going to arm themselves and defend their parents and their homesteads. He also reminded them that the Germans knew that Irishmen had gone to war with the blessing of the church so little mercy would be shown to the clergy following a German invasion.[5]

A large and enthusiastic recruiting meeting was held in Clifden on Wednesday 30 June. The chairman of Clifden Rural District Council, E. J. King, extended an enthusiastic Céad Míle Fáilte to all those present and particularly welcomed the Galway Recruiting Committee and the Connaught Rangers band. He also assured them of the whole-hearted support of the people from the district. W. Lloyd of the United Irish League then addressed the crowd, asking his fellow countrymen to rally to Ireland's defence and crush the organised attempt at land grabbing being made by the Germans.

He pointed out that a prolonged war or an inconclusive peace would mean increased taxation and general insecurity in the country. He appealed to all young men who were in a position to do so, to fight for Ireland, liberty, and the 'freedom of small nations.' He said that Ireland had already responded magnificently, and he trusted that the old fighting spirit was as strong in them as it had been in their ancestors. He concluded by saying that the unity shown by Ireland was a 'happy augury' of a united and prosperous country for the future.

The next speaker, Dr Gorham, said that they had not come to Clifden for conscription, but to ask men to fight for their country and freedom. His appeal was to the women and girls, to encourage their 'young men' to go and fight for their defence in France and Flanders, and to assure them that they would come home crowned with 'honour and glory'. The response from the crowd was incredible with people shouting words of encouragement to the speakers, resulting in several men enlisting that day.[6]

On 3 July 1915, a meeting of the Loughrea town council was held in one of the local hotels in preparation for the arrival of the Galway Recruiting Committee. In the course of his address, the chairman said that ninety-nine men in every hundred in Loughrea fully supported their brothers fighting in the trenches of Belgium and France. He told the meeting that it was imperative that more of their fellow townsmen go to the front. This was greeted with loud agreement from the floor. He said that the towns of Ireland had responded nobly to the call to arms, but rural Ireland stood paralysed, unable or unwilling to understand the doom that awaited them should the 'demon' Kaiser Wilhelm set foot on Irish shores.

He continued by saying the devil had caused the first ever war long before the dawn of civilisation and that no doubt he was behind every war since. He added that the devil appears to have set up his throne in Berlin and he, along with seven other devils have entered the body of the Kaiser and between them they have made a hell of Europe. The chairman became more and more agitated, and in a raised voice, said the Germans had soaked the earth with the blood of men and stained the oceans, 'Just look at Belgium' – whole towns and villages blotted out of existence; the

Is Ireland To Share Belgium's Fate?

Read what the Germans have done to the Churches, Priests, Women and Children of Belgium.

EXTRACTS FROM THE BELGIAN GOVERNMENT OFFICIAL REPORT.

1. "Everywhere there is ruin and devastation. At Buecken many inhabitants were killed, including the priest, who was over eighty years old.'

2. "At Wackerzeel the Germans maltreated women and children. In the same village they stripped a young boy to the waist, threatened him with death, holding a revolver to his chest, pricked him with lances, and then chased him into a field and shot at him, without, however, hitting him."

3. "The sacred vessels which had not been put in safety did not escape profanation. A priest showed us the lower part of a sacred vessel robbed from the Church of Hofstadt. The upper part, in silver, had been stolen; the lower part, copper-gilt, was found on the road. The precious stones which adorned it had been taken from their settings."

4. "A group of thirteen priests, among whom was the Curé of St. Joseph, Mr. Noel, Professor at the University, the Rector of the Scheut Monastery, were stopped on their way in the village of Lovenjoul. They were insulted in every possible way, shut up in a pig-stye from which the pigs had been driven out in their presence by the Germans. Some of them were then forced to strip themselves naked. They were all searched, and all valuables which they possessed were stolen from them. They were also brutalised and beaten."

MEN OF IRELAND

The sanctity of your Churches, the safety of your Homes, the honour of your Women can only be secured by

Defeating the Germans in Belgium

Recruiting poster, dated 6 March 1915.

(*The Galway Express*)

To the Young Women of Ireland.

Is your "Best Boy" wearing Khaki? If not, don't you think he should be?

If he does not think that you and your country are worth fighting for—do you think he is worthy of you?

Don't pity the girl who is alone—her young man is probably a soldier—fighting for her and her country—and for you.

If your young man neglects his duty to Ireland, the time may come when he will neglect you.

Think it over—then ask your young man to

JOIN AN IRISH REGIMENT TO-DAY.

Ireland will appreciate your help.

Recruiting poster, dated 3 April, 1915.

(*The Galway Express*)

homes of the rich and poor looted; women ravished, and the aged, weak and unarmed murdered. From thousands of throats the cry goes up to heaven to avenge such crimes, and Ireland has responded in a very noble manner. But the sons of tenant farmers stand alone as an exception, and like the ostrich, 'are hiding their heads' in the sand hoping the storm will blow over. When he concluded there was a discussion on how best they could receive the Galway Recruiting Committee who were to arrive in Loughrea the following day.[7]

The following evening the recruiting party arrived. They were welcomed to Loughrea by A. D. Comyn, who opened proceedings by reminding the audience there were three things vital to the war effort, munitions, men and money. He considered the principal contribution Loughrea could make was 'men' and he said that although the town had already done well in this regard, they were being asked to 'dig deeper'. He particularly appealed to the farming community to join the colours and become part of the allied success. Local politician, W. J. Duffy then addressed the meeting, describing a frightful campaign by the German army in the destruction of Belgium, and the shocking treatment of non-combatants. He condemned the torpedoing of ships without respect for humanity or nationality. Knowing that there were a number of wounded soldiers and their families attending the meeting, he also condemned the 'maiming and crippling' of their fellow townspeople. He stated that the British empire was engaged in a 'most righteous war' and that it was vital for Ireland to support its efforts and help bring the war to a successful conclusion for the allies. It was imperative that Irishmen do their duty and pledge their support with England he said, as 'today' the theatre of war was France, tomorrow it might be England or Ireland, and should the Germans succeed 'we' could bid goodbye to Irish liberty.

He urged Irishmen to fight 'now', while the war was still in France and not wait until the Germans arrived in Galway Bay. In conclusion, he appealed for the manpower to help bring a swift end to the war, adding that Irishmen should bury their past differences with England, and fight for the freedom of all small countries in Europe.[8]

The next speaker was Capt. Stephen Gwynn, who reminded the crowd that his last appearance in Loughrea was as their MP, fighting for their political aspirations, but today he was addressing them also as a captain of the Connaught Rangers. He told them he joined the army as a private the day the Home Rule Bill was placed on the statute book. The reason he had gone to war was because it was Ireland's war, and it was a war for justice. Germany, he said, had gone to war because its population had increased to such an extent that their country was 'overcrowded' and they required land for some of its surplus millions. This same threat was also used concerning the 'excess' Turkish population.

The captain then appealed to 'nationalist' farmers to send all the men they could spare, and recommended that they join the Connaught Rangers, or indeed any other Irish regiment. One of the last speakers was Martin Ward of the recruiting committee, who told the audience that Home

Rule for Ireland was assured if they fought. He reminded them that John Redmond had already pledged Ireland's loyalty and therefore the people of Ireland were already 'bound' in their support for the allies. Such tactics certainly instilled terror in many people and the fear of losing homes and land had a serious effect on the population in general.[9]

On Sunday 11 July 1915, the Irish Central Recruiting Council arrived in Galway where they held three meetings. Following these meetings, it was decided that they should travel throughout the county accompanied by the Galway campaigners. They all travelled together in a bus (known as 'Noah's Ark'). Their first venue was Moylough, where they held a meeting before a large crowd. The proceedings were much the same as previous meetings, but this one had the added attraction of a 'lantern show' illustrating areas affected by the war with a narrative by recruiting officer, Lieut Hewitt.

They travelled to Mountbellew the following day, where a meeting was held in the market area. That night, Lieut Hewitt gave his usual performance to a packed St Mary's Hall. Having spent two nights in the village, the touring party left for Ballygar, seeking support from that locality. Their next stop was Ballinasloe where they held two large meetings. They decided to make Ballinasloe their base and from there they could focus on the surrounding towns and villages. The venues included Laurencetown and Eyrecourt, at the latter they were entertained by the local landlord. The recruiting tour concluded in Portumna.[10]

The campaign was relentless throughout 1915, and to ensure that the utmost pressure was brought to bear on the public, another major recruiting rally was held in Galway. The meeting was held in Eyre Square and again the Connaught Rangers band gave a performance. Martin McDonogh, chairman of Galway Urban Council, opened proceedings. He introduced the speakers, the first of whom was Lieut Healy, who began by reminding the audience of Galway's proud history, adding that once again her manhood was required to: 'drive back the barbarians and restore the flag of liberty.' Speaking as a Nationalist, to an assembly of nationalists, he hoped the appeal being made would not be in vain. Lieut Healy said there was a promise from the British government that Ireland would be treated as a nation once the war ended, and, that would be their greatest triumph.

He asked would Ireland 'stand apart' in this war, to which the audience shouted 'never' and there was tremendous applause when he said, 'Did Ireland ever stand neutral between right and wrong? There was not a battlefield on which the cause of liberty had been waged that Irish blood had not run.' Speaking of the horrors inflicted on the Belgian population, he said if the Germans arrived in Eyre Square, they would perpetrate the same crimes, killing thousands of people. He warned that those who refused to fight would live to regret their chance to preserve Irish liberty on the battlefields of Europe.

While speaking, he noticed a large number of spilpíns (agricultural labourers) close to Eyre Square, awaiting selection for work. They became the focus of his attention and he called out, 'I will hire them' amidst loud laughter and applause, adding they would receive more wages in the army than they could ever hope to earn from the farmers of this locality.

He asked 'why won't they go to war?' and continued, 'because there were no German bullets flying across Irish farmlands', adding, there was as much danger of them getting struck by lightening, as there was of them getting hit by a German bullet. He then recalled his own mother's words when she first saw him in khaki, 'I would rather see you dead in Flanders then skulking at home.' And added 'This is the spirit in which every woman in Ireland should face the crisis.' Healy also quoted Cardinal Mercier, who had stated that every man who laid down his life in this war had also died for religious reasons, just as the martyrs of old had done. He concluded by saying this was a great opportunity to fight for liberty, justice and honour, and afterwards come home as men, rather than live in shame like those who had refused to go.[11]

Sir James O'Donohoe of the recruiting committee was next to address the gathering and he thanked the committee for the opportunity to speak. He echoed the sentiments of the previous speaker and assured them he would not ask anyone to do anything that was not honourable. No man could deny they were engaged in a war to defend their country, homes, the honour of their women, and to protect their children. He said that over the centuries thousands of their forefathers had shed blood on the hillsides of Ireland, while protecting their families and that the day will come when they may have to do the same.

Reminding the crowd he was not a prophet of evil, he warned that the authorities were watching the recruiting campaigns throughout the kingdom, and if the 'shirkers and slackers', whom he called cowards, did not respond to the call to arms, then some sort of conscription would be

North Galway Recruiting Tour.

The following Meetings will be attended by the Band of the

CONNAUGHT RANGERS

AND THE

TRAVELLING RECRUITING OFFICE

WITH

Speakers, including **IRISH OFFICERS** and well-known Public Representatives.

Sunday, 27th June - TUAM.	- 1 o'clock & 8 o'clock.
Monday, 28th June - HEADFORD.	- 1 o'clock, p.m.
Tuesday, 29th June - MAAM CROSS.	- 1 o'clock, p.m.
Wednesday, 30th June - CLIFDEN.	- 1 o'clock, p.m.
Thursday, 1st July - OUGHTERARD.	- 1 o'clock, p.m.
Friday, 2nd July - ATHENRY.	- 1 o'clock, p.m.
Saturday, 3rd July - LOUGHREA.	- 1 o'clock, p.m.
Sunday, 4th July - GALWAY CITY.	- 1 o'clock & 8 o'c., p.m.

Lantern War Pictures

Will be shown each evening.

The Tour will be continued during following week in East and South Galway.

Recruiting poster, dated 26 June 1915. (*The Galway Express*)

introduced. In conclusion, he appealed to the young men to join the Irish Brigade and help prevent the 'monsters' from invading their 'holy island'.[12]

The next speaker was Lieut Burns, of the Sixth Connaught Rangers. Having gone through the formalities of addressing the assembly, he praised the Ulster Volunteers. The message from Ulster was that both sides of the political and religious divide were united in a new future for Ireland and the Orange and Green would never be separated again. There were critics, but he would not call them Sinn Féiners, because these men were also fighting in the trenches where real Irishmen were in times of danger.

While speaking, he noticed someone in the audience who was not, it seemed, taking him very seriously. He called out to him: 'You may smile, my man, but remember that the trenches are today soaked with the blood of Irishmen in order that you may wear your collar and tie.' The crowd began to applaud again, and as it died away, he began addressing the women and girls, pleading with them not to be seen with any man unless he was wearing khaki or navy blue. As soon as he had concluded, another speaker immediately took the stand and appealed to the farming community, saying they should contribute to the defence of the country, just as the men of the towns had done. Before finishing, he said it would be more honourable for them to have a gun in their hands, rather than a spade. [13]

Yet another recruiting meeting followed later that evening in Simmons Cinema, with the same speakers taking the platform. Lieut Healy again roused the crowd with similar words such as 'Ireland is at war' and the Huns had left people with only their eyes, so they could weep. Ireland was fighting for principle and he would rather see his country doomed to another eight hundred years of slavery than loose its honour.

Quoting from the bible he said: 'What doth it profit a man if he gain the whole world and suffer the loss of his soul.' Speaking of Ireland's past and of its heroes, Wolfe Tone, Thomas Davis and Patrick Sarsfield, he said these men would have done the honourable thing. 'Today' the uniform of an English soldier is the only honourable 'suit' that man should wear, and he called out to the cheering crowd, that all Irishmen were pledged in the common cause of freedom and justice. He finished by saying these men would make history on the continent, just as their ancestors had done and they would also unite the hearts at home for the freedom of Ireland that lay ahead.

After a rousing response from the audience, Sir James O'Donohoe addressed the crowd, saying he trusted they would long enjoy the liberties granted under British rule, and that it was the duty of every Irishman to defend these liberties. He said the Germans wished to dominate all of Europe, and warned that any benefits won through the Land Acts would be swept away if they invaded Ireland. He called on all farmers' sons to show some degree of gratitude for their prosperity and join in the defence of their homes and country.

When he finished speaking, Lieut Burns took the stand and spoke at length, castigating shop assistants, bank clerks and other classes of young men who had not enlisted. While he was speaking a woman pushed her way through the enthusiastic crowd until she was in front of the stage and asked the speaker if he could give her back her son who had been killed. Members on the recruiting committee quickly, but discreetly removed the woman from the hall. As the meeting closed, a tremendous applause was heard as six young men came forward to enlist and in a show of solidarity joined the speakers on the stage. A few days later, 186 men enlisted in one morning from the Galway area alone.[14]

Shortly afterwards a meeting of women who had relatives serving at the front was held in the Cinema Theatre. Sir William Maxwell, Sir James O'Donohoe, Joseph Young and a number of others who were involved in the recruiting campaign were invited to attend. They received a very enthusiastic response from the audience, so much so, that Mrs Donovan O'Sullivan, Professor of History at University College Galway proposed setting up a women's recruiting organisation, and thus the Galway Women's Recruiting League was established, with Mrs O'Sullivan as its president. She then addressed the meeting, telling them all of her brothers and her

AY, OCTOBER 30, 1915.

THE KING'S APPEAL TO HIS PEOPLE.

More Men to Secure Victory and Enduring Peace.

DARKEST MOMENT PRODUCES THE STERNEST RESOLVE.

Below is given the text of a public appeal issued by the King to his people. His Majesty, while expressing pride in the voluntary response from his subjects who have sacrificed all in the nation's cause, and confidence that the darkest moments in the country's history have ever produced the sternest resolve, asks that men of all classes should come forward voluntarily and take their share in the fight to uphold Britain's traditions and the glory of her arms.

To make good the sacrifices already made, the appeal states, more men and yet more are wanted to keep the armies in the field, and through them to secure victory and enduring peace against an enemy who has transgressed the laws of nations and changed the ordinance that binds civilised Europe together.

BUCKINGHAM PALACE.

TO MY PEOPLE.

At this grave moment in the struggle between my people and a highly organised enemy who has transgressed the laws of nations and changed the ordinance that binds civilised Europe together, I appeal to you.

I rejoice in my Empire's effort, and I feel pride in the voluntary response from my subjects all over the world who have sacrificed home, fortune, and life itself, in order that another may not inherit the free Empire which their ancestors and mine have built.

I ask you to make good these sacrifices.

The end is not in sight. More men and yet more are wanted to keep my armies in the field, and through them to secure victory and enduring peace.

In ancient days the darkest moment has ever produced in men of our race the sternest resolve.

I ask you, men of all classes, to come forward voluntarily and take your share in the fight.

In freely responding to my appeal, you will be giving your support to our brothers, who for long months have nobly upheld Britains past traditions and the glory of her arms.

George R.I.

King George V appeals for support, dated 30 October 1915

(*The Tuam Herald*)

husband were already serving with the colours and many of her students had also gone to war. She pledged to devote much of her time to the recruiting cause.

A number of other prominent Galway women were then proposed to form a committee. On 12 January 1916, the League held another meeting in the Cinema Theatre (a venue which they continued to use), again presided over by Mrs O'Sullivan. Lieut Forsyth addressed the meeting and spoke at length on the question of the 'shop assistant class' joining the army. The chairperson suggested that those nervous of being shot could join the non-combatant corps, but the Lieut disagreed and argued that if everyone did this, they would have no front line troops.

Before finishing, he requested that the ladies continue their excellent work in canvassing for recruits, but that they should be careful not to insult anyone, or use 'white feather' tactics. This would suggest some women were resorting to intimidation in order to ensure numbers for the military. Incidentally, the film being shown on Friday of that week in the Victoria Cinema, was 'It's A Long Way to Tipperary'. The Connaught Rangers sang this song as they marched out of Boulogne in August 1914.

It was practically unknown at the time, but a reporter heard them singing, and it soon became the allies' signature tune. The Galway Women's Recruiting League continued to hold regular meetings. They were also interested in supplying men to the navy and in April 1916, Lieut Grout, of the Royal Navy Reserve, was invited to speak before a packed house. His appeal encouraged eight 'boys' of the 'required' age (eighteen) to enlist after the meeting.[15]

On 2 February 1916, the 'Great Recruiting Conference' was held in Galway. Lord Wimborne, the lord lieutenant of Ireland and John Redmond along with many other distinguished political and military figures arrived in Galway for the conference. The day was proclaimed a general holiday and most businesses closed. The route from the railway station to the town hall where the conference was to be held was decorated with flags, streamers, buntings and banners. Some of the slogans read: 'One Life, One Fleet, One Foe', 'Céad Míle Fáilte', 'The West's Awake',

'United We Stand, Divided We Fall'. The Royal Standard floated high over Eyre Square, while the Union Jack fluttered proudly in front of the Railway Hotel (Great Southern Hotel) and other allied flags hung from the windows of the houses surrounding Eyre Square.

Huge crowds gathered at the railway station well before the arrival of the lord lieutenant and his entourage. The station platform was filled with representatives of various local authorities from the city and county. Senior staff from the university and many high-ranking military personnel attended. St Patrick's Band played 'God Save Ireland' as the train pulled into the station. Having disembarked they were taken to the Railway Hotel for lunch with Martin McDonogh, chairman of the urban council.

After lunch they made their way to the Town Hall, the route was lined with cheering crowds and the National Volunteers formed a guard of honour. The Connaught Rangers and their band also turned out for the occasion. The town hall was packed with delegates for the conference, with the balcony being occupied exclusively by ladies. At 2.30 p.m. the addresses began with speakers representing the Galway Urban Council, Galway County Council, Galway Harbour Board and University College Galway. The main speakers were Lord Wimborne, John Redmond and the chief secretary for Ireland. The audience included titled people such as the marquis of Sligo, the bishop of Tuam, and many prominent MPs and businessmen. Addressing the packed house, Lord Wimborne congratulated the organisers on such a successful turnout and during his speech he expressed his gratitude to Galway for the amount of recruits they had sent to the navy. He also paid tribute to the numbers who had joined the army and stated that at this point in time over 90,000 Irishmen had enlisted countrywide.[16]

Local papers, such as *The Connacht Tribune* and *The Galway Express* carried many recruiting advertisements as well as stories from the western front. Through this medium, other Irish regiments such as the Royal Dublin Fusiliers were able to appeal for 'commercial men and farmers' to join their ranks. They also carried John Redmond's statement regarding the dishonour to Ireland if the ranks of the Irish regiments had to be filled with men from other countries. There were some reports of this happening, but it was strongly contradicted by Capt. Stephen Gwynn, who was in a position to do so, given that his duties included recruiting and training. He had also seen service at the front with Irish regiments.

Advertisements also encouraged groups of young men to join together promising them they would serve together in the so-called 'Pals Battalions'. While this boosted morale among those enlisting, it was certainly a major cause for concern. Given the devastation of so many battalions at the front, this action had the potential to wipe out the young male population of villages and towns around the country. In order to make it easier to join the army, the local newspapers also published recruiting registration forms, which were approved by the War Office. Encouragement to enlist through the media of songs and poetry was also appearing. The following is an extract from a poem published in *The Connacht Tribune* of 4 December 1915:

CONNACHT AND THE FIGHT FOR FREEDOM

Ireland, the land of the true and the brave,
The mother of honour and chivalrous hearts!

Thou to great causes thy finest sons gave,
Has felt degradation and grief's bitter darts:

Ireland has given the bravest and strong.
Brave Irish have bled 'neath the hand of the Hun.
Serbia's wrong is to Ireland her wrong.
For freedom has Ireland her bravest deeds done.[17]

Many clergymen were also encouraging young men to enlist in the military. In the 1916 Lenten pastoral letters read to the congregations throughout the city, Bishop Thomas O'Dea of Galway made special reference to the war. He mentioned the changes taking place in relations between Ireland

and England and reasoned that Irishmen should support the allied cause. He hoped that every Irish Catholic, whose politics had not been utterly perverted, would join. It was his 'earnest hope' that the contribution in blood made by Irishmen to strike down: 'arrogant militarism would not be a wasted treasure.'

The archbishop of Tuam declared: 'you will rally to the flag, not by compulsion or coercion, but from a sense of duty as becomes free men.' He said that the man, who strikes a blow against 'Prussia', strikes a blow for justice and freedom, and that every acre of land acquired by the Germans was achieved through injustice and rapine. The archbishop also mentioned that those whose political views were against England, brought disgrace upon their country and themselves.

Dr Gilmartin, bishop of Clonfert, stated at the close of a retreat that the spirit of Christ was not a spirit of aggression (boycotting or hate), but is: 'Love your enemies; do good to those who hate you'. However, this does not mean that: 'we are not to defend our rights within the laws of God'. The Rector in St Nicholas' Collegiate Church gave an eloquent sermon regarding the war and dwelt at length on the 'wicked and terrible methods' used by the enemy saying they had been: 'conceived by Satan and matured in Hell'. Many believed that such denunciations should be heard from the pulpits of all denominations, in order to make people realise the diabolic nature of German warfare. Most of the bishops throughout Ireland, with the exception of Dr O'Dwyer, bishop of Limerick, took a similar line.[18]

Some priests did stop short of telling their congregations to enlist. An example of this occurred in August 1915 when members of the recruiting committee arrived in Williamstown. Although they were welcomed and introduced by Fr Rattigan after Sunday Mass, he told Capt. Balfe of the committee that he would not tell his congregation to enlist, but would leave this decision to their own conscience. Capt. Balfe then addressed the congregation telling them he was not going to waste time with the harrowing details of the diabolical cruelty and inhumanity of the enemy.

His primary objective in coming to Williamstown was to impress upon its people with all the power at his disposal to do their duty on the part of the allies and enlist and thereby bring an early end to the war. He spoke of the heroism of the Irish troops at the front who were arousing the respect of all civilised nations. The only way to keep their homes and their island of 'saints and scholars' safe from destruction was to join the army. He hoped that every man that could be spared from Williamstown would come forward and defend their land.

Martin Egan of Williamstown then spoke and reiterated what the previous speaker had said and added a reminder of the ruthless murder of mothers, children, priests, nuns and the destruction of the churches and holy places in Belgium. Much of this recruiting campaign was again aimed at the farming community and although the authorities were constantly complaining they were not receiving sufficient numbers from the rural areas, this had certainly changed by August 1917. This is evident from a meeting of Galway Urban Council in which a member voiced his concern over the 'thousands' that had joined the army from the rural areas. He warned that if any more go to war, there would be no one left to work the land, adding that hundreds of farmers were already unable to cope sufficiently.[19]

Under the heading 'Co. Galway Farms Mapped Out in Berlin', one of the local newspapers reported that land and farms in County Galway and indeed other counties throughout Ireland were being mapped out and earmarked for German families. The report pleaded with the Irish population to face up to the reality that such events would take place should Germany win the war. It stated that the Germans would also seize the Imperial Treasury and the banks throughout the United Kingdom and they would seize all bank balances and deposit accounts. This was a reality and not a myth, as it was already happening in the German occupied territories. In rural districts, the Germans would 'levy huge cash fines' by arresting parish priests, curates and leading townspeople and holding them as hostages until the fines were paid. It would take the form of kidnapping and if the fines were not paid by a certain date, then the hostages would be shot. Reports also warned that being pro-German would not save anyone as they would simply say: 'It's your money – and your land – we want!

Hand over, and look lively.'[20]

The Royal Navy was also playing its own part in the recruiting campaign. On 15 April 1916, a meeting was held in the Cinema Theatre, William Street, under the auspices of the Galway Women's Recruiting League. During the introduction the chairperson said there was scarcely anyone present who did not have a friend, relative or acquaintance in the navy, and yet very little was known of their contribution to the war effort. Lieut T. E. Grout of the Royal Navy then spoke of 'Life on the Ocean Wave'.

He first congratulated the people of Galway for all they had done to date and then spoke of navy life in general. He emphasised the importance of the British Fleet which ensured that the army was transported safely overseas to the various theatres of war. The protection of the allied coastlines and defeat of the German navy was high on his agenda. He told of a British ship, being torpedoed while transporting Irish regiments to Gallipoli and said the survivors who were picked up after an hour or two in the water were singing 'It's a long way to Tipperary'. This received a rousing response from the crowd.

In conclusion, he requested that Galway maintain its impressive record and told the young men present that he wanted their strong hands and souls. After a vote of thanks proposed by Joseph Young, the meeting closed. Similar to the army recruiting, the navy continued their campaign for the duration of the war. The success of such recruiting drives can be judged from the fact that as late as November 1917, in one week alone, twenty-four young men from the city signed up for the Royal Naval Reserves.[21]

In August 1917, Col Arthur Lynch, MP, joined in the recruiting campaign. Addressing Galway Urban Council, he said that his connection with Galway had always left a deep impression on his mind. His name had been associated with the city for centuries and he was very proud of his ancestry. It was only after careful consideration of the extreme crisis facing the Irish people that he had joined the army. He reminded the council that America had always been a refuge for Irishmen, and he particularly hoped that Irishmen would also rally to the 'Stars and Stripes'. Lynch informed the audience that he had lived and studied in Germany for some time before the war and while he respected their science, he warned that the German system of government was the worst in existence. The only way to have Ireland's wrongs addressed was to win the sympathy of the allied countries by continuing to fight side by side with them for the common good. He added that he had not diluted one drop of his nationalist blood since wearing the British uniform. Lynch was not afraid to take up a rifle and risk his own life and had come before the young men of Galway to ask them to follow his example.

However, times were changing and when he finished speaking, Councillor Redington, challenged him saying that if England wanted Irishmen to fight, why had the government treated Ireland so unfairly. Redington pointed to centuries of mistreatment and said it was the English aristocracy who had sown the seeds of Sinn Féin. Councillor Young then interrupted him, saying he agreed that Ireland had been badly treated, but added 'two wrongs never made a right', and that he was supporting Col Lynch. Although the committee invited Col Lynch to speak to them again, the feelings of some members of the council had changed dramatically towards recruiting. Councillor Redington's out-spoken remarks would not have been heard in the early years of the war. Shortly after this meeting, the military requested an additional 2,900 recruits from the Galway area alone. The views of the council were reiterated by the councils around the county.[22]

There was no let-up in the recruiting campaign in 1918, the military took over the town hall to use as recruiting offices, but after protests by Galway County Council, they vacated the premises. In August 1918, the Galway Recruiting office was situated at Bishop's Court, in St Augustine Street. The area organiser was Allan J. J. Algie. By this time, reports warned that it was the Irish troops at the front who would suffer if there were a lack of Irish recruits.

Times were becoming desperate with recruiting officers saying that it was unfair to those who had given up everything for their country to be left exposed to more frequent and longer fighting because of a lack of support from their own countrymen. They called on all Irishmen to assist in the work of recruiting and asked for suggestions as to the most effective methods to cover every district. Recruiting was proving more difficult, and some were saying that to go to war was a betrayal of Ireland. In reply to such comments, John Dillon (he had become leader of the Irish Nationalist Party following the death of John Redmond in March 1918) said that it was a 'lie' to say any nationalist who joined the army had betrayed Ireland. On the contrary, the men who joined the army took their stand beside all the gallant Irish regiments who nobly maintained the traditions of a patriotic race. Men who used intimidation to discourage people from joining the forces were acting falsely for Ireland. Although he was disappointed with the government over Home Rule not being enforced, he did not wish to see the men at the front forgotten and he tried to ensure they would be fully supported. He said that although he had never been involved in recruiting, he was opposed to the anti-recruiting lobby.

Dillon continued by saying Ireland could not abandon the war now and lose the support and sympathy of the other nations involved. In conclusion he said that in this war Christian principles were at stake, and the Irish would always do battle in defence of Christianity. Considering he prided himself on not becoming involved in recruiting, his speech certainly made a good argument in its favour. The recruiting drive continued right up to the end of the war and it was reported that on Armistice Day, Galway ranked third in the country, behind Dublin and Cork for recruiting numbers. [23]

CHAPTER IV

THE CARROT AND THE STICK
CONSCRIPTION AND HOME RULE

Among the reasons for the shift in attitudes to the war, were conscription and Home Rule. There was also of course the change of ideals following the 1916 Rebellion and the enormous death toll on the western front. One could well argue that these were the main reasons, but even before the rebellion there was a change in opinions among some who had initially supported the war. There was growing concern among nationalist politicians and the people over the conscription question and Home Rule. The government had been very cunning in some methods of recruiting in Ireland, and the old 'carrot and stick' approach, was put to use, the carrot being Home Rule, and the stick, conscription. In March 1915, it was reported in the strongest possible terms, that if the government could not encourage enough men to join the ranks voluntarily, then conscription would have to be introduced.

The argument continued throughout the year and in October, the attitude of the Irish Nationalist Party to conscription was made perfectly clear. John Dillon, speaking for the party, told the House of Commons that his party was totally opposed to conscription in any form. He said that Ireland had already given the best of her manhood to crush Prussian military domination and was still willing to supply 'voluntarily' her quota of men.

In November 1915, it was reported that the conscription scare had caused large numbers of young men to emigrate. However, upon investigation by the local authorities these allegations proved to be almost totally unfounded. There were some instances of parents forcing their sons to leave the country because of the threat, but these were very few.

On 7 November 1915, a train arrived in Galway carrying thirty young men, who were returning from Liverpool after an unsuccessful attempt to emigrate to America.

When they were questioned on the matter, some did say they had been forced to leave by their parents, while others said they were simply seeking employment abroad. When the emigration authorities were approached regarding the issue, they stated that those concerned about young men of military age leaving the country could have spared themselves the trouble, as bookings had never been as low. They confirmed that the official emigration figures for 1913 had been the lowest on record, and those for early 1914 were no higher. The authorities also declared, that at 'this' point in time the emigration tide had fallen away almost completely, with the greatest reductions being in Munster and Connacht.

Despite this disclosure the threat continued but the Irish Party stood firm, even against pressure from Ulster. The successful stance of the Irish Party was highlighted at a meeting of the Tuam United Irish League in January 1916. The secretary, Thomas Sloyan, stated that the meeting should not close without congratulating the Irish Nationalist Party on securing exemption for Ireland from conscription. He also said there had been an outcry from northern unionists in favour of conscription, but his reply to this was simple; it would be more honourable for them to enlist voluntarily.

Many of the people attending the meeting felt that conscription should not even be on the agenda as Ireland was already well represented in the armed forces. It was well documented that Ireland had suffered considerable losses since the war began, and that this sacrifice had been given generously, 'freely, fully, fearlessly and unflinchingly'. The regiments that suffered the fiercest onslaughts at Mons were the Connaught Rangers, Munster Fusiliers and Irish Guards. These men had displayed the same courage at every battle since, and were still doing their duty nobly. The Irish won the admiration of all who witnessed the Gallipoli landings. Relative to population, Ireland had already sent more men to the front than England and Wales. These were the views expressed by the committee and they also wished to remind the government, that if

England, with its teeming millions had answered the call to arms as well as Ireland had done, there would be no need to introduce such measures as conscription. They concluded by proclaiming the loyalty and bravery of the Irishmen already serving at the front and reminded those in authority, that these men would fight for a just cause, but warned that they would not be driven by a 'whip'.

If conscription had been introduced it would have totally depleted Ireland of all men of military age. This was of serious concern to many people, particularly among those with separatist ideas. One of the effects that conscription would have in Ireland was immediate rebellion on the part of the extreme nationalists. The Irish Republican Brotherhood Military Council had already taken this decision. They felt urgent action would be required while there were still men of military age, ready to bear arms for the Irish cause.

Following the 1916 Rebellion, there were calls from some English politicians to introduce conscription immediately. They believed the time was right because most of the rebels had been removed from the political arena. In a bid to show the government the manpower still available in Ireland, the authorities had 'war planes' circle over Sinn Féin gatherings to photograph the crowds. The War Office was alerted and the government was urged to enforce conscription immediately.

However, they were very wary of the disastrous results that such a venture might have. Most people in Ireland agreed the only way conscription could be averted was through the Irish Nationalist Party. As long as they remained united and strong against its introduction, then the 'English extremists' would not have their way and plunge Ireland into an even deeper legacy of bloodshed. Nevertheless, once conscription was introduced in England, it would likely be only a matter of time before it was extended to Ireland.

In July 1917, Capt. Stephen Gwynn addressed a meeting of Galway Urban Council and voiced his opinion on the question of conscription in the strongest possible terms. During his very lengthy talk, he said that when conscription was introduced in Britain, the government, although under extreme pressure, had refrained from extending it to Ireland. In order to avoid conscription, Ireland would have to produce another 50,000 recruits immediately, and in addition to this, between two and three thousand men per month would be required to support those already in the field. Gwynn went on to say that the other allied countries would not be offended by the introduction of conscription in Ireland. Regarding Home Rule, he stated that Ireland could not expect any support from these countries if she was not willing to fight now, when she was needed most. He spoke at length on both subjects, but had overlooked or forgotten Ireland's, and indeed Galway's remarkable contribution in troops thus far.

One member of council, James Redington, reminded him of this fact. Councillor Redington also reiterated the general opinion of most Irish people at the time – that they would not be threatened or forced into conscription. He reminded Gwynn that the Home Rule Act which had been promised so many times in the past, still had not been delivered. He asked what guarantee they had of its implementation, given that the government had previously held 'Home Rule' in their hands, and like 'a puff of wind' it was gone. Even the King's signature made no difference, because once Carson and the unionists were against the act, it would not be introduced. In conclusion, Councillor Redington pointed out the differences in the populations of the other allied countries in comparison to Ireland and added that the male population of the country was already totally depleted and it could not afford to send any more troops.

By 1917, there were two schools of thought among Irish nationalists on the question of Home Rule. Some favoured total independence and were striving for an Irish Republic, while others would have been satisfied with Home Rule. At a meeting held in Kilronan on the Aran Islands in June 1917, the United Irish League representative urged support for Home Rule. He stated that an Irish Republic was not realistic, as the country would require a large army and navy to protect itself. He said Ireland's greatest misfortune was that Irishmen could never agree when it came to politics, and pointed out that it would be more beneficial and practical to attain what was possible and within reach.

He also warned that England would rather lose all its other colonies than part with Ireland. Nevertheless, support for independence in one form or another was growing stronger and it was too late to reverse the cycle. It is interesting to note that even Capt. Gwynn was in favour of Home Rule by 1918. He was asked to speak on the subject before a meeting held under the auspices of the Galway National Club in April of that year. Gwynn said that he believed self-government for Ireland would be established within five months. He believed that it would become a reality, because it was the wish of the people of Ireland, England, America and Australia. On the question of total independence, he said that this was up to the people to decide, but warned they were likely to sweep away any investment planned for Ireland. Thus the town's 'progressive' development would suffer and would hinder Galway's chance of becoming a great seaport and gateway to America.[5]

An excellent example of the total change in attitudes to the war occurred in August 1918, when Stephen Gwynn was refused permission to deliver a speech to Galway County Council. Before the meeting began, the chairman announced that Capt. Gwynn, Col Lynch and Sgt O'Sullivan, who were in the adjoining room, wished to address the meeting on the issue of voluntary recruiting. He asked the council if they would listen to what these men had to say, to which someone quickly shouted 'No, we won't'. Another member of council said they had already been 'humbugged' by Lloyd George, Carson and others, adding that they had been promised Home Rule, and 'now' it was not even in the plans, instead there was a conscription act being forced upon them.

Martin McDonogh voiced his opinion in favour of the recruiting officers, but was unable to convince the others. Obviously people were not as naïve as they had been in 1914; in fact they were saying that Gwynn's 'goose is cooked' and making other such remarks. This was very different from the early days of the war. Letters and poems such as the following did not help the government's cause either. These ditties left people in no doubt as to the unionist stance on the question of Home Rule. The letter castigating Carson and the government was published in *The Tuam Herald* in April 1917 and stated that 500,000 Irishmen were already at war. The poem appeared in *The East Galway Democrat* in May 1918:

NEW RALLYING SONG FOR CARSON

Oh, Ulster she will fight
And Ulster will be right,
Rally, boys, rally!

We do not hate the Hun
But the Popish priest and nun.
Rally, boys, rally!

Haig's back is to the wall
But 'No Popery' is the call;
Rally, boys, rally!

We won't fight the Kaiser Bill
It's Home Rule we've got to kill
And perhaps the Kaiser still
Will be our ally.

Sir – One of the most sinister figures for the allies that this war has brought to the front is Sir Edward Carson. Carson had a large share in bringing on the war, for it was Carson's threatened rebellion against Home Rule that made Germany believe that England would be so occupied putting down the Carson gang in Ulster that she would not go into the Continental war; and now that 500,000 Irishmen are giving their lives to help save civilisation from the Huns, it is again Carson and his English supporters, Lords Lansdowne, Middleton and Beresford, who are preventing the Irish from getting one of the rewards of their sacrifice. The right to have a legislature and power to rule themselves in local matters had been promised to the Irish by England. From Gladstone on, every Englishman of real vision has seen that the way to dispose of the Irish question was to give Ireland Home Rule. And now, at this crucial time, we are again having an illustration of the kind of English-Ulster revolution. 'Rather the Kaiser than the Pope', was what Ulster men said prior to the war and it apparently is still their frame of mind. For their own happiness, that they might get the Pope rather than the Kaiser, is the sincere wish of one who is not himself a Papist.

Lawrence Godkin, New York, March 8.[6]

The question of Home Rule and conscription was also being raised by front line troops. One Irishman in the American army wrote a letter in the strongest possible terms to the authorities in Galway, saying that he believed that America was the only country in the world that could force Irish independence. He could not understand why this had not already happened, given that Irish-American soldiers were laying down their lives to crush the common enemy, while British authorities succeeded only in: '… crowning their follies by endeavouring to force conscription on a separate nation'.

Although they were aware of the strong opposition to conscription in Ireland, the English press continued to call for its introduction. A reporter with *The Connacht Tribune* again pointed out the dangers of such an event. In his opinion, this stance by the British, was proof of the 'ignorance and stupidity' of Englishmen, about the true state of affairs in Ireland. He also felt that these people were shrewd enough to realise that to force a conscription bill in Ireland against the wishes of the majority of the people and the Irish Party would be foolish in the extreme. So, was there a hidden agenda?

In April 1918, the nationalist MP Joseph Devlin, reiterated the Irish Party's position and warned all concerned that his party would never permit such an act, and would oppose it: 'as long as they had breath in their body'. He also described conscription as a 'blood tax'. But despite all this opposition, the issue remained on the agenda and was raised again in May of that year during a debate in the House of Commons. Devlin again argued strongly against the act and in an extremely heated moment, he offered to enlist in the army himself. He said other Irishmen would follow his example, if the government would abandon the idea of trying to force them to fight its 'battles' and guarantee freedom for Ireland. Devlin then declared that Ireland had given more to the war effort than any of the other allied countries, because it had done so of 'her own free will' and that whatever she gives in future will be given as a gift of an Irish nation which is free, not just in name, but in reality. He concluded by making it clear that any blame for a disastrous outcome on this issue should be placed firmly on the 'right shoulders' as it will do much to avert the: 'mischievous delusions which our rulers utilise for nefarious ends.'

As far as most local politicians were concerned, the government was prepared to use 'Prussian' methods of force, to supply their armies with men. In spite of all that had happened, the government still did not, or could not, see any betrayal in the promises made since the war had begun.

Many believed at the time that the lack of action on Home Rule simply meant that the 'carrot' was gone, but the 'stick' would more than compensate if used to its fullest capacity. To many Irish people, the only thing that protected them from a bloodbath was the Irish Party's refusal to bow to the wishes of the government. It is clear that relationships between the party and the government had changed dramatically since the beginning of the war. The clergy also supported the Irish Party's stance – as can be seen in the following letter written by the bishop of Galway, to Galway County Council:

Mount St. Mary's, Galway, 19th April, 1918.

Dear Sir – I cannot come to the County meeting on Monday, but I approve and bless, with all my heart, the purpose for which it is being held. My view on conscription is exactly that of my brother Bishops. I believe that this law, as forced upon Ireland, is oppressive, inhuman, and impossible, and therefore, in my judgment, the Irish people have a right to resist it by what ever lawful means. I rest this view chiefly on the aggregate of the past and present relations between the two countries, which it is impossible even to summarise in a letter, taking into account also the objects of war, both real and ostensible and the moral atmosphere in which it is being waged. May

God be with his faithful Irish people in this crisis of their existence, and may they all prove true to Him, and to one another in the struggle. – Faithfully yours,

Thomas O'Dea, Bishop of Galway.

Despite all this opposition, the threat continued and in July 1918, the Irish Party made a strong appeal to the American government for support against conscription. In a speech to the House of Commons the following month, Joseph Devlin pointed out the vast numbers of Irishmen that had joined the army since the war began. He told them the Irish Recruiting Council were at present touring Ireland, in an effort to encourage more nationalists to join the army.

He explained that the attitude of indifference 'now' taken by Galway County Council was typical of the overwhelming majority of councils throughout the country and said this atmosphere was the creation of the government. He said that Lloyd George ran away from an Irish debate on Home Rule when the League of Nations was mentioned, but his 'henchmen' on the ministerial bench indicated, that 'no policy save coercion' would be used. Behind this lurked the threat of conscription and the Irish Recruiting Council were making this very clear when pleading their case to the general public. Devlin continued, by saying the government should end its threats and honour its pledges to Ireland, and then a free people of Ireland would assist them just as they had done in the: '... days before Redmond was betrayed'. He told them Ireland could be led, but not driven. In conclusion, he said that Ireland would respond generously in manpower, but would not be cajoled, coerced, nor 'conscripted'. While conscription remained an issue, it did not materialise and gradually subsided, as an end to the conflict loomed.

CHAPTER V

GOD SAVE IRELAND
GALWAY'S OPPOSITION TO THE WAR

From the beginning there was some degree of opposition to the war, but this was mainly from the Sinn Féin movement. Contrary to popular belief at the time, there were those who did not believe that Ireland would gain Home Rule through supporting the war against Germany. They deemed that in the fight for the freedom of small nations, Ireland was well and truly forgotten. They began making their presence felt by protesting and disrupting recruiting meetings. During one meeting the power was cut and sulphuric acid was squirted at the speakers. This was totally condemned by the authorities and those responsible were compared with 'the most brutal Germans to invade Belgium'. The Sinn Féin protest marches gained little or no support from the public. There were serious scuffles and name-calling between them, and those supporting the war. Fights became commonplace and bottles were sometimes thrown during large demonstrations.

In October 1914, Sinn Féin called for an anti-recruiting meeting to be held in their drill hall, in Williamsgate Street. After the meeting got under way, a large crowd of pro-war supporters gathered in the street outside. Stones were hurled through the windows of the building and a short time later, members of the Irish Volunteers and Sinn Féin marched out of the building in military formation. The first four men were armed with rifles and bayonets, while the remaining sixteen had wooden rifles. As they marched towards Shop Street, the crowd followed, jeering and shouting abuse at them.

A series of clashes began and as they reached O'Gormans (present-day Easons), bottles were thrown at the 'Sinn Féiners'. They turned and faced the crowd and began to swing their wooden weapons in a threatening manner, which at first had the desired effect.

However, one man stepped out from the crowd, Pte Joe McGowan from Prospect Hill, who was home after being wounded in action at the battle of Mons. Some said he was simply going for a walk and had nothing to do with the attack on the anti-war protesters, but nevertheless, he received a broken wrist when he was struck with the butt of a wooden rifle. The man who delivered the blow was James Carter, a clerk with Galway County Council (he was later fined £10 by the courts). By this time a much larger crowd had gathered and the attack on the Sinn Féin members intensified.

The Sinn Féiners made a last stand at the Shambles Barracks near O'Brien's Bridge, by which time many of them had already been disarmed. The crowd surged forward and the Sinn Féiners had to make a hasty retreat towards Nuns Island and New Road. In the aftermath, the crowd marched throughout the streets of Galway in triumph, brandishing the captured trophies (wooden guns). They sang 'A Nation Once Again', and 'We'll Hang the Kaiser From A Sour Apple Tree' and proceeded to attack the homes of known Sinn Féin members in Dominick Street, Merchants Road, Mary Street and other areas of the town, smashing the front windows of the houses with stones and bricks. It was described as 'Galway's first engagement with the enemy'. Despite such incidents, the anti-war movement continued to make protests in the face of a very strong pro-war movement.[1]

Shortly afterwards a 'German-looking Sinn Féiner' arrived in Ross, armed to the teeth with pro-German material, and it seems he had a lucky escape when some of the 'best men' in the locality followed him, with the intention of 'sorting' him out. In University College Galway, students verbally attacked a certain professor because he had shown support for Sinn Féin. They jeered at him, and shouted their support for John Redmond and the war and began singing 'God save the King' and 'God save Ireland' forcing the man to make a quick exit.

In Dublin, two men who later became famous Irish historical figures were jailed for a number of months hard labour for campaigning against the war. They were Seán McDermott and Francis Sheehy-Skeffington;

both men had addressed anti-war meetings, the former in Tuam and the latter in Dublin.

Seán McDermott's speech in Tuam was important, because it left the authorities in no doubt of the nationalist's attitude towards the war. The Tuam meeting was held on 16 May 1915, and although only a small crowd turned out, McDermott spoke out passionately against the British authorities. During his speech, he referred to the open condemnation of German atrocities in Belgium and reminded the gathering that this same government had suitably forgotten 'their own' atrocities committed at Bachelor's Walk. He was referring to the Irish nationalists who were shot dead by British troops following the Howth gun-running episode. He told the audience that he had just returned from England, where he saw much employment created for young men there, but in Ireland the only employment available was to join the: 'Army to get killed fighting for England'. Regarding conscription, he said that the Volunteers would fight this at any cost, adding that they were neither pro-German nor pro-British and would fight against either side to protect Ireland. In conclusion he said that England's 'difficulty' was Ireland's 'opportunity' and this should be acted upon. Nevertheless, much of the anti-war lobbying was ignored. Poems and songs were also composed and written to criticise all those opposed to the war. The following poem was published in *The Galway Express* in October 1914:

THE FIRING LINE – AT HOME

I won't go to the front, he said
To see the real fighting and brave dead;
I'm safe from shrapnel, steel and lead
In the firing line – at home.

Tis easier to march and drill,
On some green Irish field or hill,
Where talk is cheap and foes are nil

Poster of Ireland embracing Sinn Féin while telling John Redmond to leave.

(The Allen Literary Collection)

At the firing line – at home.

I'd hate to meet with any harm,
Perchance a wound in leg or arm,
I much prefer the safe alarm
Of the firing line – at home.

Let others go defend our shore,
On foreign plains mid cannon's roar,
I'll rant and spout of ancient lore
In the firing line – at home.

At soldiers true I'll scoff and jeer,
At valiant deeds I'll calmly sneer
For well I know there's naught to fear
From the firing line – at home.[2]

Opposition to Sinn Féin and an independent nationalist Ireland changed dramatically after the 1916 Rebellion. An example of this occurred in June 1916, when a row broke out between two soldiers and two former sailors from the Claddagh. They were having a drink in Michael Walsh's bar in Eyre Square, when the soldiers, one a recruiting sergeant and the other a private, walked into the premises. One of the sailors said to the sergeant that he, being a Galwayman, should be ashamed to wear the king's uniform. The sergeant reacted by saying he was proud to fight for 'King and Country', which resulted in one of the sailors attempting to strike him. The sailor then shouted 'God bless Germany'. The police arrived and took both sailors into custody.

While in the cell, one of the sailors requested a drink, when the constable returned with the water, the sailor told him that he had been in Boston when John Redmond was there collecting for the war. He said Redmond had collected $3,000 in three-quarters of an hour, but added that if Redmond were there now, the people would shoot him. Another incident occurred in early July when some members of the Seventh Battalion Sherwood Foresters who were stationed in Oranmore, arrived in town. After a few drinks they got into a number of arguments with several people around Eyre Square.

In one incident, a soldier walked up to a civilian and demanded to know why he was not wearing khaki. Because the man did not give a satisfactory answer, the soldier punched him in the face. The incident was reported to the police, but because the man could not identify the soldier who committed the offence, nothing could be done. Others were similarly confronted, but because the soldiers were armed, people felt intimidated and did not react to the abuse. The military were becoming anxious over such incidents, as it would have a serious effect on their continued recruiting drive. This seems to have been an isolated incident with the Foresters, as later that year they were complimented on their overall good behaviour upon leaving Galway. Although the government and the military did not wish to have any ill feelings between themselves and the people, times were certainly changing.[3]

In a letter to the editor of the *East Galway Democrat*, Professor Joseph Longford, complained bitterly of the 'incredible breaches of faith' on the part of the government, the 'tyranny' of military agents and the utter ingratitude shown for 'Irish blood' which had been shed in the war. He said that Lloyd George would do well to bear this in mind when making statements regarding Ireland. The government were championing the 'wrongs of Belgium, Serbia and Poland, while people in Ireland had to take matters into their own hands, resulting in an armed struggle during Easter 1916.

During the Easter Rising, Irish rebels occupied many of the most prominent public buildings in Dublin city and stood defiantly for the cause of Irish Independence. There were also pockets of resistance in Wexford, Cork and a large show of strength in County Galway, where at least 500 rebels came out, prepared to fight. They occupied areas around Oranmore, Athenry and Moyode and at one point made an attempt to march towards Galway City. According to one report, it was shelling by British war ships in Galway Bay that prevented this attack.

The rebellion collapsed after a week and there were hundreds of arrests, as rebels and those suspected of involvement, were rounded up. While there was little support initially for the rebellion, once its leaders had been executed public opinion changed dramatically. In July 1916, solemn high mass was celebrated in the Augustinian church, for the: 'repose of the souls of the Irishmen who lost their lives in the recent Rebellion, but more especially for the fifteen leaders from whom the extreme penalty had been extracted.' The church was packed to capacity and public sympathy was now turning in favour of the rebels.

More and more, people were beginning to voice their opposition to the war and incidents between the authorities and the public were becoming more frequent. In February 1917, three men were arrested near Oranmore for shouting slogans such as: 'To hell with England', 'Up Germany', 'To hell with King George', 'Up the Rebels', and 'Up the Kaiser'. All were charged under the defence of the realm act and convicted. In another incident, recruiting officer Capt. Stephen Gwynn, was struck with a goose egg as he tried to address people leaving Sunday morning mass at Castlegar church. The man responsible was charged with the offence as the authorities said he had brought the egg to mass with the intention of using it against the officer who was simply doing his duty.[4]

The first anniversary of the rebellion did not go off without celebration or incident. In May 1917, tricolour flags hung from buildings in Francis Street, Lombard Street, Forster Street, Nile Lodge, Raleigh Row, Lynch's Castle, St Nicholas' pro-Cathedral and O'Brien's Bridge. As soon as the authorities were informed, the police flocked onto the streets to remove the 'offending flags.' In the Claddagh, a large republican flag floated from a telegraph pole in full view of shipping in the bay. A woman who noticed it, procured a ladder and proceeded to pull down the flag with the aid of a boat hook, amid the almost deafening sarcastic cheers from the crowd that had gathered.

A large number of police arrived, but simply watched proceedings with amused interest as the crowd although supportive of the flag, were not hostile. As the woman reached the safety of the ground, the flag was grabbed from her and carried in triumph around the town by a youth followed by cheering women. Later, the flag was returned to the Claddagh, where it was erected on the roof of a house. Again the woman ascended a ladder and proceeded to remove the flag, but while she was engaged in this activity, the ladder was taken away, leaving her stranded on the roof to the amusement of the crowd. She had to remain there until she was rescued sometime later. That night a bonfire was lit in the Small Crane and decorated Sinn Féin banners spanned the roadway. The British red, white and blue banners were equally prominent at Spanish Parade. There were a number of minor scuffles between both sides, with most of the hostilities occurring between the womenfolk. The following morning a procession of women passed through the streets carrying Union Jacks to show their support for the men at the front.

The anniversary of the rebellion resulted in similar scenes throughout the county with republican flags inscribed with slogans such as 'In Memory of the Dead 1916' appearing. Such flags were displayed in Barna, Gort, Ardrahan, Kinvara and in many other towns. In Shantalla, an 'Anti-British Dog' was sentenced to death, following attacks made on Sgt McGlynn who was cycling through the area. The owner of the dog, Timothy Molloy, made no attempt to stop the animal as he attacked the sergeant, while on his journey, both to and from the area.[5]

By July 1917, those in opposition to the war were getting more daring and in some cases, protesters were turning up outside urban council meetings when recruiting was on the agenda. At one such meeting, chaired by Martin McDonogh, a number of young men gathered outside the building. As soon as the committee members made their appearance, someone shouted 'Up de Valera,' while abusive name-calling was directed at Joseph Young. Worse was to follow with the meetings themselves being disrupted. One such example occurred at a Royal Air Force recruiting lecture which was held in the town hall on 1 October 1918.

This meeting created much hostility and resentment among protesters, many of whom had obviously attended with the purpose of disrupting the event. The talk was delivered by Capt. Alston of the Royal Air Force, on

Capt. Alston

ROYAL AIR FORCE,

WILL

Lecture

ON

His Experiences in the Air

ILLUSTRATED BY LANTERN SLIDES,

AT THE

Town Hall, Galway

ON

Tuesday, October 1

AT 8.30 P M

ADMISSION FREE

Captain Alston Lecture advertisement, dated 28 September 1918.

(*The Connacht Tribune*)

the subject of his experiences in aerial combat, and was illustrated with lantern-slides. A party of Sinn Féin members proceeded to the town hall and shortly after taking their seats, stood up again and began singing 'The Soldier's Song,' much to the annoyance of the organisers. When the band of the Connaught Rangers entered the hall there was a great applause from the majority of the crowd.

The Sinn Féin members at last sat down, but then began booing. The band played a number of popular tunes, during which there were shouts of 'Up Redmond', 'Up King George', with the odd shout 'Up de Valera'. When the band finished playing, the Sinn Féiners began singing songs in defiance. The military ignored them and took their seats on stage accompanied by Capt. Alston. Martin McDonogh who was presiding over the lecture began to address the audience, but was immediately shouted down by one section of the crowd, and the uproar continued for about fifteen minutes.

When the shouting stopped, Capt. Alston took centre stage and began his address. It was received with a mixture of applause and hisses. He was then subjected to physical abuse, when potatoes, onions and 'empty' packets of cigarettes were thrown at him. The people on stage appealed for calm and asked the protesters to give the speaker a chance to talk. Capt. Alston made another attempt, but as he began to speak, he was again interrupted. Soon a party of policemen arrived and lined up in front of the demonstrators.

Those in favour of the talk also stood with the police, and the authorities removed one individual who continued to disrupt proceedings. His colleagues also left the premises but continued their demonstration outside, throwing missiles at the windows to the sound of high-pitched shouts of protest and singing. Nevertheless, the lecture went ahead with the approval of almost ninety per cent of the audience.

Meanwhile more demonstrators were beginning to gather outside the building. The police soon became targets for the demonstrators, who began throwing stones, mud and other missiles at them. Reinforcements arrived and a baton charge was organised which left a number on both sides injured. The crowd was forced to flee towards the police barracks in Eglinton Street.

As they were running past the building, a number of stones were hurled at the barracks breaking some windows. The police inside reacted immediately and appeared on the street armed with rifles. They were soon joined by the military from Renmore Barracks and order was restored in the streets.[6]

By 1918, those arrested in the aftermath of the Easter Rebellion had been released from prison and most had returned home. This was a major boost to the Sinn Féin movement and the Irish Republican Army as many of them became involved with these organisations. With the growth of such movements, the seeds for an independent Ireland were well and truly sown. Some of the soldiers returning from the war in Europe also joined the IRA.

An example of this was John Joe Leonard from Prospect Hill, who had served with the Black Watch, and was severely wounded at the battle of the Somme. Upon his return to Ireland in 1917, he joined Sinn Féin and later the IRA; becoming one of the ten most wanted men in the country. Such men made welcome additions to the republican movement, as they were already well-trained soldiers. The increased nationalist manpower was also a major contributing factor to the growing opposition to the war.[7]

CHAPTER VI

FUEL TO THE FIRE
SUSPICIONS & RUMOURS

Shortly after war was announced, strangers in Galway City and County were viewed with suspicion. Rumours of a German invasion were also circulating, particularly along the west coast and people felt threatened by such gossip. Reports of people suspected of spying were appearing in the newspapers regularly, adding 'fuel to the fire.' While these reports proved to be unfounded, people were still worried that at some stage they would become a reality.

One incident took place in August 1914 near Cleggan, where a man was arrested on suspicion of being a German spy. Locals later said it was his foreign appearance that attracted the attention of the police, however, it turned out he was an American journalist. In Galway City a week later, two men were stopped in separate incidents. The first man was observed at the end of Nimmo's pier painting the landscape. He was promptly arrested as a spy, but released a short time later, when he was able to prove that he was an artist from Dublin and had no German connections.

The second incident occurred in William Street, when a constable in plain clothes, stopped a suspicious looking motorcyclist. After the man had convinced the policeman of his innocence, he was allowed to continue on his journey. On 19 September 1914, *The Galway Express* reported that there were a number of 'German-Irish' spies hovering around Galway. It was suggested that any persons found undermining British interests, should have their 'venom' permanently extracted. There was no time for sentiment as they were fighting to the 'death'.[1]

On 14 November 1914, reports of German troops landing along the west coast were circulated at a fair held in Galway City. A number of Aran men attending the fair said they heard the sound of artillery fire coming from the Clifden direction on the previous night. Although they were of the opinion that the Germans had indeed landed, it obviously did not deter them from attending the fair. Similar telephone messages were also received from several towns and villages along the coast.

Although it was later confirmed that three British battleships were responsible for the rumours, it did not alleviate the fear of invasion. In a separate incident, the people living around Maam reported hearing the sound of aeroplanes flying over the area. Their concerns were later put to rest, when they were assured that they were English planes patrolling the coastline. At a Galway harbour board meeting in December 1914, Joseph Young proposed a vote of sympathy for the victims of German Zeppelin raids on England. He added that the threat of attacks on Galway were very real and should be taken seriously. The raids over England continued with incendiary bombs being dropped in various parts of the country.

These reports were of course exploited by the 'scaremongers'. In January 1915, the Galway police were warned to: 'hold themselves in readiness' in the event of German troops landing along the coast. They were also told to warn all non-combatants to move inland in the event of such an attack. It seems that the people of Tuam and other outlying areas were warned first, which caused some resentment in the city, as they were living closer to the danger. People were obviously worried, and there was a certain degree of paranoia among the locals. An example of this occurred in the Claddagh in January 1915. Although humorous, it gives some idea of the unrest. A woman was suddenly awakened during the night by an 'almighty crash' and in panic she called out to her daughter: 'Get up quick, Mary, the Germans have dropped a bomb on us.' Upon investigation, it was discovered that the cat had knocked a jug of milk off the dresser.[2]

In January 1915, the British Admiralty decided to establish a naval base at Galway for coastal boats and mine sweepers. Initially, there was an air of secrecy about the scheme, but soon people were talking about the potential base. Some people were concerned about such a development, as they felt their town would then pose a worthwhile target for the Germans. When Lieut Holmes of the Royal Navy arrived in Galway for a visit, he was questioned by reporters regarding the issue, but would neither confirm or deny the reports.

Nevertheless, the plans went ahead and Galway became one of six Royal Naval bases set up throughout Ireland. Various British war ships were already appearing in Galway Bay, and to add to the excitement, *HMS Saxon* and *HMS Guillemot* arrived in Galway docks during the first week of February 1915.

The patrol vessels also brought business to the town; Griffin's Bakery secured a major contract to supply bread to the entire patrol fleet off the west coast. The patrol boats were required as there was a real threat to shipping off the coast, and because of rumours regarding the enemy making contact with people in remote areas of the coast. It was reported that large containers of petrol had been discovered after being hidden at various points along the coast for use by German submarines. It had been suspected for some time, but it was only when these discoveries were made that the reports were taken seriously. British patrol boats were also visiting a number of islands off the west coast, where they believed that trade in petrol and poitín was being carried out between the locals and the Germans.[3]

Negative rumours of how the war was going were also prevalent about the town and were taken very seriously by the authorities. Indulging in, and spreading such rumours carried a substantial fine and a jail term. Local postman, John Burke, became the first man in the west of Ireland to be charged under the defence of the realm act for: 'unlawfully spreading false rumours in relation to His Majesty's ships which was likely to cause alarm to members of His Majesty's subjects', particularly around the Claddagh, as this community had so many men serving in the navy. It seems that on 22 January 1915 during his postal delivery round, the postman told several people, including a police constable that a number of British ships had been sunk by the Germans. The authorities felt that only people with pro-German tendencies would spread such malicious rumours, and so the postman was arrested and charged. In his own defence, he said that he had simply heard these rumours while on his way to work earlier that morning, but admitted he had been indulging in a bit of 'gossiping'. His defence told the court the original source of the rumour could not be traced, especially in Galway where rumours were rampant. In passing sentence the judge said that because there was no evil intent on the part of Burke, he would not be sent to jail, but instead was ordered to pay a fine of £1, plus costs.

The German admiralty announced that from 18 February 1915 the waters around the Irish coast were being included in the military area and that all merchant ships of the allies would be destroyed irrespective of the danger to their crews. This caused concern in Galway as many of the merchant seamen were from the city area and of course the Claddagh.

To give some degree of assurance to the people, the British admiralty revealed they would have six heavily armoured vessels patrolling the sea around Galway Bay within weeks. The purpose of these would be to support the smaller ships already engaged in such exercises. In April 1915, the Germans announced that their submarines were laying mines around the coasts of England, Ireland and Scotland.

The first known encounter around Galway occurred almost immediately when a number of Aran men making their way to Inishmaan in a currach, struck a mine with an oar. Fortunately, it did not explode, but it was proof of the very real danger that was facing Galway. A short time later, there were reports of a German submarine making its way towards Galway. One of the Royal Navy ships left the harbour to confront the enemy, a short time later gunfire was heard off the coast, and the submarine disappeared out to sea. These statements and actions by the Germans removed any sense of security and isolation felt in Galway during the war.[5]

In March 1916, it was reported that a German invasion was imminent, as Ireland and more importantly Irish ports, were vital to the German war effort. From these strategic locations, the Germans could control with ease any merchant shipping coming from the United States to England. Thus, cutting off supplies and bringing the British to their knees.

It was believed the Germans had already prepared elaborate plans for the 'invasion, conquest and occupation' of Ireland. The authorities

GROW MORE

FOOD!

Do more than your Tenth !

You will not lose ! and Your country will gain!

EVERY man of good will has already ploughed or arranged to plough the extra tenth required of him.

But all the food that can be grown will be needed.

Grow more than your tenth, if it takes you night and day to do it.

Remember the man who has no land; remember the poor in the towns and cities who depend on you.

Don't mind the slacker.

Do your own part well

If the food supply is short of the need, no man who failed to do his best will be happy.

Grow more than your Tenth !

Advertisement appealing for people to grow more crops, dated 10 March 1917 (*The Connacht Tribune*) reported that some years earlier, the German fleet had visited Ireland and taken soundings, photographs, and made plans and drawings of many Irish ports, particularly the ones around the west coast. It was announced that German naval officers had been continually visiting Ireland in the guise of tourists and that the country was teeming with German spies. The authorities were becoming increasingly worried about up-to-date plans and drawings that might have been already made of western ports.

Under Regulation 19 of the defence of the realm act no person had the authority to record in any manner the navy and military bases, docks or harbours around the country. People were warned of the serious consequences of any infringement of this act. Such reports certainly helped fuel rumours of the Germans landing to support the 1916 Rebellion.

On Easter Monday morning, a young worker in Oranmore informed his employer that he was leaving to join the 'boys'. When questioned as to why he was joining the rebels, considering he had two brothers fighting in France, he replied by saying that eight thousand Germans had landed in Clifden. He added that he was going to join them and march on Belfast: 'to do away with the Orangemen.' However, this young man never got to march on Belfast, as he was serving time in Galway jail within twenty-four hours. In an attempt to keep people away from the coast, the military authorities even placed an embargo on excursion tickets to Salthill, much to the disapproval of the local business community.[6]

The threat of invasion was not the only enemy posing a menace to Ireland. As the war dragged on, there were reports that the country could face food shortages and detailed the misery that would result from such an occurrence. The Great Famine of the 1840s was still within living memory, and whilst most people did not believe that such a catastrophe could re-occur, they were still worried about food shortages. By 1917, the need for local food production became essential in order to avoid the danger of privation. The government acknowledged this danger and the department of agriculture took special steps to alleviate the threat. Many areas of Ireland were supplied with seed, manure and implements for extra tillage.

The government were also making special loans available for the purchase of such commodities through the rural and urban district councils. People who owned ten or more acres of land were required to cultivate one tenth more arable land than they had done the previous year. Advertisements and reports were published in national and local newspapers advising people of the dangers ahead and ways of avoiding hardship. Compulsory rationing was also on the agenda and with the announcement of a 'world shortage of cereals' there was a warning that unless the consumption of food produced from wheat was reduced, drastic measures would have to be taken. Suggestions were put forward on how to reduce the consumption of bread, meat and tea by increasing the production of other home-grown foods such as potatoes and various types of vegetables through the development of garden allotments.[7]

The Urban Council Land Cultivation Committee was established and acquired forty-eight acres of land around the city area in order to develop about 300 allotments. It was reported shortly afterwards that Galway City was surrounded with garden allotments, which could produce a rich harvest for the 'needy' in the days ahead. Many people in the town became almost self-sufficient using their newly developed skills. As sundown approached it became a familiar sight to see men, women, and even children working away in their allotments. It was also a place where many of the rumours originated, and were spread, as passers-by stopped to say 'God Bless the Work'. People from every walk of life, policemen, shopkeepers, traders, clerks, mechanics, and tradesmen were involved in this industrious work. Allotments were established in Woodquay (Plots), Dyke Road, College Road, Shea's Field at Shantalla, Munster Lane, Salthill Park, and fields close to South Park were also cultivated for such use. Sections of University College Galway and Galway Golf Club along with some other areas were also utilised for this purpose. It was hoped that with proper management, these allotments would produce a thousand tons of food per year. The results were exceptional and people benefited greatly from them. The success of the allotments was such that this type the cultivation continued for many years after the war.[8]

CHAPTER VII

MESSAGE IN A BOTTLE
GALWAY SEA WAR

Because of their close proximity and association with the ocean it was inevitable that Galwegians would be lost to the sea, particularly during war. By April 1915, the situation was becoming alarming, with an announcement that 104 British merchant vessels had already been lost to the enemy. The following are examples of sea tragedies that affected Galway during the Great War.

In March 1915 the *SS Atlanta*, left Galway, bound for Glasgow. When the ship reached the island of Inishturk, a submarine was sighted in the distance. The submarine sent up three rocket signals and the ship halted, unsure of the identity of the other vessel. As it approached, marine gunners William Gunn and Michael Kilgannon of the *Atlanta* observed the German ensign and immediately opened fire on the submarine. The submarine returned fire sending two shells in the direction of the ship before submerging. After a few minutes it resurfaced and again began firing at the *Atlanta*, wounding Kilgannon. The Germans pressed home the attack and as they closed on the stricken vessel, the crew were ordered to abandon ship. The ship was then set alight and drifted towards Cleggan while her sixteen-man crew headed for Inishturk in the lifeboats. Upon reaching Inishturk, they were then taken to Clifden and from there were brought to Galway by train. The crew were given accommodation in the Skeffington Arms Hotel, Eyre Square. Incidentally, the *Atlanta* did not sink and was later towed into Cleggan Harbour.

This was the first recorded enemy attack off the west coast and the furthest recorded distance of a German submarine from its home base. Two months later in May 1915, the *SS Fulgent* with its cargo of coal left Cardiff for the Orkney Islands, never to complete its journey. It encountered a hostile German submarine and suffered the consequences. Some of the crew who survived the initial attack also had to endure fifty-one hours adrift in a life-boat, until a steamer, the SS *Tosto*, came to their rescue and landed the survivors safely in Galway. The manager at the port, Mr Witcher, made them welcome and gave them accommodation in the Seaman's Memorial Home at New Docks. Witcher later joined the forces and served on the western front. The Seaman's Memorial Home continued to accommodate many fortunate sailors rescued from torpedoed ships throughout the war years.[1]

On 7 May 1915, a German torpedo struck the ocean liner *Lusitania*. One witness recalled: 'as strollers gathered on deck after lunch to watch the approaching green fields of Ireland, disaster struck'. It had been a pleasant uneventful crossing from New York and the ship was just passing the old Head of Kinsale, when it came under attack. The *Lusitania* went beneath the waves within eighteen minutes, taking with her 1,198 lives, among them 128 Americans.

In Galway City, people mourned for Maggie L. Boyd who lost her life on board the ill-fated liner. Another Galway woman who went down with the ship was Bessie Hare from Tuam, she was on her way home to visit her mother having spent eleven years in the United States. Mary Kelly from Kinvara was also lost to the sea, while her prospective husband awaited her arrival at Queenstown.

Another victim connected with Galway was Sir Hugh Lane, honorary director of the Dublin Municipal Art Gallery. His mother was a member of the Persse family of Roxborough and the news was received as a personal blow to Galway. Two other victims of the *Lusitania* were buried in Killeaney cemetery on the Aran Islands. However, it was later decided to have the bodies exhumed and reburied in a more 'appropriate' place, as the denomination of these unfortunate victims was unknown.

On 19 May, the body of another female victim arrived in Galway docks having been picked up by a trawler. A number of baby items were found with the remains and according to the reports, it was evident from the position of her arms, that the woman had died while clutching a baby.

Following the tragedy, the flags of the harbour board were flown at half-mast as a mark of respect. There were also calls for Galway to be developed as a much larger port, capable of accommodating ocean liners, as it was felt that Galway was unrivalled as a potential harbour and could be protected from the Aran Islands. It was also the shortest route from America.[2]

On 13 August 1915, the SS Royal Edward was sunk by a German submarine, with terrible loss of life. Corp. R. Mackensie, a former manager of the Galway Granite Works, wrote the following very graphic description of the sinking ship. He wrote the letter to his friend, Mr E. Wallace, manager of the Galway Woollen Mills. It gives some idea of the horrors on board a stricken vessel in its last moments:

Doubtless you have by this time read the fate of the transport, Royal Edward, on the 13th inst (unlucky thirteen!). She was torpedoed and sunk when within a few hours sail of her destination. I was one of the passengers, and one of those lucky enough to escape. It was a most terrible experience. To think of all these poor fellows! – I imagine now that I see them all on deck just as they were, at one moment in the best of spirits and within five minutes afterwards a thousand of them gone to the bottom, without being given the slightest chance to defend themselves. Could we have seen the perpetrators, we should have seen them viewing their handiwork and dancing with joy. The whole thing was over in such a short time that one had scarce time to realise it. Although the lifeboats were swung clear ready for lowering at a moment's notice should anything happen there was not even time for the crew to get up on deck and loosen the ropes. Only about three of the lifeboats got clear, while eight of the unsinkable boats, which lie on the deck and are not tied down, floated off.

I got overboard and swam clear of the ship as soon as she was struck, not even taking time to get a lifebelt; and I got a fine view of the Royal Edward as she was going down. It was awful to see that mighty ship standing, as it were, on end, and then plunging stern first to the bottom amidst the roar of bursting boilers, etc. There was not even a wireless message sent out, although we had the installation, but as luck would have it another ship laden with troops was within sight, and she sent out the message being unable to come to the rescue herself for fear of sharing the same fate. The message was picked up by a hospital ship, which arrived on the scene about two hours afterwards. After my first half-hour in the water, I got into a boat, but it was not seaworthy and sank before long. I had just time to get off all my clothes though, and I then felt quite at ease, as I could, with the assistance of bits of floating wreckage, keep above the surface for hours. When I saw the hospital ship coming in sight, I got off and swam towards her, getting aboard shortly after noon, having been in the water since 9.15 a.m. The hospital ship was making for Alexandria, with a load of wounded, so we, about 500 of us, were taken back to port. We have had a good fortnight's rest now, and expect to go off on another attempt to reach the firing line to-morrow. I hope there are no more torpedoes for us. There were about 400 K.O.S.Bs. on board, of which about 40 were left. But some detachments suffered more. In my own section of twenty-five men – fellows who have enlisted and been training along with me – only six remain.[3]

On 29 February 1916, the British auxiliary cruiser, *HMS Alcantara*, was sunk in combat with a German ship, which was masquerading as a merchant ship and flying the Norwegian flag. When the captain of the *Alcantara* sighted the disguised German ship, he became suspicious and sent a small craft out to investigate. As soon as it drew close, the suspicious looking vessel dropped its bulwarks and immediately revealed its true nature, with guns of various calibre opening fire on the small boat sending it to the bottom of the sea in minutes. The *Alcantara* engaged the German ship immediately, inflicting severe damage and sent it to a watery grave, but not before the Germans managed to return fire resulting in the British ship also being sunk. Four of the crew were from Galway, they jumped over-board and were later rescued and taken home. They were Martin O'Donnell and Stephen Curran from the Claddagh and Colman Flaherty and Martin Walsh from Long Walk.

There were a number of other attacks on shipping off the Irish coast in 1916, with many of the survivors being taken to Galway. In March 1917, two ships, the *Dunbar Moor* and a Norwegian ship the *Silas*, were sunk within days of each other. The crew of the *Dunbar Moor* managed to get into lifeboats before the ship went down. They drifted for four days with meagre rations, until they were picked up by a passing ship and taken to Galway. However, the skipper, Capt. Collins had already died of exposure. He was buried in the New Cemetery following a funeral service at St Nicholas' Collegiate Church at which a band played the 'Flowers of the Forest'. The crew of the *Silas* were also taken to Galway after being rescued, it seems the Germans had given them time to abandon ship, before sending it to the bottom of the sea.4

In June 1917, it was reported that German submarines were destroying Irish fishing fleets from Kenmare to Howth and boasted that they could sink all Irish fishing boats in a month. Although this was not accomplished, many vessels did in fact end up at the bottom of the sea because of submarine attacks, and some because of mines. One such tragedy took place near Inverin on Friday, 15 June 1917. On that day two local fishermen, Patrick Folan and Edward McDermott, were fishing from a currach when they spotted an object in the water some distance from the shore. It resembled a barrel with irons protruding from it. Not realising it was a mine, they attached a rope to the object and towed it to within four or five feet of the shore. Patrick Folan then went to inform the police of its presence, during which time the tide turned leaving the mine stranded on the beach.

A group of local men who had observed what was happening decided to investigate. McDermott asked them to help him roll the mine up the beach towards the headland. As they rolled the object up along the beach a number of the men became somewhat nervous and began to run away from the area, but it was too late, the mine exploded with devastating consequences. Nine men were killed, they included Peter Folan, Tim Keady, Thomas Hopkins, Joe Flaherty, Coleman Feeney, Edward McDermott, Manus Flaherty, Edward Lee and Pat Lee. The explosion was heard in Galway and the carnage was horrific with portions of human remains being found up to sixty yards away. Three people, Lord Killanin, the local doctor and priest, were quickly on the scene to try to comfort the weeping women. Some of them were in a hysterical condition, after witnessing the sight of blackened flesh and human remains that lay strewn across the beach. An inquest was held the following day and the question arose was it a German or British mine? It was never adequately answered, but the feeling was that it was German. In June 1970, a memorial to the nine victims was unveiled at the beach in Inverin. Relatives of the victims attended as did the only survivor, Joe Flaherty.[5]

Another tragedy involving a mine occurred on 17 December 1917 when a party of four fishermen and a boy left Galway on board the fishing trawler, *Neptune*. The crew included Martin McDonagh, Buttermilk Lane, William Walsh, Quay Street and his sixteen year old son Patrick, Bartly Gill also of Quay Street and Stephen Melia, Church Lane. The forty-five ton trawler was described as one of the finest in the Claddagh Fleet and was owned by Martin Ashe. Before the trawler left port, the skipper, Henry Connell, an experienced sailor, refused to take the boat out because of a suspected problem with the vessel.

FISHERMEN.

GERMAN SUBMARINES have attacked and sunk Irish Fishing Vessels and murdered Irish Fishermen. Many hundreds of Irishmen have recently joined up to avenge these crimes against their fellow countrymen—Join the Trawler Section of the Royal Navy and show that you remember the victims of these outrages belonging to

Carna, Howth, Annalong, Kilkeel and Portavoghie.

There are still vacancies for Men with sea experience. GOOD PAY, FREE KIT, SEPARATION ALLOWANCE, all found. Do not delay. Join your Comrades already serving. Apply to any of the Irish Recruiting Offices. Naval Recruiting Offices, Coastguard Stations, and to—

LIEUT. A. F. SPRY, R.N V.R.,

R N.R. RECRUITING HEADQUARTERS,

98, AMIENS STREET, DUBLIN.

Also, to the Customs House, Limerick, Galway, Waterford.

Fishermen warned of German submarine attacks, 28 September 1918.

(*The Connacht Tribune*)

Nevertheless, it went to sea. By 2 p.m. they were fishing some three miles off the Spiddal coast, when a mine became entangled in the trawler's net. The crew were unaware of the danger lurking beneath the waves and continued operations, believing that the additional weight was a piece of old wreckage. The crew continued to fish for another hour by which time they were approximately a mile off the Spiddal coastline. They then proceeded to raise the net. When the mine came in contact with the trawler, it exploded with devastating consequences. The force of the explosion shattered the trawler, splitting it in two and hurling the crew into the sea. *The Neptune* sank within four minutes. At the time of the explosion, a naval motor launch was patrolling the sea about five miles off the coast, and on hearing the explosion, dashed to the scene immediately.

Upon reaching the area, they found Martin McDonagh clinging to a piece of wreckage. A dinghy was lowered and he was rescued while Stephen Melia, who was also supported by wreckage was pulled to safety by a trawler that had also come to their aid. Martin McDonagh was placed in the officer's quarters of the launch, but despite the best efforts of the crew to save him, he died about thirty minutes later. The trawler searched in vain for the other fishermen, but was forced to abandon the search with the onset of darkness.

News of the tragedy reached Galway when the motor launch arrived that evening with the remains of Martin McDonagh. Painful and pitiful scenes were witnessed as family and friends of the ill-fated crewmen began gathering at the quayside to meet the rescue trawler, which was carrying the only survivor, Stephen Melia. Again there was a question over who was responsible for the mine. During the inquest, held the following week, the British naval representative, Commander Hanan stated that there were no British mines laid in, or near Galway Bay, therefore, the mine was undoubtedly of German origin. By March 1918, the Galway Bay Mine Disaster Fund was set up. [6]

A man named Laurie Curtis whose ship was torpedoed by a German submarine on 30 May 1918 wrote the following notes. The attack took place some 300 to 400 miles off the Irish coast. Along with a number of other seamen, he managed to survive the initial attack and escaped in a lifeboat. However, there was not enough drinking water to sustain them on their journey to find land. It is not known how they met their deaths, but it was believed that sometime after they had exhausted their supply of fresh water, a severe storm destroyed or capsized their boat resulting in the men being thrown into the sea.

There was a storm recorded for 16 June 1918, which could account for the tragedy. No one will ever know exactly what happened, but what is certain is that there were no survivors. The body of Laurie Curtis was washed up on the beach near Carna sometime later and was discovered on 21 June 1918. Two young men, named Kelly and Conneelly, who were walking along the beach that evening, found his remains. They noticed that attached to his lifejacket, was a crucifix and a bottle containing the very poignant notes included below. They were written on two small postcards:

(1) At Sea, 6th June 1918.

My Dear Wife – The – was torpedoed last Thursday evening at 5 p.m. over 300 miles from Ireland. The escort had left two days before and I managed to get away on a boat, but there was no navigator, only a compass and a couple of seamen. Our water (drinking) is now getting very low, also our spirits seem dead and the thirst is damnable so I am writing the last good-bye in the hope that it may be picked up and sent to you. Much love to you and my pets, also my mother – from your poor broken-hearted

Laurie XXX

Will the finder of this card kindly forward to the address on the other side, Mrs. Curtis, 8 Thomfield Road, Orrell Park, Liverpool, England.

(2) Good-bye mother dear, pets and all, God is love. If this falls into the hands of any kindly person please send it to my wife at 8 Thomfield Road, Orrell Park, Liverpool, England. Dear Elie – The – was sunk by a submarine on May 30, 300 or 400 miles from Ireland. I got away safely in a small boat, but unfortunately got lost and have

been drifting for seven days, and cannot find the land, so in case you don't see me again this is my last good-bye, dear, to you and my children – Your loving husband, Laurie.

(3) Last drop of water gone, all hands dying with thirst

– Laurie XXX.

In June 1918, a German submarine off the west coast sank the fishing boat, *Pretty Polly*. According to one report, the German vessel approached the helpless fishing boat and upon reaching it, placed a bomb on board. After a few minutes the bomb exploded killing some of the fishermen, those who escaped the explosion were left to drown in the sea. Among the seven victims was the owner of the boat Thomas Canavan, and his two sons. All the fishermen were from the Carna area. The Carna Disaster Fund was set up and received very generous support from businesses and individuals from Galway City and county and various parts of Ireland.

A number of fundraising events were held in the city and while all this was going on, malicious rumours about the unfortunate fishermen were circulating throughout the county. It was alleged that the fishermen who had supposedly lost their lives, were actually in Germany, safe and well, having been rescued by the enemy sailors. *The Galway Express* newspaper referred to the story, but this was immediately challenged by a reporter from *The Connacht Tribune* who called it an 'absurd lie'. Fr M. McHugh, Parish Priest of Carna was also furious and contradicted the allegations. He said that it was German sympathisers who were 'industriously' spreading these stories. According to one of the rumours, Michael Hurney of Claddagh Parade had a brother, who was a prisoner of war in Germany. He had allegedly written to Michael informing him he had seen the crew of the *Pretty Polly* in Germany and that they were all well. However, when Michael Hurney was approached and questioned about the story, he was completely surprised and replied that he never received such a letter, adding that he had no brother or indeed relative in any German prisoner of war camp.[8]

On 10 October 1918, the *SS Leinster* set out from Dun Laoghaire under the command of Capt. William Biech. It was one of four large ferries (*Ulster, Munster* and *Connaught*) which operated between Dun Laoghaire and Holyhead. Despite the dangers from German submarines frequently sighted in the area, the ferries travelled without military escort. *The Leinster* had carried thousands of military personnel and civilians across the Irish Sea during those years.

On that fateful day there were 771 passengers and crew on board, including about 300 soldiers on their way to the western front. Approximately sixteen miles out to sea the first of three German torpedoes was fired at the ferry from submarine *UB-123*, which was under the command of twenty-seven year old Robert Ramm. The first torpedo missed its target, but the second one struck the port bow area. The struggling vessel was then hit by another torpedo close to the engine room on the starboard side. The result was devastating with the ship sinking in minutes, causing the deaths of 501 men, women and children.

There were a number of Galway people lost when the ship went down including Nurse Sophie Barrett, Ballintava, Helen Jameson, Menlough, Joseph Robinson, Killimore, Henrietta Kirwan, Tuam, Nora Kirwan, Spiddal, Sir William Henry Thomson, Pte John Loughlin, Ballinasloe, Pte John Coyne, J. Shaw Jones, Pte Martin Flaherty (Irish Guards) and Elizabeth Ellam, great-grandmother of Ronnie O'Gorman, (Galway Advertiser). There were also a number of Galway people among the survivors. One of them, Martin Flaherty, a sailor with the Royal Navy, saved the life of Mrs Plunkett, the wife of one of the officers. He heard shouts of alarm from the officer as his wife was being swept into the sea. Flaherty grabbed the woman as she was being carried away and managed to remove his own lifebelt and secure it on the woman. He then fastened her to a raft from which she was later rescued. Another survivor, Able Seaman Folan of Quay Street, was returning to Liverpool to take up his post with the Royal Naval Reserve when the Germans struck. Having been rescued he was taken to Kingstown where his son John awaited him. He was then removed to hospital in Renmore where he recorded his experiences:

MEN OF GALWAY

Aven~e the loss of your 500 countrymen, women and children cruelly murdered by the Huns, in the Sinking of the " Leinster," on Thursday, October 1Oth, 1918.

Show your disapproval by immediately joining the Navy, Army or Air Force.

Full Particulars at

THE RECRUITING OFFICE,

Bishops' Court,

GALWAY.

Galwaymen asked to avenge the sinking of the SS Leinster, 12 October 1918.

(*The Connacht Tribune*)

I was down below when the first torpedo came. I immediately came up on deck to see the people rushing around on all sides. I asked my mate, Langely, to wait a bit; and we sat down and took our boots and collars off. Langely went looking for a lifeboat, as he could not swim, while I waited for a raft. They were trying to lower the port lifeboat at the time. There was a big crowd of people, and the weight jammed the fall, so they could not lower it any further. The Leinster swung around after being hit, and blew her siren, and the crowd on board thinking it was a cruiser coming to the rescue, cheered, but a few moments afterwards they saw the mistake. My pal jumped for a boat; just then a woman handed me a child, saying, 'Save it for me if you can.' I said, I cannot save it now, as there is no boat. I saw a man trying to get into a boat that was already crowded. I asked him to ask them to make room for the child, and put it in. I looked around but the mother was gone, and a lot of people had been knocked down against the side of the ship with the second explosion, and the boilers, funnels, and masts had come up. Many of the people were thrown into the sea from the roll. I jumped for it, and clung on to a raft, which was taken under with me; by the time I came up again the ship was gone. Everything was gone but pieces of wreckage, and dead and struggling bodies floating everywhere around. There was nobody with me when I got hold of the raft, but when I came up to the top again the raft came up under seven men. There were eight of us on it for a time, but only three others and myself were able to cling on. Four of them were washed off and drowned, or died from exhaustion. The raft was not riding well to the heavy sea, and these men, as they would get cold and stiff, kept altering their positions. I told them to keep a hold of the little grey home, and when land hove in sight I sung it out to all on the raft, and to any who were floating near, in order to give them courage, and the cry was taken up by other sailors. After over two hours we were picked up and landed in Kingstown. The sights we saw were beyond description.[9]

A few days later, the funerals of two other Galway victims of the *Leinster* took place amid touching scenes in the town. They were Capt. Edward (Ned) Milne DMC of the Canadian Expeditionary Force and Claire McNally, daughter of Major McNally of the Connaught Rangers. Although not a native of Galway, Capt. Milne was viewed by all who knew him as a Galwegian. Born in Montrose, Scotland in February 1888, the family moved to Galway when he was six years old. He was educated at the Model School and later the Grammar School. He joined the staff of *The Galway Express* as a journalist, and in 1908 left Ireland for Canada where he worked on a farm for some years before joining the army. Both Capt. Milne and Claire McNally shared the same solemn requiem funeral mass held in the pro-Cathedral which was presided over by Dr O'Dea, bishop of Galway. The church was packed to capacity and following the mass, the funerals of both victims proceeded through crowded streets to the New Cemetery in Bohermore.

Former colleagues of Capt. Milne from *The Galway Express* offices attended and the boys of the grammar school marched in military formation. Capt. Milne had been wounded in action a number of times during the war and on this occasion was at home in Galway, recuperating and spending some time with his wife. Milne was returning to a London hospital when disaster struck. Officers and the band of the Connaught Rangers, as well as members of the Surrey Yeomanry also accompanied the funerals which were met by a military firing party at the graveside of Capt. Milne. He was later posthumously awarded the Military Cross for the courage he displayed at Amiens on 8 August 1918, when, despite being severely wounded, he still managed to carry out his objective with exceptional bravery. The ceremony took place in Renmore Barracks where the commander, Col Chamier, pinned the Military Cross on Capt. Milne's infant son while the troops formed a guard of honour.[10]

Following the tragedy Galway Urban Council expressed their condolences to all the families of the deceased, saying it was the worst disaster since the sinking of the *Lusitania*. All the allied countries condemned the atrocity. Cardinal Logue came out in the strongest possible terms, castigating Germany for their unprovoked barbarity and callous disregard for innocent people. He also warned people not to listen to the 'diabolic agents', who do Germany's dirty work for them in Ireland by spreading sinister rumours that German torpedoes were not responsible for the loss of the *Leinster*.

The sinking of the *Leinster* had a profound effect on Ireland, and the recruiting campaigners in Galway certainly lost no time in exploiting the atrocity as can be seen by the accompanying poster. It also triggered the setting up of the 'Mansion House "*Leinster*" Fund,' to raise finance for the bereaved families. In Galway, a hugely successful concert was organised by Mrs Hanan, wife of Commander Hanan of the Royal Navy. The concert opened in early December with a performance by the band of the Connaught Rangers which was followed by many of the top local entertainers performing to a packed hall. Incidentally, the German submarine which sank the *SS Leinster* struck a mine in the North Sea while returning to Germany on 19 October 1918. There were no survivors of the thirty-five-man crew, all of whom, with the exception of the commander, were between the ages of nineteen and twenty-five. The sinking of the *SS Leinster* was the last sea tragedy to affect Galway during the war.[1]

CHAPTER VIII

IT'S AN ILL WIND
GALWAY WAR INDUSTRY

With the male population of the town diminishing many of the women began filling the vacant positions in the workplace. Although the Galway Woollen Mills at Newtownsmith had been providing much needed employment for many years, it had struggled to stay open before the war. However, business changed immediately with the announcement of war. In September 1914, the War Office placed a large order with the mill for khaki uniforms. All concerned welcomed the additional work, as this was the first of many orders that provided continued employment in the town. The mill stood on the site which is now occupied by the Convent of Mercy Secondary School. The working hours were long, from 6 a.m. to 6 p.m., with two breaks, one in the morning and one in the afternoon.

After only five months, the shareholders, who were now reaping the rewards of their investments, quoted the time worn proverb 'It's an ill wind that does not blow someone some good'. By early 1915, the company was in a position to purchase additional machinery, and the workforce also increased in order to meet the demand. Record profits were announced, and the workers benefited from the military orders. In September 1915 as the male population continued to diminish a meeting was held in the Cinema Theatre, William Street under the auspices of the Galway Women's Suffrage Society. The title of the talk was 'Women and the War', and it was given by Mrs H. M. Swanrick, MA.

The purpose of the meeting was to highlight the additional work that women were being called on to do, because of the reduction in manpower. The woollen mills provided a good example for this talk with the increased responsibility placed on women. The women in the woollen mills had certainly risen to the challenge and were producing the 'goods', with an excellent record in productivity, a trend which continued throughout the war years. In March 1917, the annual sales amounted to £50,828.16s and a year later, had increased to £60,777.4s.7d. Because profits were reaching an all time high, it was decided to increase the annual salary of the six company directors from £25 to £50. There was only one cause for concern and that was the supply of wool, but over time they managed to overcome this problem.[1]

Another area of employment that served the troops, and the families at home, was the munitions business. In March 1916, Lloyd George held a meeting in London at which most large towns and cities in the United Kingdom were represented. The meeting was in connection with munitions production, which would be very beneficial to the communities chosen to carry out this work. Galway had not been represented at the meeting and because of this, the local authorities were severely criticised.

The Galway newspapers reported on the meeting and complained of the unemployment situation in the town, making comparisons to its healthy position some forty years earlier. Munitions factories had already been established in many of the large industrial centres in England. There was also much criticism over this, not simply because it was effecting local employment, but also because it was drawing much of the Irish labour force overseas to carry out work, which could be done in Ireland. Less than a week after these issues were highlighted, members of the urban council began campaigning to have a munitions factory opened in Galway. The Midland Great Western Railway Company agreed to release their chief locomotive engineer, Mr Morton to help in this regard, as he was a munitions expert. It was agreed that he would be taken around the town with a view to choosing a suitable site. However, before approaching the war office on this matter, the local authorities were required to have certain issues addressed and completed.

There was the question of a company being formed, with the necessary funds secured, machinery had to be installed and skilled workers needed to be available. By July 1916, it was announced that plans for the munitions factory were almost complete and that John Redmond was also lobbying the government on Galway's behalf. Eventually, with strong support from the Irish Party it was agreed that Galway City would indeed be the location for a new national shell factory. The minister for munitions announced the decision with the support of Lloyd George before an All-Ireland Committee. They had investigated other suitable sites around the country accompanied by John Redmond and members of the Irish Party, but a site at Earl's Island was eventually chosen. Although there was some difficulty regarding the site and the deeds, these obstacles were overcome by Christmas 1916.[2]

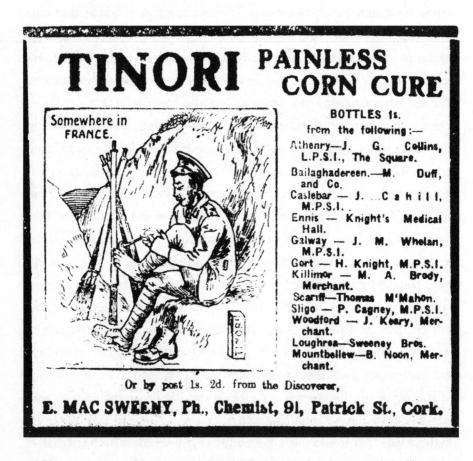

The war also created opportunities for other businesses. An advertisement for Tinori,

a treatment for corns, dated 13 November 1915. (*The Connacht Tribune*)

In January 1917, the machinery for the production of artillery shells arrived in Galway. It was installed in the new factory on Earl's Island within a month. A lady superintendent from the Dublin National Shell Factory also arrived in Galway to interview a number of girls for employment in the local factory. The successful candidates were then taken to Dublin for training, with a number of them being sent to London to complete specialised training. The authorities were determined to have a fully trained and efficient workforce prepared and ready when the factory opened. The plan was to produce 1,000 '18 pounder' shells per week – of course this was confidential information at the time and protected under the defence of the realm act. In addition to the other overheads, the factory was expected to pay between £300 and £400 in wages. It opened as the Galway Munitions Factory, much to the disappointment of the local pessimists, who had been continually critical of the idea, saying, among other things, that it was just a political stunt by the government to keep the local authorities happy.

Shortly after opening, Capt. Downie, an expert in the production of munitions, was sent to Galway to evaluate the new factory and also to carry out an investigation regarding the capability of the workforce. In his report, he stated that the Galway factory was sufficiently laid out and well capable of producing its quota of shells required for the front, and that it would be doing so within two weeks. Nine lathes for boring out the shells were in place to get production going, with capacity for additional machines if they were required. The work of producing the shells included boiling them to ensure that all traces of oil was removed. They were then lacquered on the inside to eliminate rust, which could cause a premature explosion. The finished shell was painted khaki and finally, the appropriate coloured stripes were added to indicate high explosives.[3]

The factory employed mostly women and ran three eight-hour round the clock shifts. The company policy with regard to the production of the shells, stated that it was more beneficial to use shift work rather than to work overtime. It took two girls to work each of the nine lathes and their duties also included the training of new personnel. Additional staff were

Summit Flour advertisment, dated 1 May 1915. (*The Galway Express*)

taken on as required. None of the girls were allowed to work more than seven and a half hours without taking a break. The wages per week were between 10s.6d and 17s depending on experience. Employment in the factory was through the labour exchange as it was also company policy not to employ workers from any of the other industries around Galway. There was also a trained nurse on site. The local traders experienced a considerable increase in business almost immediately, thus, all were pleased with the opening of the new factory. Having opened, the question was asked in the House of Commons if the shell factory established in Galway was turning out shells as efficiently and affordably as those set up in England. The question was directed at the minister for munitions, who believed it was too early to comment.

However, he informed them that the waterpower and workforce was sufficient to meet the present requirements and that there was capacity to introduce additional machines when necessary. The quality of the shells produced was obviously of the highest standard, because in June 1917 the Dublin authorities reported that the Galway Munitions Factory was already turning out excellent work. Electrical power became a problem for the factory in September 1918. To alleviate this dilemma the ministry of munitions issued orders that no new electricity users were to be connected unless sanctioned by the director of the Electricity Company. The Galway Munitions Factory was later converted into a Jute factory and in 1934, the Irish Metal Industries Ltd., opened on the site.[4]

A medical supply industry was also developed in the town when the Galway branch of the Irish War Hospital Supply Depot was opened in October 1916. Initially it opened for two days a week, Mondays and Thursdays with over forty workers turning out the much-needed hospital items each day. It produced a variety of emergency field dressings, sponges, eye bandages and many more items of first aid. It was run mainly by voluntary workers and cost £26 per month to produce 1,860 various types of dressings. One hundred yards of gauze was required every day from the Galway branch.

University College Galway provided the grounds on which fetes were

SUNLIGHT SOAP

A GREAT ALLY OF OUR CLEAN FIGHTERS.

THE quickest and most pleasant route from the Black Sea of dirt to the White Sea of cleanliness is via SUNLIGHT SOAP.

That's what Tommy says in praise of a British product which has established and maintained a reputation all the world over. He also states that his great ally will "freeze on" to Sunlight because it is as pure as the driven snow of his own country. Sunlight Soap saves all the hard labour of the wash—all the wear and tear of the clothes.

The 1d. size will be found convenient for including in your parcels to the front.

£1,000 GUARANTEE OF PURITY on Every Bar.

The name Lever on Soap is a Guarantee of Purity and Excellence.

LEVER BROTHERS LIMITED, PORT SUNLIGHT.

Sunlight Soap advertisement, dated 25 May 1916. (*The Irish Times*) held to raise funds to support the work of the Galway War Hospital Committee as they did for the many other support organisations. These 'comforts' were sent to military field hospitals on the western front and many other military hospitals, including Malta. The Galway War Hospital Supply Depot remained in operation for over two years during which time they produced some 45,768 articles for the troops. Many young women working there were also turning to nursing, and the need was so great by October 1916, that appeals were made for those in the profession to volunteer for service in the war zones.

One of the nurses who left Galway to work at the Batterick Military Hospital was M. A. Tonry from Briarhill. A year later she was commended by the secretary of war for her excellent work in caring for the wounded. Another Galway nurse who gave excellent service was nurse Sister Daly, daughter of the archdeacon of Gort. She was awarded the First Class Honour of the Royal Red Cross Order. Two other Galway nurses who served with distinction were Violet and Ethel Cloherty. The Galway War Hospital Supply Depot and indeed other support groups took full advantage of the nurses serving in the various theatres of war, by having them distribute parcels to the 'local' wounded soldiers.[5]

Although there was a lot of employment for young women in the Woollen Mills and the Munitions Factory, and of course other industries that benefited indirectly from these companies, there were many others leaving the country to secure employment abroad. This became a major concern in December 1917, when it was reported that up to 3,000 young boys and girls from around the country were travelling to England every month to take work in munitions and nursing.

Complaints and concerns were again raised by local authorities throughout the country against a system which denied these youngsters employment at home. They stated that with the exception of a few minor munitions factories and some other small industries, very little had been granted to Ireland. The government was accused of not having provided Ireland with an adequate share of the employment created by the war. In reply to these accusations, the government promised they would employ thousands of workers in the aviation business early in the 'New Year', 1918. In order to soothe relations with the local authorities in Galway, the government released information which indicated that aviation stations would be set up around the country, with one planned for the 'heart' of County Galway. However, this failed to materialise.[6]

Another area in which Galway people could benefit financially from the war was through investments in War Savings Certificates. It was announced at a meeting held in the town hall in July 1918, that people could gain financially from the war. The purpose of the meeting was to establish a War Savings Committee in Galway.

The gathering was addressed by the commissioner of the National War Savings Committee, whose duty it was to encourage the setting up of such committees throughout Ireland. The minimum subscription for each member was 6d, and when the committee had collected 15s.6d, they could purchase a War Savings Certificate, which at the end of five years would be worth £1. All were eligible for membership, but no one individual or group could hold more than 500 certificates. The certificate increased in value at the end of each year and could be purchased at any Post Office. They could also be cashed before maturing, but a few days notice had to be given. The new War Savings Committee included Dr O'Dea, bishop of Galway, Dr Plunkett, bishop of Tuam, Lord Killanin, Lord Clonbrock, Martin McDonogh, Lady Ashtown, Professor Anderson, president of University College Galway, and a number of other leading figures from the town and university. It seems that this idea was also welcomed by the various support groups in Galway.[7]

CHAPTER IX

GONE BUT NOT FORGOTTEN
GALWAY SUPPORTS ITS TROOPS

Concern for the welfare of the troops at the front was immediate in Galway and fundraising began in order to support these servicemen. A 'Subscription List' was opened in September 1914 for the Connaught Rangers Comfort Fund, which was the first of many such funds to be established. The committee published the list of donations weekly. All contributions were sent to members of the finance committee, which included Miss Josephine Murray, Mrs Wilson Lynch, Mrs Moon and Mrs Young, wife of Galway Urban Councillor Joseph Young.

Most of the women involved were the wives of leading businessmen of the town. Madeline Persse was possibly the most prominent and active member of the war support movements in Galway. She was a member of the famous distillery family and lived at 3 The Crescent. Madeline was totally committed to the war effort from the beginning, and was also very concerned for the women and children of the servicemen. As early as 15 August 1914, she had a letter published in *The Galway Express*, voicing her concern over the financial well-being of the wives and children of: 'our gallant countrymen' at the front.

She helped with the foundation of the Connaught War Relief Fund and requested that donations be sent directly to herself or the manager of the National Bank, Galway. She was commended many times by the troops for her generous support and the success of the fund raising is apparent from the many letters of gratitude received by the committee. The following is an example sent to Josephine Murray, treasurer of the Connaught Rangers Comfort Fund. It was written by Ethel Hamilton, the wife of a Connaught Ranger officer, in grateful appreciation for the excellent support:

Derrycassan, Granard, 17th November, 1914.

Dear Miss Murray, – I heard from my husband at the front to-day, and he asked me to thank you and the committee so very much on behalf of the Rangers for all the splendid things which have arrived and which are very much appreciated by the men. They have been having a dreadful time, in dirty wet trenches for five days and nights at a stretch, then only one night off and then back in the trenches again only 30 yards from the German lines for six days and nights with no rest. They have lost seven officers, killed or wounded, and 300 men since they have been in this last battle, and five officers have gone on the sick list. Major Alexander, who is now in command of the Second Battalion, and my husband are the only two officers who went from Aldershot. He says the shelling is incessant, day and night, and that our men are simply splendid; so it is a great thing that we can do anything to help them bear it all, and they are very grateful for the parcels sent from Galway.

– Yours sincerely – Ethel Hamilton.[1]

Other concerned groups and individuals also got involved in fundraising. A flag day was organised for 8 December 1914 to try to raise £630 for a 'Motor Ambulance' which would be sent to the front. Lady Clonbrock of Ahascragh was a leading force behind the idea along with the County Galway Red Cross. The Industrial School Band marched through the town playing 'It's a long way to Tipperary' until they reached Eyre Square where they entertained the crowds while officials collected for the flag day. The Royal Hotel at Eyre Square provided a venue for the collectors and organising committee for the day.

The success of the event was obvious from the sheer numbers of people wearing the emblem, and it was alleged that to see someone without a Red Cross flag in Galway that day, would have been like seeing a soldier at the front without a uniform. The event was not limited to Galway City, many other towns and villages around the county also supported the fundraiser. It proved so successful that the ambulance was sent to France by 20 February 1915. A brass plate was attached to the ambulance and was inscribed as follows:

For the Connaught Rangers
And Their Comrades
From The People Of The County Of Galway
December 1914.[2]

In 1914, the wife of a private soldier was entitled to a separation allowance of 7s 6d per week and if there were children an additional 2d per day for each child was paid. She was also entitled to 5s. for one child, 3s.6d. for a second child and 2s. each for any others. The soldiers were being paid 7s. per week and if a man was married, 3s.6d. was deducted and added to his wife's allowance. Soldiers could also have additional deductions made from their wages and forwarded to their wives. If a soldier was fully disabled from wounds in battle, he was awarded 25s. per week. In some cases, there were reports of drunkenness among the wives of the servicemen while they were away at war.

In December 1914, Dora Mellon, secretary of the Irishwomen's Suffrage Federation, voiced the organisation's concern about such allegations. They were also outraged because the home secretary had placed the wives of some servicemen under police supervision, and made public houses off limits to the women. The Suffragettes felt it was an absolute disgrace and called for the immediate removal of such policing. The various associations and individuals involved in the support groups in Galway also took offence to these allegations and the measures taken by the authorities. The local newspapers joined in support of the accused women and recorded the reports of excessive drinking among the wives of soldiers and sailors had been grossly exaggerated. Some said that the rumours originated through jealousy over the women's new-found wealth, and it was those who would not go to war that were spreading such gossip. The following letter was written by Capt. Waithman of Merlin Park, defending the reputation of the women of Galway:

Merlin Park, Galway, 25th November 1914.

Sir – I see so much in Irish and English papers about the increase of drunkenness amongst soldiers' and sailors' wives that perhaps I might be permitted to say something about our Galway ones. Since the various allowances have been granted to them, not one case of drunkenness of a soldier's or sailor's wife has been before the bench of magistrates in Galway. The women are spending their money on bedding and clothes for their little ones and themselves; and the children who never wore boots are now wearing them. The children who go to the Lady Philippa's tea-room are a pleasure to see – kept cleaner and more warmly clad than they have ever been during the last four years. I am sure everyone will rejoice with me that our Galway women are conducting themselves so well and putting their grants to such good purposes.

Yours. etc.

W. S. Waithman, Hon. Sec. Soldiers and Sailors Families Association.[3]

The Soldiers and Sailors Family Association mentioned in the above letter, was another organisation founded to provide additional support for the families of the men on active service and those killed, wounded, in prisoner of war camps, or missing. Mrs Waithman of Merlin Park was president of the first Galway branch. To encourage contributions, the organisation regularly published the sums donated and the names of the subscribers. Operatic concerts were organised by the association and with the funds raised, the organisers were able to provide additional relief (an average of 5 shillings for each family) to over 200 Galway families during Christmas 1914.

The war was also making its presence felt in the nursery that year. German toys, which were normally a favourite and were commonly purchased at Christmas in those years, were declared contraband and replaced by toys from England and France. Dolls dressed in khaki, highland costumes, etc. replaced teddy bears and other old favourites. There were also dolls dressed in French and Belgian uniforms armed with miniature '12-inch guns' and other weapons of war.

On 9 December another group, the Local Representative Relief Committee issued a statement requesting that lists of names, addresses, ages and sex of children of soldiers and sailors killed, missing or on active service, be submitted to them. The children were to be given gifts received from the United States. Entertainment was also provided for the children in venues such as the town hall, where in addition to the amusements, hundreds of packets of sweets were distributed.

Christmas 1914 also saw an upsurge in gifts sent out to the troops, among them Christmas puddings, balaclavas, body shields and Holloway's Pills and Ointment. Advertisements instructed people to be practical when buying presents for the troops, advising them to be aware of the health needs of the soldiers. Many other items were also sent and all carried the message 'From Friends in Galway.' Supplies of various types of clothing had begun arriving from Canada to be sorted and then sent out to the troops. To keep the soldiers informed of events at home, copies of *The Galway Express* and *The Connacht Tribune* were also sent.[4]

Support from local people was not just limited to the troops and their families, it was announced in October 1914, that Galway was preparing to accommodate Belgian refugees. The first group were looked after by the nuns in Seamount House, Salthill. Accommodation was also being prepared in the town for additional arrivals. It was made clear to anyone interested in providing accommodation for the refugees, that they would have to accommodate an entire family rather the split the families.

They began arriving in December 1914 and were made welcome by the people of Galway who gathered at the Railway Hotel. Some of the local businessmen, J. J. Ward, A. Simmons, Jack Meldon and J. C. Gardiner provided transport for the refugees. There was much sympathy for these people, particularly because they had to take refuge so far from home just before Christmas. The plight of these people inspired greater co-operation and solidarity among those promoting the war effort. The support continued and sometime later, a Belgian Soldiers' Comfort Fund was founded by Lady Ashtown of Woodlawn House.[5]

In January 1915, a meeting was held in the Railway Hotel to form a committee to establish a reading and recreation room for soldiers and sailors, who were sent home wounded, invalided or 'otherwise'. The River

What is the Value of a Life?

WE can't reply to that, but we have evidence that the LIFE-SAVING BODY
SHIELD has saved the lives of many of our braves fighting at the front.

It will stop a Revolver bullet at six yards' range, Flying Shrapnel at a velocity of
750 ft. per second, Bursting Grenades, Bayonet, Sword or Lance thrust.

It has no metal in its construction, is light and keeps the body warm.

What Better Present

For your Relative or Friend? Imagine being able to say in the future: "There he is
and my Gift saved his life."

We are the sole agents for Galway and district. Apply to us for full particulars of
this wonderful invention.

HILL & CO., Galway.

Advertisement for the Life-Saving Body Shield, dated 23 December 1916

(*The Galway Express*)

Plate Meat Company on the corner of Shop Street and Lower Abbeygate Street provided two rooms. The manager, Mr Gallagher, was responsible for the facility. Refreshments were donated by various interested groups and individuals, including Lady McCullagh, Lord Killanin, Lady Ashtown and Miss Burton Persse. Donations of games, cards, draughts, puzzles, newspapers and books were made. Businessman Philip O'Gorman, provided stationary, calendars etc, with various other items being provided by other local business people. A billiard table and gramophone were also secured.

The Soldiers and Sailors Reading Rooms were formally opened on 3 March 1915. The centre proved to be a huge success and organisers were delighted with the amount of 'boys in khaki' that were using the facility from the beginning. The servicemen were also entertained regularly by local singers and musicians. In a concert held in February 1916, two talented local ladies gave excellent and memorable performances. Winnie Tolputt sang 'A Little Bit Of Heaven' while Lady McCullagh brought the audience to its feet with her rendering of 'One, Two, Buckle My Shoe'. A number of other performers also took part while refreshments and cigarettes were given out to the soldiers. The management of the facility was then handed over to yet another new organisation the Soldiers' Recreation and Refreshment Committee.

Support organisations were also springing up throughout the county, with similar concerts and events being held at various venues. In Ballinasloe, Lady Clancarty was to the fore in organising such events. One particular concert she held in Garbally Court, was such a success, that it prompted many of those attending to become involved in the support movements. The Ballinasloe concert raised £90 some of which was donated to provide furni-

A Balaclava Cap or Campaign Helmet.

Illustration of a knitted balaclava. Women were advised to knit such items for soldiers and sailors on active service. This advertisement is from *Practical Knitter.*
(Courtesy of Helen Spelman)

ture for a reading room already set up in the town. The Ballinasloe War Needlework Guild was founded and as well as working from home, the ladies met once a week in a hall that was provided by a local businessperson. This insured that quotas of clothing and other items required by the troops were completed in a timely manner. All the items were valued by the troops, and for the wounded, soft felt slippers were extremely welcome as many of them suffered from frostbite, chilblains and other problems associated with the feet, the result of standing in waterlogged trenches over long periods of time. Meanwhile many of the newspapers were publishing a 'Roll of Honour' recording the names of those killed and wounded, which helped keep the tragedy fresh in the minds of the people.[6]

The Galway branch of the National Society for the Prevention of Cruelty to Children was established in 1911, thus by the beginning of the war it was in a strong position to help and support families in need. Their office was at 8 Eyre Square and they immediately took on the additional task of supporting children whose fathers were serving at the front. The society also placed its premises at the disposal of the Soldiers' and Sailors' Committee for meetings. This experienced organisation was well equipped with trained personnel to deal with child-welfare and their involvement was extremely welcomed by the other organisations.

On 6 May 1915, the organisation blitzed Galway for support under the banner of 'Children's Day'. With the aid of a specially decorated sponsored tram, they filled the collection boxes with badly needed funds. Again, there were allegations of women taking to the 'drink' and neglecting the children while the men were at war, but when the society investigated the reports, they again proved to be false. The organisation did confirm that there were some cases of women drinking and neglecting their children, but these were simply the 'usual culprits' and most of them were not the wives of servicemen. Many of the male members of the organisation were not content with staying at home looking after children and instead joined the military believing their priority was on the battlefield. By 1915, fifty-six of the organisation's inspectors were on active service.[7]

By early 1915, the war had become a stalemate and the trenches were taking their toll in killed and wounded. Many of the wounded troops, or those who were strong enough to travel, were beginning to arrive back in Galway to be cared for at home. Because of the substantial numbers involved, support for these men became essential, thus concerts were organised to aid those convalescing in the Renmore Hospital. By May 1915, the British military were obviously very concerned about accommodation as they requested that the Railway Hotel be converted and used as a military hospital. The Soldiers and Sailors Association also got involved in securing accommodation for the troops, and even approached people living outside the city. One of the ideas they came up with was to have the soldiers housed in the country, where they could recuperate in 'peaceful surroundings'. The following letters requesting support for such accommodation were written by K. E. Persse of Roxborough House to Martin Farrell a local farmer in the Craughwell area:

(1) Mr. Farrell, – Would you feel inclined to take in a convalescent sailor, soldier – Irish – or whomsoever you like. The Soldier & Sailor's Help Society has asked me to send up names of any who are willing to do so – and especially people living in the country, where the poor invalid could have fresh milk, eggs – and food, air etc. We are taking in four here – 2 men and 2 officers. If you know of any families near you who would also do it, please let me know the names. There are some nice farmhouses around Gort neigbourhood, but I do not know the owners names.

– Mrs. K. E. Persse.

The idea was to relieve the hospitals and keep the men until they were fit to go back to and fight.

(2) Roxborough, Mr. Farrell, – I am much obliged to you for the form, which I have forwarded to the Head. It will be interesting to see who they send us.

– K. E. Persse.[8]

The prisoners of war were also in need of support and although people were concerned about them, the troops in action seem to have been the priority. This was the case until local newspaper editors began receiving letters of appeal from soldiers in prison camps. The following are examples of letters received, the first of which was from Pte M. Connors. It was written in February 1915 and was addressed to the editor of *The Galway Express*. He obviously felt that as prisoners they had been forgotten in their home-town. The second and third letters were from Pte P. Cavanagh, and were received by the editor of *The Connacht Tribune*. His first letter was written in March 1915, requesting cigarettes, a commodity that was high on the list of required items among many of the troops. So much for the present-day smoking ban, one wonders what Ptes Connors and

Cavanagh and indeed their comrades would have thought of it? By all accounts, the appeals proved very successful and a 'Cigarette Fund' was opened. The full details of subscriptions were published each week and the first consignment of cigarettes was shipped out to the prisoners on 19 April 1915:

(1) Dear Sir, – Just a line to let you know that we are prisoners of war in Germany, and would be thankful to you if you could assist us in some way, as every regiment gets a lot of stuff from different persons. So the Connaught Rangers asked me to write to you and ask you to help them. The Dublin evening papers send a lot of things to the Dublins or the R.D.F., so if you ask the people of Galway to help you to send us some things they will assist you. Ask the Officer Commanding Depot, and he will do some good for the old Connaughts. They say, 'Dead, but not forgotten', but – alive and forgotten! I ask you once more now to help us in the hour of need and God will reward you for it. I finish up now hoping I will hear from you soon, and don't forget the old Connaught Rangers, the sons of old Connaught – I remain your obedient servant.

(2) Sir – I beg to announce to you that we have come to the conclusion that we, Galwaymen, who are prisoners of war here in Germany, should write to ask for your assistance, if you can possibly do anything for us. You might send, if you can, some boxes of cigarettes to myself and Seaman Fitzgerald, of the Claddagh who will undertake to distribute them amongst others. We hope that some day we will be able to return thanks personally for your gift.

– Yours faithfully.

P. Cavanagh.

(3) 20th May 1915 – Sir, – I have received your two parcels, for which I am very thankful. I return my gratitude, and the gratitude of my fellows to you for your kindness in sending them to us, for we generally get them here in good time. There are very few of our countrymen here, only about 14 or 20. If you send anything in the line of cigarettes or tobacco only send them to my address, and to the men from the country. Would you please send me personally a parcel of bread, tea, sugar, milk

and a tin of meat, and I will myself see you to thank yourself and your readers when I get back? I know it is very hard to be asking these things, but nevertheless, we must be excused, as we are prisoners of war. We are kept very clean here in clothing and washing. If you can send the eatables it will be alright.

– Yours respectfully.

Pte. P. Cavanagh, Irish Guards.

The support did not end there, the Connaught Rangers Comfort Fund committee organised a 'bridge drive' and various other types of competitions to raise finance to support the prisoners of war. Some of the events were held at the Bank of Ireland, Eyre Square and contributions of all kinds were received from around the town. They were very well attended and the competitions, with categories including advertising, spelling, war-games and cake-weighing contests provided much of the entertainment. Soon consignments of mufflers, socks, mittens, towels, pencils, notepaper, cigarettes and matches, as well as many other commodities were being sent to the prisoners of war. 'Gone but not forgotten' was the order of the day.[9]

Although much had already been done, it was time to elect a committee and form an official association to unite and organise the efforts of all interested parties. On 19 June 1915, a meeting was held in the town hall in Galway, the purpose of which was to decide on the most efficient way to support the troops.

Lord Clonbrock, presided over the meeting and his wife, Lady Clonbrock, was elected president of the newly formed County Galway War Fund Association. The aims of the association were as follows:

A. Provide comforts for the Connaught Rangers on active service, and prisoners of war.

B. Support for Galwaymen serving in H.M.S. Navy.

C. Support for Galwaymen serving in corps having no territorial connection.

D. Support the sick and wounded troops.

The town hall was placed at the disposal of the committee and it was agreed that they would meet there once a month. The committee was also given a room at the Railway Hotel for the packing of provisions, which were purchased locally and sent to the front every fortnight. They also secured a large storeroom from Joyce & Mackie at Eyre Square where most of the goods were received, stored and eventually packed for shipment. The committee then joined forces with the Irish Women's Association, a national support organisation that was in a position to purchase provisions at much lower rates because of the vast quantities involved.

By September they were providing items such as socks, shirts, handkerchiefs, towels, mittens, tobacco, sixpenny novels, draught sets etc. to all Connaught Ranger battalions throughout the various theatres of war. They received donations from numerous sources and organised fetes and other such events to raise the required finance. In conjunction with the Irish Women's Association, the committee appointed 'godmothers' for members of the Connaught Rangers who did not have anyone to support them from home. These women ensured that gifts and letters were sent to these men. In addition to this and the other provisions, blackberry-picking parties were organised and from the harvested berries, jars of blackberry jam were produced and sent out to the troops.

Setting up the County Galway War Fund Association proved an immediate success and by July enough funds had been raised to ensure that another ambulance was sent to the front. The Galway Race Committee donated a third of the finance towards the purchase of the vehicle.[10]

The following is an example of just one of the events held by the committee. On 16 September 1915, a fete was organised in Renmore Barracks and the main prize for the raffle that day was a very ornate clock presented by Thomas Dillon of Galway. There was a 'Fancy Stall', which contained a variety of useful household objects and items of an ornamental nature. Some Galway craft firms donated various samples of their needlework.

The Galway Restaurant Company provided a large cake, which was used in a competition, with a prize being presented to the person who could guess its correct weight. On the 'Country Produce Stall' the salmon, grouse and flower arrangements sold out extremely fast, as did the contents of the 'Sweet Stall'. Both the brass and pipe bands of the Connaught Rangers provided entertainment throughout the day. Local groups and individuals displayed their talents in singing, dancing and acting. All performances were given in the Variety Hall, followed by a concert which was held in the army gymnasium. The Galway Gas Works donated a new state-of-the-art cooker for the tea rooms, in order to accommodate the large crowds who turned out to support the event. The proceeds from the event were in excess of £159, and the money was added to the Connaught Rangers War Fund. Again Madeline Persse was one of the most successful ladies involved in the fete, selling well over her quota of goods.[11]

In April 1916, University College Galway actively showed their support for the men in the trenches when its president, Professor Alexander Anderson, made an appeal for books. People could send books to the university where they would be consolidated and prepared for shipment to the Connaught Rangers at the front, and those wounded and convalescing in hospitals. A University Support Committee was set up to carry out the work and included Professors Anderson; Rishworth (treasurer); Donovan-O'Sullivan (secretary); and Professors Kinkead; Senior; Mahon; Griffith; McElderry; Howley (committee members). They worked in conjunction with the County Galway War Fund Association who gratefully accepted all assistance and acknowledged their support at their Annual General Meeting held in the town hall in June 1916.

At the meeting, the chairperson thanked all sections of the community who had been involved with the support groups and both the secretary and treasurer's reports testified to the success of the committee's efforts over the previous year. However, it could not be a once-off endeavour, as continued assistance was vital to the war effort and more people were required to help. They announced that a three-day fun and entertainment event was planned for August. It was called the 'Great Galway Carnival' and was organised in aid of the Connaught Rangers & Prisoners of War Fund. It was held in Eyre Square and included fancy dress competitions, which displayed brilliantly all the allied colours. A gymkhana was held during which the excellent horsemanship of officers and men of other ranks, encouraged youngsters to join the cavalry.

Another event that attracted a lot of attention was a bicycle parade in fancy dress. All the young ladies of the town were requested to take part in this event. Various types of races and other competitions were also held and Eyre Square was awash with colour. The Midland and Great Western Railway Company provided extra train services in order to accommodate those attending the event and many of the Galway hotels provided additional accommodation. The bands of the Connaught Rangers and the Sherwood Foresters entertained the crowd. The troops fighting in the Middle East were not forgotten either, with fundraising events held during 'Mesopotamia Day' for the soldiers in that theatre of war. The efforts continued and increased as Christmas loomed. Items sent to the Connaught Rangers for the season of good-will in 1916, were; 480lbs. of plum puddings, 500 cakes, 480 soup rolls, 10,000 cigarettes, tobacco, 100 pipes and a number of footballs.[12]

The success of the County Galway War Fund Association was proven repeatedly. At the annual general meeting of 1917, a report was read thanking the women of the United Kingdom, and in particular the women of Galway for the patriotism and self-sacrifice they had shown since the war began. After the committee expressed their deepest condolences to Lady Clonbrock on the death of her husband, Lord Clonbrock, Capt. Stephen Gwynn was invited to address the meeting. He had just returned from the trenches and had witnessed first hand the benefits of the association's work. He explained the relief that the troops felt upon leaving the trenches, bitterly cold, wet, covered in mud and feeling absolutely miserable, to find fresh, clean, dry clothing, sent by their 'Friends in Galway'. He told them of life in the trenches, and explained how important their work was to the men in the field. He said it was not only the dangers of war that affected the men, but also the continuous hardships and he thanked the committee for bringing 'a ray of comfort' into the lives of the troops. Gwynn then emphasised the importance of continued support.

This was still evident in June 1918, when the committee expressed their gratitude to all their supporters and mentioned in particular, twenty-four ladies who ensured the Connaught Rangers prisoners of war received their fortnightly parcels of provisions. By this period, it was costing £106 per month to supply all the commodities required for these parcels alone. The methods of raising the much-needed finance continued along much the same lines throughout the war. Additional finance was secured through large contributions from organisations such as the Tuam Race Committee, who contributed £144. That year they also introduced an extra race to their programme by establishing the Galway War Plate.

Organisations in Oughterard, Gort, and many other towns throughout the county also made valuable contributions through hosting various sporting events, with Tennis Tournaments alone raising almost £82. The Victoria Cinema was placed at the disposal of the fund raisers and well-attended concerts were held there to the delight of all those involved, particularly the local artists and singers who took the opportunity to display their skills and talents. Wounded soldiers were invited to take their place among the audience.

The events were always well advertised and appeared under various headings: 'Connaught Rangers Comfort Fund', 'Soldiers And Sailors Comfort Fund' and the 'County of Galway Naval & Military War Fund'. The County Galway War Fund Association remained active until the war ended and at their last meeting in June 1919, they announced that £12,330-7-7 had been raised since its foundation. Lady Clonbrock addressed the gathering and gave examples of contributions throughout the county, such as one lady from Gort who had knitted a pair of socks every week for three years. Upon hearing this, the hall erupted with applause. Long lists of contributors and organisations were read out before the large audience. A number of military personnel also attended and Capt. Chamier, representing the army, congratulated all those who had supported and helped alleviate the sufferings of the soldiers in the trenches.[13]

CHAPTER X

ALL QUIET ON THE WESTERN FRONT
AFTERMATH

On 5 October 1918, the successful progress of the allies was reported in Galway. While this was welcome news, people remembered its cost in human terms. As trench after trench yielded, the ground behind the allied armies revealed some terrible sights among the skeletal remains of cities and towns. The great houses of the noble and those of the poor had all suffered the same fate. There are few things that arouse more melancholy than the sight of a ruined habitation, a derelict dwelling and a discarded item belonging to someone who once lived, but was now gone, such as a child's toy discarded near a shattered house. Such sights are monuments of departed joys. The scarred roads, camouflaged positions and hidden dugouts all revealed their own horrors as the troops moved forward through the destroyed barbed wire defences, passing discarded machinery of destruction as they went. Abandoned vehicles some on fire, dead men and horses, all bore testament to the grim reality of war. Miles upon miles of devastated countryside signified the western front and a ghastly uncanny wasted atmosphere marked the battlegrounds.

When the shadows of evening fell, this landscape took on a freaky, eerie quality, where soldiers had once gazed out from their trenches into no-mans-land and wondered what the morning would bring. Hundreds upon thousands of little wooden crosses stood as silent witnesses to those who had lost their lives. In one sector, a crucifix stood stark against the sky, where throughout the fighting soldiers on their way up to the trenches had prayed as they passed. The following poem was written by Mme Loir (nee Mary MacHale), sister of a Lieut J. R. J. MacHale who was killed in action:

WOODEN CROSSES

The battlefield is silent; there are no Germans there;
The smell of smoke and powder still lingers on the air;
The shades of night have fallen, and little can be seen,
But simple rude white crosses with narrow space between.
An eerie sense is stealing along this silent plain –
The hour when spirit mothers pay tribute to their slain;
How quietly they're gliding – these phantoms of the night
With shattered hopes, broken hearts – their guerdon of the fight!

From England, Scotland, Ireland these spirit mothers come
To moisten with their weeping this graveyard of the Somme;
From Canada, Australia, from India – everywhere
Are mothers – spirit mothers – of heroes resting there.
From grave to grave they wander, from cross to cross they steal
Until each finds the one of all that makes direct appeal;
And through each night throughout each year while soul to body clings,
They'll hasten surely hither on swiftest spirit wings.

A Wooden Cross. Beneath it an English 'Tommy' sleeps,
And here the spirit-mother her lonely vigil keeps;
Her heart with grief is broken, her eyes are blind with tears,
And as she vents her sorrow, his voice she thinks she hears;

'Be brave, be brave, O Mother; cease weeping for your son,
Who has but done his duty and bids you carry on.'

A Wooden Cross. Beside it a mother on her knees
And from the cross a plaidie – bloodstained – floats on the breeze
Its folds she kisses, kisses, in agonies of grief
Until her bitter anguish in words finds some relief:
'My bairnie, my wee bairnie, – ye'll no come back again

To the Hielands, and the heather – to you homestead in the glen?'

A Wooden Cross. The tenant who 'neath its shadow lies
Came from the hills of Connacht, young, strong, with laughing eyes.
The spirit-mother near it is training shamrock there
While blending with her wailing a rosary of prayer;
'Mo leanb boct, mo cuirle – 'Naoim Muire Matain De,'
'Ta lan do trár an lora' – ir nuan do'n leaba é'

A Wooden Cross. Beside it a comely dame of France;
Her weeping now abandoned, she seems as in a trance,
When from its spell she awakens, her words are winging afar
Votre pauvre moce qui á vous parles, mon chez, mon petit gar;
Loin de chez nous, et de la Ferme, et de la Normandie
Tu fais dodo, mals pour toujours – toujours' – tourjours, Ah, oui.

And so to this rich harvest of crosses planted there
The faithful spirit-mothers from regions wide repair;
Red, white, and blue; bleu, blanc, et rouge; and so on to the end
The Shamrock green, and purple heath with fleur de-lis shall blend
For mothers' hearts are all akin upon the stricken field,
Each yearning for the touch of him whom Death shall never yield
Until the Dies Irae – the Day of God – shall come
To reunite the Mothers and Heroes of the Somme.[1]

On 31 October 1918, Turkey signed the armistice and by 3 November, Germany stood alone. To avoid total catastrophe, Kaiser Wilhelm II appointed Prince Maximilian of Baden as chancellor with the task of seeking an armistice. He then abdicated and fled to the neutrality of the Netherlands. On 11 November, German delegates led by Matthias Erzverger walked through drizzling rain and entered a railway car in the Compiégne Forest to sign the armistice. Marshal Ferdinand Foch signed for the allies and ordered that the fighting was to stop on all battlefronts at 11.00 a.m., thus ending the First World War. This ended over four horrific years of the most bitter fighting in history, at last all was quiet on the western front. People rejoiced throughout the allied countries, not so much in victory, but because the appalling slaughter had ended.

The effects of the intense bombardment in areas of military operations had destroyed the industrial and commercial lives of many towns and cities throughout Europe. Schools, factories and homes had been destroyed leaving people very dependent on government food supplies in the effected areas. The estimated military casualties alone were enormous, with some 5,232,788 allies having lost their lives, while the central powers' losses were estimated at 3,947,495, with millions more wounded. Civilian deaths were estimated at 5,000,000, with millions more dying of Spanish influenza, which many believed was a direct result of the war. In financial terms the war had cost in excess of $337 billion.[2]

News of the armistice reached Galway in the afternoon of 11 November, and as the report circulated, people began to rejoice. The bells of St. Nicholas' Collegiate Church rang out across the town in celebration. Flags were hung from all the public buildings and people gathered in the streets expressing the overwhelming joy they felt. Aeroplanes flew over the town in the brilliant sunshine. The Connaught Rangers procured tar barrels and bonfires were lit at Eyre Square and Middle Street. A 'peace dance' was immediately organised for the town hall that night and the venue was lavishly decorated within hours. The dance was packed to capacity and proved a tremendous success. The band of the Connaught Rangers ended the night with a very appropriate air, 'The Perfect Day.'

But for hundreds of Galway families peace had come too late, for them it was also a day of great sorrow, thinking of their loved ones who would never return. One of the most welcome sights for anxious mothers was the closure of the recruiting offices, which occurred over the following days. The sub-offices also closed in Tuam, Ballinasloe and Clifden, and it was announced that the staff were returning to England.

The newspapers celebrated the peace, but also recorded the horrors of a war they had fully supported with recruiting advertisements and glorifying accounts of various battles, to encourage young men to join the army. *The East Galway Democrat* reported that after four years, the devastation of countries, human life and property, unparalleled misery and suffering, the martyrdom of two nations and the ruin of several: 'the greatest war the world has ever seen is over – thanks be to God.' *The Galway Express* newspaper had also supported the war, but on 13 December 1918, the offices were seized and occupied by a detachment of armed Surrey Yeomanry and police. The seizure caused a sensation in the town and large crowds gathered to watch as the military cordoned off the front and rear of the building and began loading the machinery onto army lorries.

It is not known for certain why this occurred, but in August of that year, the editor had been arrested as part of countrywide swoop on people who were suspected of involvement in the so-called 'German Plot', an alleged plan to help the German war effort. However, it is more likely that the newspaper office was closed because it had switched its allegiance to the nationalist cause.[3]

The end of the war signalled an increase in unemployment with the reduction in munitions and uniforms. There was also an increase in manpower as soldiers and sailors began returning home which added to the problem. Although circumstances in the town were worrying, the situation in the Claddagh was desperate. Major investment was required to rebuild the fishing fleet and provide modern housing for its inhabitants. Before the war, Galway Urban Council had expressed the idea of building new houses in the Claddagh and developing South Park as a municipal 'pleasure-ground'.

However, only preliminary steps had been taken when the war broke out. The government and the urban council were severely criticized by local groups for lack of action, saying that there was a tendency in Ireland to neglect the neglected places, such as the Claddagh. The fisher-folk of this ancient village had taken their stand on the battleships, and as a result, the little measure of prosperity they possessed before the war vanished during their absence.

Now with the war over, 'Claddagh's Magnificent Response' was all but forgotten. *The Connacht Tribune* reported that the Claddagh had voluntarily given more men in proportion to its population than any other community of similar size in Great Britain or Ireland. Almost every day men were returning to their old homes and once their twenty-eight days leave was completed, they were demobilised, thus finding themselves unemployed. They had no means of obtaining employment within their own community and very little possibility of finding employment in the town.

By June 1919, there were over 400 demobilised sailors in Galway, the vast majority of these men being from the Claddagh. Most were former fishermen whose boats had become un-seaworthy during the war years and many more fishing boats had been sold off to support the needs of the families. The fishing equipment had also been sold, or was lost. Many of the houses required immediate repair and there was little or no finance available to carry out this much needed maintenance.

There was also discontent among the fishermen because the fishing industry had developed exceedingly well on the Aran Islands during the war, because the male population had not been decimated there, as it had been in the Claddagh. Indeed there was great dissatisfaction expressed among most of the ex-servicemen throughout Galway because of the lack of action by the government and indeed the lack of information available to them upon their return. All of this left the survivors with a feeling of resentment towards the government, after all, many promises had been made to them when they were going off to war, but now the politicians and authorities were suffering from convenient memory loss.[4]

The ex-servicemen continued to voice their disappointment and eventually efforts were made to support the men. A meeting was held in the Claddagh hall in 1919 to discuss methods of reviving the fishing industry. It was announced that the gross turn-over for the Aran fishermen the previous year had been £40,000 through cooperative methods. This method and a number of other suggestions were put forward, with the priority being a new fishing fleet.

There was also some assistance available through support organisations similar to those that had been established during the war years. One such organisation, was the Discharged Soldiers' and Sailors' Society. Various branches of this society had been set up throughout the county. By the summer of 1919, the Galway branch of the society was well established. At a meeting held in the Court Theatre, a letter was read by the secretary, regarding funding and employment. Enclosed with the letter was a 'handsome' donation from Commander Hanan. The commander, who was present, expressed his pleasure in having joined the committee and also stated that the admiralty was interested in providing temporary employment for the demobilised men.

During his address, Commander Hanan suggested they put a plan in place, and draw up a list of demands they could submit to the authorities. He told them that the Congested Districts Board were already sparing no effort in developing the fishing industry and were in the process of having new boats built for the sailors. The first of these vessels was expected to arrive in Galway within two months. Hanan told the meeting that the men would be informed of all developments, including any relative information about the housing act, which was to be passed within a few days. He told them that realistically, all of the men could not be re-employed in the fishing industry immediately, but said he had already sought employment for them with the naval architects and shipbuilders in Dublin. The company was willing to employ the men until their boats became available.

When Commander Hanan concluded, Joseph Young thanked the speaker and added that he was delighted to see the work that was in progress and the increase in the society's funds. He said it was time to have a memorial erected to the men who died. He felt sure if they appealed to a sympathetic public that additional funds could be raised. Many at the meeting believed that the living should be remembered also and felt the most appropriate way to honour them, was to provide new housing. In response to all the pressure, Galway Urban Council announced they had ear-marked £500 for developing South Park. They also stated that any opportunity to develop the Claddagh would not be missed, saying it could be transformed into one of the most attractive areas in the city.

Eventually this issue was somewhat solved during the mid-1920s, when houses for the ex-servicemen were provided at Beattystown and Frenchville. Work on demolishing the old Claddagh houses and rebuilding the new ones would not begin until the 1930s, even though the living conditions had been condemned in 1927 under the terms of the Health Act.[5]

There was also much discontent among the officers who had returned and they began to question the validity of the war. On 15 March 1919 a letter outlining the: 'treachery of the British Government' was sent to King George V. It was signed by 150 officers, all Irish, who had served with the British army throughout the war. The contents of the letter are extremely interesting and the King was left under no illusion as to the displeasure of the men.

They demanded that the sacrifice they had made on the field of battle be recognised, and the pledges made by the British government be honoured immediately. The letter informed the King that for four years they had worn his uniform and saluted his name. Month after month with little rest day or night, they had led their own countrymen into danger and death and had seen hundreds and thousands of their fellow officers and men killed in Flanders, France, Italy and the far off shores of Gallipoli.

Having come through the 'fiery crucible' of the most hellish conflict in history, they said that the time had come for them to reap the reward of their own harvest and not be undermined by unscrupulous politicians. They said their patriotism was sacrificial and sublime, and had been there in 'abundant measure'. They warned they would challenge any government that would betray Irish soldiers, both living and dead. As far as they were concerned, every Irishman who fought did so for world freedom and this included their own freedom. The letter continued, stating that no matter what the propagandists might say and no matter how much the political circumstances had changed in Ireland, the undeniable fact was that Ireland gave as many men 'voluntarily' per head of population, as any country in the empire.

Now they had returned, they were demanding as the king's officers, that the pledges made to them and their troops, be implemented. They expressed a wish that Ireland's case be referred to in the forthcoming Peace Conference and that the country's future be 'moulded' with the principles promised. The Irish representatives had been driven out of the House of Commons, not because of 'inherent perversity' of their own people, but simply because of the 'treachery' of Liberal statesmen, who nullified all their efforts. This, they said, was an appeal to the king, to whom they had been faithful even unto death, to ensure freedom for the land for which they had fought. They concluded by saying that no statesman could deny their claim and only a 'knave or a fool' could stoop to betray them and their kinsmen who had paid the supreme sacrifice that Ireland might be free.[6]

Even Capt. Stephen Gwynn, who had done so much for the war effort was extremely disappointed in the government and in a letter to the king, he also requested that the issue be raised at the Peace Conference. He felt that their judgment would be more acceptable than the decision of English politicians who had betrayed them. He added that the Westminster politicians strive to control the destiny of Ireland in their own 'hatchery of intrigue' and that it was because of this that the Irish nation had been cursed for so long with conflict and strife. In conclusion, he asked if these statesmen were still going to deny Ireland the: 'fruits of a victory that the Irish regiments have helped to win?'

By voicing his disappointment in government policy, he earned some respect from those who had opposed him during the war. His views were also welcomed by several of his fellow officers. Many of these officers also wanted their fallen comrades to be remembered at home. On 9 June 1919, the 'Friends of the Grammar School' held a meeting at the school to consider methods of perpetuating the memory of twenty-one former students of the school who had lost their lives in the Great War. Several ideas for a memorial were proposed, but they had to be abandoned until funds could be raised to carry out any plans. The committee included H. J. Anderson, Headmaster, Major Frank Purser and R. B. Tivy of the Provincial Bank.[7]

Because of the change in the political climate, there was resentment at home towards the disbanded soldiers. They found themselves returning to a very different Ireland from the one they had left. The 1916 Rebellion had taken place, and its leaders executed, for the same principles (freedom of small nations) along which the Great War had been fought. Most people had forgotten that these men went off to war with the promise that this was the path to Home Rule. The critics had also conveniently forgotten the intensive recruiting campaigns, which had used every means at its disposal to encourage, lie and threaten young men into joining the forces.

Despite all the problems facing them, the survivors continued arriving home, after all, what could be worse than the western front? Some of the lucky ones returned to take up old positions with former employers. Others spent time looking for work throughout the city and county, while many more left for the United States, Australia and England. Those who did remain at home tried to organise support for themselves and established a branch of the British Legion. Their hall was situated opposite the present day fire station, approximately where Yeats College is located today.

On 1 July each year, veterans would march from their headquarters to Eyre Square where they honoured those left behind on the old battlegrounds. All wore poppies and a two-minute silence was observed in memory of those who lost their lives. The poppy was also sold openly on the streets of Galway up until the 1930s and similar to the anniversary parade, both practices ceased about that time.

Regardless of criticism, these men simply got on with their lives and the daily routine of providing for their wives and children. There was little or no psychiatric counselling to help them as they re-adjusted to normal life. As time went by and months turned to years the horrors of the war were all but forgotten, except by those who had witnessed the terrible slaughter. Today the old newsreels takes one back to the smoke and gas-filled bloody battlegrounds of Europe, where millions of 'Willie McBrides' lie among the poppies.

Even these images fall short of displaying the full horrors of a lost generation and the terror they endured before their young bodies were torn apart by the weapons of an insane war. In the cemetery memorial books of the First World War, there is a word that continues to appear: 'why?' What was it all for? After all, the 'War to end all Wars' fell miserably short of its promise, to the men who lost their lives and youth on the western front.[8]

CHAPTER XI

THE BATTLE & RETREAT FROM MONS

On 19 August 1914, the reconnaissance aeroplanes of the Royal Flying Corps gave the first indication that thousands of German troops were sweeping across Belgium. By 22 August, the British Expeditionary Force was positioned along a line running between two Belgian towns, Mons and Conde. A short time later, the first shots discharged by the British took place along the road between the Mons and Soignies. It occurred when a patrol of the Fourth Royal Irish Dragoon Guards encountered some German troops, the short engagement proved successful for the British. It was along this route that they were supposed to be joined by the French troops.

The plan was for the British to attack the Germans with the French supporting both left and right flanks and possibly envelop the enemy. In the early morning of the 23 August, Sir John French visited the area and informed his troops that the enemy would have little more than one or two corps with perhaps a cavalry division, he then departed. By 9 a.m. German field guns had begun to shell the British lines and almost at once the sky exploded with shrapnel, shells and bullets all raining down on allied positions.[1]

The German commander at Mons was Alexander Von Kluck, he had joined the Prussian Army in 1865. By 1914 he was an experienced soldier, having fought in the Austro-Prussian and Franco-Prussian wars. The German troops, estimated at 160,000 men thrust forward and caused a split between the British right flank and the French Army. As the attack gathered momentum, six German divisions, supported by cavalry were employed in attacking two British divisions along a twenty-one mile front.

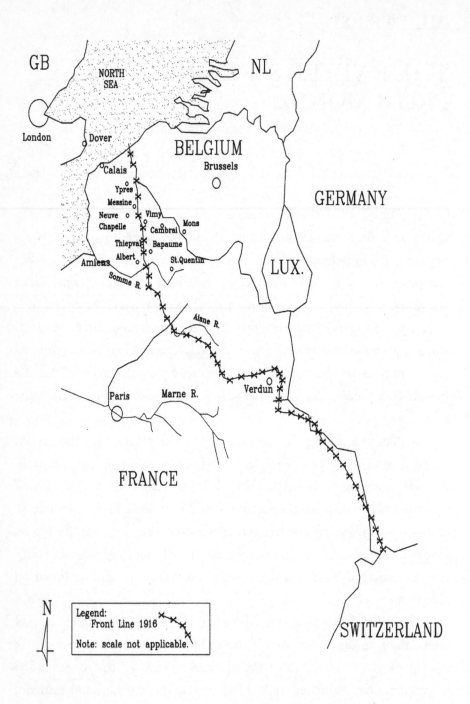

Map of the Western Front.

(Courtesy of Eamonn O'Regan & Michael Conneely)

The French began to fall back, leaving the British open to encirclement.

Assuming the French would return, the British dug in and resisted the German attack. The fighting was intense as the German troops continued to press forward in dense formation, however, this extraordinary bravery proved extremely costly against the British riflemen. The Royal Irish machine-gunners also caused carnage among the German cavalry. The assault continued throughout the day until eventually the German columns staggered, lost their cohesion and the attack gradually halted. As darkness approached, the Germans began to fall back leaving heavy losses on the field. The British welcomed the German bugles as they sounded the cease-fire, and they gave the enemy time to gather their dead and remove the wounded. Later that night the Germans were heard singing *Deutschland uber Alles*. This was the beginning of a long and bloody war and it signalled the ferocity in which it would be fought. Recording his experiences at Mons, one British soldier later wrote:

> They advanced in companies of quite 150 men in files five deep... We could steady our rifles on the trench and take deliberate aim. The first company were simply blasted away to Heaven by a volley at 700 yards and, in their insane formation, every bullet was bound to find two billets. The other companies kept advancing very slowly, using their dead comrades as cover, but they had absolutely no chance.[2]

Shortly after dawn on 24 August, the Connaught Rangers were informed that they would act as a rear-guard when the order was given to retreat. It had become obvious that there would be no French counter-attack to try to halt the German advance. At 11 a.m. the German artillery opened fire and the allies began to fall back. The Rangers became one of the last regiments to leave their post as they made their way across open wheat fields.

Although there was no sign of the enemy advancing the following morning, the shelling continued. By late afternoon, the Rangers had caught up with the First Irish Guards and First Grenadier Guards, who took over the rearguard. There were a number of Irish regiments represented at Mons and the subsequent retreat. The Second Royal Irish Rifles' withdrawal from Mons had cost them over 300 men. During the retreat the Second Connaught Rangers were surrounded at Le Grand Fayt and although most of the unit escaped, a number of them were either killed or captured, including Lieut Col Abercrombie, who had earlier, in the midst of the German shelling, called out: 'Rangers of Connaught, all eyes are upon you tonight. While you have fists and hearts within you, charge them. If you don't, never face me again in this world, or the next.'

There was also confusion in the ranks, with company commanders at times not knowing the location of each other. The Germans continued to press forward and about forty miles from Paris the Irish Guards lost Lieut Col George Morris. It was in the Villers Cotteret area while riding from one section of the fight to another, encouraging his men, that he was fatally shot. Col Morris was from Spiddal, County Galway and was a member of one of the old tribal families. Despite the pressure from the Germans, the Guardsmen displayed a great air of calmness during the retreat. Some even stopped to pick berries, a favourite pastime back home. Once they reached the River Marne, they were ordered to halt, thus ending their retreat.[3]

The Munster Fusiliers also suffered severe losses, but for the most part stood their ground in the face of a strong enemy attack. The Germans even resorted to rounding up cattle and driving them towards the Munstermen, but this also failed to make any impact on their formation. Although they were eventually forced out of position, their rearguard stand at Etreux had gained valuable time for the allies.

By 28 August, the entire British Expeditionary Force was in full retreat, they had little to eat or drink and were exhausted due to the fighting and lack of sleep. Day after day, the sun blazed down on the retreating troops as they made their way along the dusty road towards Paris, continually harassed by the enemy. The German advance continued until they were some fourteen miles from Paris by which time their supply lines were fully stretched, caused by their swift progress. The initial over-confidence of the German leadership changed to doubt as they manoeuvred before Paris. In a bid to destroy the French Fifth Army and the British Expeditionary Force, Von Kluck's army crossed the River Marne, leaving only a reserve corps to guard its Paris flank. The Schlieffen Plan, envisaged by the Germans to envelope the French and British was not effective, thus a gap appeared between the German armies into which the British Expeditionary Force and the Fifth French Army stepped. The allies Sixth army reinforced by the Paris garrison attacked and defeated the surprised German reserve. This gave the British time to regroup and counterattack, forcing the Germans to retreat. Both sides faced each other again on 5 September at the battle of the Marne. This battle is sometimes overlooked, but it was a turning point in the very early stages of the war, as it resulted in a full retreat by the Germans. However, on 12 September the German retreat halted behind the River Aisne, where they had constructed a line of entrenched positions.[4]

The following are examples of letters and interviews recording the experiences of some Galway soldiers who fought at Mons. This interview was given by Corp. Stokes, while he was at home recovering from an accident. He also had two brothers, both sergeants serving with the Second Connaught Rangers. Their father was from Athenry and during his military career, had seen action in the Zulu Wars. He had attempted to enlist for the Great War, but he was over the age limit:

(1) He said at about 2.30 p.m. that Sunday a small party of mounted cyclists (about 40), with two troops of cavalry, guarding the right flank of the allies, were entrenched on the right of Mons, holding in check a small force of German cavalry. On the right of them were about 100 of the Royal Irish, with one machine gun and over 30 more mounted cyclists guarding a bridge. 'All of a Slap,' he continued, about 500 German infantry with one or two large guns, came up. The Royal Irish and the cyclists with them opened fire on the enemy, while we got the word to retire behind a village in the vicinity to make trenches, so as to be able to cover our comrades' retirement. We took up a position on a hill about a thousand yards behind the village, and the German artillery opened fire on our comrades at the bridge, but no lives were lost. The enemy then opened fire with their large guns on our fellows holding the bridge, with the result that their one machine gun was silenced and the company of Royal Irish were

all wiped out, bar four or five who returned to tell the tale. The Germans afterwards opened fire on the village, and very soon their shrapnel shells left it in a heap of ruins. A little church in it was the first to be destroyed, and, of course the inhabitants did not escape the awful destruction of the shells. Then their aeroplane [sic] hovered over us for a while, and, returning gave the enemy the range. Immediately a very large shell fire was opened on us and as we had no big guns we could not respond. Capt. Hall of the King's Own Liverpools gave us the order to retire from the trenches. The men made the best of the order, but of course some of our men suffered from the shells. Private Flack, who was close to me, was wounded in the hand. Pte. O'Toole was on my right, about the third man from me, and he was also wounded. Lieut. Blacker, in retiring was hit by a shrapnel shell which burst behind him, and he received several wounds, from which the poor fellow has since died in hospital. But the worst case I saw was that of Pte. Hill. He was quite close to me when his left arm was completely blown off by a shell. He staggered a few hundred yards, but fell from the loss of blood, and I did not see him after that, as every man had to look to himself.

When I pointed to Cpl. Stokes right leg, as showing signs of having received an injury, he admitted with some hesitation that a splinter from a shell struck him there. 'In the course of my retirement, he added, a shell came whizzing over my head, and I threw myself down. I got up again and ran about 100 yards, when another shell burst in front of me in the air. Another one burst behind me and made a large hole in the ground. On looking back to see if there were any more 'favours' coming towards me, I accidentally fell over a cliff, fourteen feet of a drop fracturing my spine. I lay there for about ten minutes unable to move, and had given myself up for lost, when a cavalry man came along, took me on his horse and brought me to a village about a mile away, where he left me. Pte. Young, of the Berkshires then assisted me to the Red Cross Hospital there, where my wounds were attended too. After a couple of hours the military ambulance brought Capt. Hall, Pte. Flack and I away to a Field Hospital, a circumstance which was lucky for us, for the enemy some hours afterwards shelled the hospital. A detachment of our artillery passed the hospital about 20 minutes after I was brought in, but I don't know what took place, though I heard plenty of shooting going on.

(*The Galway Express* 19-9-1914)

The following interview was given by Sgt Stephen Shaughnessy of the Irish

Guards, who was a native of Tuam. He also gave accounts of the battles of the Aisne and Ypres, which are included in the relevant chapters:

(2) We marched from that day until we came to Mons. The battle was in full progress when we reached the latter place, on the Belgian frontier. We were on the reserve on that day, and on the next morning, at 2 o'clock, the retreat of the first troops began, and the fighting was taken up by the rearguard. We continued fighting, and marching day and night, until we came to Andrecies. The Essex Regiment and French were on our right. The British, as you have seen in the Press, suffered heavily at Mons. The town of Mons was completely in flames when we left in the morning. The whole Expeditionary Force, believed to be 150,000 strong, was engaged in the battle. Andrecies, where we arrived on the 25th, is a town of about 10,000 population. The people were pursuing their ordinary occupations on our entry into their midst. We were billeted in stables, barns, archways, etc. on straw. After an hour our rations (a biscuit and a half and a pound of bully beef) were issued. In the midst of the meal, the first in 48 hours, the order, 'Stand to arms' rang forth. We fell into line at once, and after spending half-hour in preparation for action, it was found to be that a false alarm had been given. We were dismissed, and returned to our billets, where we resumed our consumption of the rations. In about twenty minutes afterwards the order 'Stand to arms' rang out again. At this time the Germans were within a mile of Andrecies. They advanced on the town in thousands, on motor buses. Two army corps (80,000 men) were afterwards mentioned as their strength. At this time the Guards' Brigade comprised two battalions of the Coldstreams, one of the Irish and one of the Grenadiers.

When we retired from the town, the inhabitants became panic stricken, and fled from their homes, leaving their property at the mercy of the Germans. Roughly, about 5,000 of us were there to meet the advance of the enemy's 80,000. We were ordered to barricade the streets of the town. We tore up the streets and took possession of everything available, including household furniture to make the barricades. The Germans were then in full action about a mile from the town. The Coldstreams were the first of our Brigade to come into action with the enemy's troops. They checked the advance of the German column until 4 a.m. In the engagement the casualties were terrible, the troops being mowed down as the Germans advanced in close formation. The Coldstreams fell back, and the Germans entered the town. The retreat began, and we marched day and night in the direction of Paris, resting whenever the advanced guard of the Germans stopped marching. The longest day's march of the retreat was Aug. thirty-first when 35 miles were covered with very little food during the journey, as our transport had to keep far in advance of the column in order to avoid being captured. In the march, only five of the Irish Guards fell out from exhaustion, whilst 40 per cent of other regiments in the Brigade succumbed to the fatigue. The news was intimated to us by the commanding officer on the following morning, when we suddenly received orders on the road to 'Fix bayonets'. At this time we were lying on the roadside at Villiers Cotterets, a thickly-wooded country. We only advanced through the wood one hundred yards when the first German bullet whistled over us. Ourselves and the enemy engaged shots without any idea where we or they were situated. We were ordered to retire and for the first time, caught sight of the Germans through the trees. Our commanding officer, Lieutenant-Colonel Morris, mounted on horseback and smoking a cigarette, was on the road giving orders. He was accompanied by Major Crichton, Captain Tisdall, and company and platoon officers. We lost sixteen officers including Colonel Morris, and 150 rank and file. In that engagement, Private John Ryan, who, I think came from Lavally, Tuam, was killed. Private Ryan was in the Birmingham Railway Police, and rejoined at the mobilisation. In the height of this attack we attended our wounded and dying and, having placed them in safety, continued our retreat.

The Germans arrived and attended the wounded, removing those capable of walking and attended to the badly wounded in churches and convents, which were converted into temporary hospitals. At the end of six hours' march we were relieved in the retreat by fresh troops, we had a quiet time with the exception of continuous matching, until Sept. 6 when we reached the neigbourhood of Meaux. The advancing Germans slackened about this time, and on the morning of the 7th the Guards' Brigade were ordered to advance in artillery formation for the purpose of ascertaining the position of the enemy's artillery. The Germans opened artillery fire on us. After marching for three hours our artillery found their range, and silenced them in about ten minutes. The 11th Lancers at this stage, charged and captured two German battery corps and six guns, compared to which our losses were only four guns. This was the turning point in the retreat and reinforcements came from Paris by taxis, and converted the retreat into an advance.

(*The Connaught Tribune* 6-11-1915)

Lance Corp. Wilson of the Second Connaught Rangers, who received an ankle wound at Mons, gave this interview:

(3) On Sunday evening, the 23rd August, the Connaughts made their trenches, but at daybreak on Monday they got the word to retire without having occupied the trenches. It was fortunate for them that they did so, for the Germans found their range just after they left, and continued to shell the trenches for three hours, believing the Connaughts were there. They had to fight a rear guard action during the retreat, and naturally their losses were not slight. The French reinforcements did not come up until the British were about two days on the retreat, and the appearance of the former was greeted with a hearty cheer. At a place called Morbey, the Connaughts met with bad luck in having over 300 of their number captured. A mistake was made somewhere, said Cpl. Wilson who, before the capture, saw Lt-Col. Abercrombie walk down the road from where the men were resting, and he knew the Commander was walking into the German ranks. He did not see the Lieutenant after that, for he, with Lieut. Barker and the number already stated were taken prisoners, having been surrounded on all sides, and completely cut off. Corpl. Wilson's Company, 'D,' had a narrow escape from being captured, they had left at dusk from Morbey, and very shortly afterwards the others were captured, along with two maxim guns, thus leaving the other portion of the Battalion without a machine gun.

About three days after our evacuation of Mons, a remarkable instance of bravery on the part of the Connaughts was shown. We had been on the march all day, and suddenly, without the slightest warning, we observed a whole regiment of Uhlan cavalry bearing down on us. We got into formation at once to meet the onrush. We fixed bayonets, and immediately as we swept up the road to meet the Uhlans, you could hear nothing but the wild cries of 'Come on, the Connaughts'. We dashed up the road, out pacing all the other British regiments, and charged the Uhlans. But they did not wait long enough to make our thorough acquaintance, for they turned around and fled. Nothing could stop us, despite our severe day's marching, and we pursued them through the village. We would have killed several with our rifle fire, but there were women and children in the village, and we were ordered by Cpt. O'Sullivan not to fire, lest we might kill them. It was marvellous the way the fellows fought that evening. Pte. Hayes succeeded in pacifying the terrified women and assured them that we were friends. The only chance, we had of sleep was in the middle of the day, when a halt would be called, and then all hands would throw themselves on the side of the road and go to sleep. On every occasion on which any important engagement was fought, 'D' Coy. was sure to be in it. Eventually, the allies found themselves within eight or ten miles of Paris. It was enough to break our fellows hearts, to hear the order given continually to retire, and at first we did not understand it, but eventually we found out it was part of the scheme to drive the Germans into a trap. Then the allies got the enemy on the move, driving them back the same road whence they came.

(*The Galway Express* 14-11-1914)

Lieut W. G. Barker of the Connaught Rangers wrote this letter to Lieut Col Jourdain in Renmore Barracks. Lieut Barker was taken prisoner after being wounded at Mons. Pte Molloy's military number was recorded incorrectly in the letter, but it has been corrected for this publication:

(4) Festungsalazarett, Ehrenbreitstein, Bei Coblenz, 15-9-14,

Dear Major – Just a line to ask you if you got my report of a small fight poor Leader, (Capt. F. W. M. Leader), Turner (Lieut. C. A. C. Turner), and I got mixed up in, in which ten men were killed and many wounded and the rest taken prisoners (I also was wounded and Turner very seriously). I sent you the names of the men so you might let their people know. If you could also let them know that personally I saw them decently buried and that I had Masses said for them afterwards by a Catholic priest, it might comfort them a bit. I regret that Pte. Molloy (7277) who lives in Ballinasloe, and who was doing quite well in hospital in the bed next me, suddenly showed signs of tetanus, and died two days later. He was a very decent and plucky fellow and, I am sorry to say, was married. I am here in hospital with some French officers and soldiers, and its better than where I was last week, in a cell in the Castle of Siegburg, near Cologne. They won't ask for our parole, I don't know why. Have you any news of the Regiment?

– Yours Sincerely, W. G. Barker.

(*The Galway Express* 24-10-1914)

Pte Duffy of the Second Connaught Rangers was wounded at Mons and following a short stay in a Brighton hospital, he was sent home to Abbey Lane, from where he gave the following interview:

(5) The fighting at Mons started early on Sunday morning 23rd August, but it was not until evening that the Connaughts were called into action. Then at about seven o'clock on the Sabbath they got the word to get into the firing line. Pte. Duffy can amply corroborate the statements which have now passed into history as to the overwhelming majority of the enemy, their terrible artillery fire, weak rifle fire, and the havoc wrought by their shrapnel shells. But there was another thing to which he could testify – his opinion being no way partial – namely, the remarkable bravery, coolness, and marksmanship of the British. All that memorable Sunday they fought in the trenches, without support from any of the other allies, and against an army six or seven times as large as their own. The most disconcerting thing was that when they mowed down one company of the enemy, there was another company to take its place. The superior numbers told, and at 2 o'clock next day, they got the order to retire, which they did so in good order. It was Tuesday before they could get time to eat a meal, having fallen back on a village in the neighbourhood.

It was on Tuesday that Pte. Duffy was injured and he was taken by the Brigadier General to a place of safety until he was attended to. 'They made the Germans sit up' was his brief epitome of the British fighting. The enemies' gunners were, he said, very accurate in finding their billets with the shrapnel shells, but their rifle fire was very poor. 'It is only by chance they get you,' he added. The German aeroplanes [sic] helped the enemy find the allies' range. It is unnecessary to repeat at length the history of the struggle at Mons as told by Pte. Duffy, it has been told and retold. Lieut. Col. Abercrombie was in command of the Connaughts, but he is now numbered among the missing. A fortunate circumstance, as far as these three days' fighting was concerned, added Pte. Duffy was that very few of the brave Connaughts were injured, though the Munster Fusiliers paid a dreadful toll, as did also the Irish Guards. So heavily did the former suffer, that one of them informed Pte. Duffy that his regiment was wiped out, as the German cavalry cut them off. 'Cold steel' was the treatment meted out to the wounded allies by the Germans, and Pte. Duffy fears for the worst for those who are numbered amongst the missing. The allies' wounded who fall into German hands may expect no quarter. Private Duffy was all through the Boer War, saw service at Colenso, Spion Cop, and the relief of Ladysmith, but he says, no comparison could be instituted between those engagements and the present ones. It is simply dreadful when a deluge of lead and shells comes pouring all around one. It requires a marvellous presence of mind to keep cool.

Pte. Duffy relates that Lce-Cpl. Flynn of the Connaughts attached to the cycling corps had a miraculous escape from death; he and a comrade were standing together when a shell burst between them, but neither was injured to any extent. The treatment of the British soldiers by the French and the Belgians was splendid. 'You would insult them' he said 'if you offered them money or anything.' As a contrast to that he had nothing but condemnation for the awful treatment meted out by the Germans to the old men, women and children whom they came across. Pte. Duffy will soon rejoin his regiment at the front. He was informed, when in hospital, that the Russians passed through Brighton on their way to join the allies in France.

(*The Galway Express* 12-9-1914)

This brief letter was written by Pte George McGowan of the Royal Army Medical Corps. George was one of five brothers from Prospect Hill, who served at the front. Their mother, Catherine, received a letter of congratulations from King George V, for having five sons serving in the army. George McGowan was taken prisoner during the retreat from Mons and his experience was in total contrast to the previous interview:

(6) Sennelager, English Camp, Paderborn, Germany.

Dear Mother,

I am a prisoner here. We are treated very well. We are allowed to receive parcels up to 10lbs. Could you send me some butter, cakes and jam now and again? Don't fret for me, as I am in the best of good health, thank God. Hope all is well at home. Tell Joe I was asking for him.

(*The Galway Express* 31-10-1914)

Joe McGowan, brother of George was wounded at Mons and gave the following interview while recovering at home. He was later awarded the

Distinguished Conduct Medal:

(7) He was five hours in the trenches keeping off the Germans, who vastly outnumbered the British, when he was struck in the leg and rendered hors de combat. But during those five hours he saw some of the fiercest fighting recorded in history. The coolness and courage of the small force of Britishers was, he said, remarkable, considering the unceasing attention which the enemy paid them with their 'Jack Johnsons' artillery fire, etc. He corroborates the statements already made by soldiers at the front as to the inefficiency of the enemies rifle fire. The struggle he witnessed was terrific, and the scenes he saw around him have left an indelible imprint on his memory. Beside him he saw a corporal's head blown off with a shell, while he was also witness to the horrible scenes of dead, dying and wounded all around him … Pte. McGowan gives a humorous account of the soldiers, especially the Irish singing all sorts of songs in the trenches and their apparent unconcern about death was inspiring … An incident he relates should give the lie to the Pro-Germans, who regard with scepticism the stories of German atrocities. Journeying home with him was a young lady, a native of Ballyglunin, who had been at school in Belgium and who had to flee from the place. In the town which she was in she saw the Germans murder women and children, and she was horrified to see a German soldier run his bayonet into a child's body. While she, with other members of the household in which she was, were in the cellar hiding their jewellery from the marauders, the Huns entered the house, ransacked it, and subsequently levelled it to the ground. She was lucky to escape from her hiding place.

(*The Galway Express* 10-10-1914)

The following interview was given by Pte Tully after returning from action at Mons where he was wounded:

(8) The Connaughts, with other regiments had to march 500 miles in 18 days after landing in France so as to reach the scene of the battle. The Irish regiments engaged included the Connaughts, Irish Guards, Munster Fusiliers, Dublin Fusiliers and the Royal Irish Rifles. The action commenced on Sunday morning 23rd August. For the first five or six minutes after the shells began to drop in and around one … one would

experience some nervousness, but after that one took everything coolly, and ones only desire was to get at the Germans. The enemy far outnumbered the British, who did not receive the reinforcements they expected from the French and consequently they had to retreat, though in good order. The Germans were as thick as the leaves on the trees in autumn. The Connaughts must have had someone's prayers during the engagement, for they came off very lightly, but the other Irish regiments suffered terribly. The enemy never cared for cold steel and ran when the Irishmen introduced the bayonets. Incidents occurred in which German officers shot their own men for cowardice. The enemy's rifle fire was very poor; it was the shrapnel shells and artillery which did the most damage ... About half way between Paris and Mons, a Belgium woman came to the Allied lines in a – terrible state. She had her two breasts cut off and had nothing on her save a short skirt. All English medical corps attended her subsequently.

(*The Galway Express* 3-10-1914)

The letter below was written by Sgt William Glinn, to his sister in Taylor's Hill:

(9) I don't know if you received my P. C. or not. I wrote you over a week ago, when I was on the way to hospital with a shrapnel wound I received in the right thigh on 15th (Sept.). It is a rather nasty wound, and yesterday I went through a great deal of pain getting a piece of the bullet out. The doctors probed at my wound for nearly an hour feeling for it; then they took a piece out with a forceps. There is some more to be taken from it yet, and I expect to go through great pain with it. We are in a French convent (Catholic) which has been turned into a temporary hospital for British wounded. The people are very kind, but the Customs are strange and we cannot understand the language. We are attended by French doctors, assisted by Nuns and priests. I was rather unlucky to get the wound as I did. We were after getting through two hard days of fighting, and were taking a rest for a day, after handing over 256 German prisoners we captured, when a stray shell came over our way, and I was the only one of the Regiment hit. Afterwards, when getting carried on a stretcher to hospital, I had a marvellous escape. A shell dropped under my stretcher, took the arm off one bearer and injured the other about the head and body, and only threw me into

a ditch. My Company lost 2 officers killed, 2 wounded, and 76 N.C.O. s and men killed or wounded on the 14th. A bit warm for one day's fighting. Sammy Stokes was killed with a shell.

The war is not expected to last very long. They expect out here to have it finished by Xmas. My opinion is that it will last for 18 months at least. We can safely say our army will more then hold its own. The Germans won't have any of us – they're off! Johnny Carty is missing since the battle of Landrecies; he must have been captured. I don't know how long we are going to stay in this hospital. We expect to be sent to England soon. The majority of us are wearing whiskers and hair like poets. I do look a sight with a whisker! I'm like a tramp! I have no clothing, only a pair of kid boots; our Drum Major got me them in a house where our wounded were. If I get the chance they will do great for swanking! When you are writing, do you mind sending me about three packets of Woodbine cigarettes, and I will repay you when I get home! French tobacco is black and not nice for smoking.

P. S. – Major Sarsfield was wounded in the knee the day after me.

(*The Galway Express* 17-10-1914)

CHAPTER XII

THE BATTLES OF THE AISNE

There were three battles of the Aisne fought between September 1914 and June 1918. The first battle took place from 14 until 20 September 1914 along a one hundred mile front between Compeigne and Tahure near Reims. By 12 September the First, Second, Third and Fourth German armies had entrenched themselves north of the River Aisne, where they had considerable artillery support. The allies crossed the river in the Soissons area, and while advancing up the wooded slopes on the far side, they came under heavy artillery fire. It soon became apparent to the allied commanders that this was more than a rearguard action. Ahead of them the Germans had already begun constructing a series of elaborate trench systems, honeycombed with deep underground areas, capable of housing men and in some cases, horses. Storerooms and minor headquarters were also set up, and their trenches were deep enough to provide protection from rifle and machine gun fire, and wide enough for two soldiers to pass each other.

During the battle, the Germans took the offensive and attacked allied positions. At one stage of the engagement the Irish Guards had taken and cleared an area of woods when the enemy displayed a white flag, as some of the guardsmen stepped into the open, they were fired upon by the Germans causing several casualties among their ranks. The British pressed on with the attack over the following days, but realising it was 'fruitless', began 'digging-in'. From then until March 1918, trench warfare became the order of the day. Further allied gains on the Aisne were prevented because of poor artillery support. Both sides also became embroiled in what became know as the 'race to the sea' in an attempt to out flank each other. By December 1914, the western front had been established and consolidated with hundreds of miles of trenches running from the North Sea to Switzerland.[1]

The following are examples of letters and interviews from Galway soldiers who saw action at the Aisne. This 'well embellished' letter was written by Pte Michael Hayes from Prospect Hill to a friend in Forster Street:

(1) The battle of the Aisne, which we are at, is the longest ever known; we are at it since the 12th September. Of course we do not want to advance any further for a while. We could have been in the German trenches days and days ago, but it is our policy not to do so, as we are waiting for our troops and the French to get around to their right and left wings, a scheme which will take a long time. We are only joking with them yet, taking down 700 or 800 a day. In the first big battle on the Aisne we (the Connaught Rangers) were fighting an advance guard action. We halted at a farmhouse to make some tea, but before we had it the Germans let us know they were coming with a volley from the woods. We number only hundreds, but we turned against nine German regiments and held them there for a good few hours, until our regiment was getting so weak that we were being forced back. We have to thank the Coldstream Guards, however, for being alive today, for they reinforced us in the nick of time, and then I tell you we let them have it. We were only getting hot at it when they showed the white flag. The firing on our side ceased, and when we advanced to take them prisoners and were within a hundred yards of them, the cowards opened fire on us again. Well, such 'a gait of going' we gave them! We charged them furiously, drove them back and took nearly 300 prisoners. The battle then ceased, and at night we left the German corpses four feet high on the field of battle; there were thousands upon thousands of them killed.

When we had done, after fasting the whole day, we had breakfast, dinner and tea together, we got plenty, and tobacco and cigarettes. The next day the General gave us a rest, and as we rested along a canal bank the Germans shelled us out of it with their big guns, and we had to take cover under a high bank. After a good night's sleep we had to make trenches on a hill the next day, to protect us from the enemy's shells, because it is their artillery that is doing all the damage; the infantry come out now and again, but only to meet their doom, and when the trenches were made the enemy made a night attack on us, not thinking that we were waiting for them, or that we sleep with one eye and one ear open. We drove them back after a tussle, and the next morning (Sunday) our breakfast was a good fight with the Germans, lasting all day. We had another hard day's fighting on the twenty-first September, the enemy kept coming and going all day long, and they were tripping over the piles of their dead. They had the cheek to make another night attack on us, but we charged them with the bayonet, but when they saw that useful weapon they did a right-about turn, and ran for all they were worth, and some of them surrendered. I tell you we do give them what ... I do enjoy it myself. The best sport I ever had is taking them down, I can't half shoot, either. They might as well try and bring their dead to life as try to get through the British lines, and they would sooner meet d – I then us.

We are living the life of rabbits for we have burrowed ourselves in trenches, in which we have remained for over a fortnight in rain and cold at night. The bursting of shells overhead was continuous, and after a while it became monotonous. To the youngsters it is an awful experience at first, but even they became accustomed to the roar overhead that they raise a cheer each time shrapnel or shell spoke, and make such remarks as 'There's another rocket, John.' We had as companions some of the King's Liverpool Regiment, most of whom are Irish like ourselves, and we spin yarns about the dear homeland. Sometimes to kill time we play 25's – an Irishman's game – which we play for cigarettes, papers, etc. Sometimes we discuss the prospects of our favourite hockey team, and on one occasion when on that topic, a shell burst near us, striking one of our chaps on the knee. He calmly remarked, as we bandaged his knee for him 'I won't be able to play on Christmas Day for the Connacht Cup.' We are all a lighthearted lot, and so are our officers, for whom we dug out a kind of subterranean mess room, where they take their meals, and which is decorated with cigarette pictures etc. The food they get is not exactly what would be supplied to them in the Railway Hotel. A jollier or kinder lot you would not meet than the officers. One officer who was well stocked with 'fags' divided them among his men and we were able to repay him for his kindness shortly afterwards by digging him out from under his mess room, a shell having tumbled in the structure like a house of cards.

During the time we were in those trenches over 500 shells burst over our heads, but thanks to the protection afforded by the trenches, not a single man was killed, and less than a dozen wounded. When we got into the open we realised what we had been subjected to, for the ground was literally strewn with burst shells, one of which would make a hole big enough to bury a horse. On the 24th September the enemy came on in large numbers and tried to get through the British lines, but they might as well try to get to Heaven. It was here I was wounded in the hand, and the only officer (Lieu. Benison) who was left in my Company fell that morning by my side. I looked to see if I could do anything with his wound, but it was no use. His last words were 'Take me to Major Hayes.' I, with two others, carried him to our headquarters, amidst the terrible fire from shot and shell, but we had somebody's prayers that saved us from being blown to pieces. Back I went again under awful fire to the trenches, to which I had to lead a fresh Company up, as my Company was not strong enough to keep the enemy back. With the reinforcements we beat the Germans back, and in the evening I had to go back to the village, where the medical staff was, to get my wound dressed, as it was terribly painful. They sent me back to England against my will, as I did not want to leave my chums, and I wanted to have another slap at the Germans.

(*The Galway Express* 14-11-1914)

This letter was written by Pte Michael Ward, a Connaught Ranger from Ballinasloe. Pte Ward received a gun shot wound to the right eye, but survived and was invalided out of the army:

(2) We were in every fight there was from Belgium to Mons and since Mons. There are only about 170 of us left now, and we went out 1,300 strong and had 800 men in reinforcements sent out to us. We took part in several bayonet charges, and the sight of dead Germans in some of the trenches we took was awful. I was wounded on Friday week in Belgium; we were in the firing line there again. The Dublins and the Leinsters were fighting with us. I was eight days in flooded trenches, and then I got this wound in my head. The food was all right, we were getting plenty, biscuits principally. One good bayonet charge we had was at Soupier with the Irish Guards, the Leinsters Second Battalion and what was left of us (Rangers). In the first bayonet charge the Rangers had at Mons there were 700 of us, and there at the last charge we had only 400. After that charge there were only 270 of us left – out of 1,300 strong and the reinforcements of 800 we had got all told. The Irish Guards did great work out there two weeks ago in a place called, I think, Moussy. They captured a battery with a bayonet charge, and after the charge they were asked to go back for a rest, but

refused to rest, and went on to the firing line again.

(*The Galway Express* 14-11-1914)

Gen. Sir Horace Smith-Dorrien wrote the letter below in tribute to the men who fought under him at the battles of the Aisne and the Marne. It was directed towards the Soldiers and Sailors Families Association:

(3) Knowing as I do that you are striving to help the wives and families of the brave soldiers who are fighting under me in this glorious war. I should like you to tell them, when you have the opportunity, a little about the doings of the husbands, brothers and sons, so they may learn to appreciate them at their true value. Never has an army been called on to engage in such desperate fighting as is the daily occurrence in this present war, and never have any troops behaved so magnificently as our soldiers in this war. The stories of the battles of Le Mons and Le Cateau are only beginning to be known, but at them a British force not only held its own against a German Army four times its own size, but it hit the enemy so hard that never were they able to do more than follow it up. Of course our troops had to fall back before them, an operation which would demoralise most armies. Not so with ours, however. Though they naturally did not like retiring for twelve successive days, they merely fell silently back, striking hard whenever attacked, and the moment the order came to go forward, there were smiling faces everywhere. Then followed the battle of the Marne and the Aisne.

Tell the women that all these great battles have, day after day, witnessed countless feats of heroism and brave fighting. Large numbers will be given Victoria Crosses and Distinguished Conduct Medals, but many more have earned them, for it has been impossible to bring every case to notice. Tell the women that, proud as I am to have such soldiers under my command, they should be prouder still to be near and dear relations of such men, and they can show their pride by their behaviour. Let them think of their husbands and brothers undergoing the greatest imaginable fatigue, often cold and wet for days together and through it all though in constant danger, performing deeds of which any country might be proud.

Tell the wives to talk to their children about their brave fathers, and for themselves never to do anything in full account of which they would shrink from giving their husbands on their return from war. Tell the women and girls they can serve their country best by leading quiet lives, thus setting an example of self-restraint and uprightness at home, which equally with the bravery of their dear ones in the war, is necessary to bring the country through this great national crisis with credit to those who have the good fortune to live under the Union Jack.

(*The Galway Express* 12-12-1914)

The following extract is taken from the interview with Sgt Stephen Shaughnessy from Tuam, who was serving with the Irish Guards:

(4) On crossing the river the battle of the Aisne commenced. We took the offensive, and drove the enemy through several towns, and advanced eight miles. We entrenched ourselves for the night on the roadside. The Germans were forced back to the heights over the Aisne, where they had dug trenches. At this point trench warfare, for the first time since the beginning of the war, began and continued for a month. On October 15 we were relieved by the French territorials, and two days were spent travelling in cattle trucks, each bearing a freight of 42 men. We arrived in Haslebruck, from where we marched for three days and nights towards Ypres. We were two days in the train, at the end of which we reached Ypres, and took possession of a salient outside the town.

(*The Connaught Tribune* 6-11-1915)

This is an extract from an account that was given by Pte J. Sweeny of the Second Connaught Rangers, while he was recovering from wounds at his home near Creggs:

(5) My regiment took part in numerous other engagements during that retreat; and although a good many British were killed and wounded, still we counted for a good many Germans. We made an exceptional stand against overwhelming numbesr on the banks of the Aisne. For nine weeks we were entrenched along the river side, and notwithstanding the fierce attacks both night and day by the Germans, we held our own. The heavy artillery fire by the Germans was very effective, and the accuracy with which they found range was most remarkable. With the rifle they are practically useless, and the British troops score wonderfully in bayonet charges. The Germans

have a holy horror of the bayonet, and fly in the most cowardly manner when charged. I took part in the battle of Sedan. For several days there was continuous fierce fighting. The Germans are constantly dropping their shells in our midst, our positions being accurately gauged by their aeroplanes. These aeroplanes are damnable things, and it is extremely hard to evade them. Many of them were brought down, but it was no easy task to do so. It was subsequent to the battle of the river Marne, while on the march, that I got wounded by a shell bursting close to our ranks and a portion of which cut me badly on the thigh. In hospital, both doctors and nurses were very kind. I was in active service for about sixteen weeks, and can bear personal witness to the fact that the Scots' Greys, the Coldstreams, the Connaught Rangers and the Irish Guards acquitted themselves with great bravery on the battlefield.

(*The Tuam Herald* 21-11-1914)

The second battle of the Aisne took place between 16 April and 20 May 1917. The French, under the command of Gen. Robert Nivelle, planned to attack the German lines with twenty-seven divisions. However, the plans were compromised when the Germans intercepted a copy of the orders and immediately began reinforcing their positions with both infantry and artillery. Although they were also hampered by weather conditions, the French still went ahead with the attack, but machine gun fire from the German lines thinned their ranks. They were initially to have the support of tanks, but this did not materialise due to the late arrival of these 'new war machines'. Nevertheless, the French managed to penetrate some four miles into the German positions before being stopped. Both sides suffered severe losses, the French casualties were some 187,000, while the German losses numbered about 163,000. The heavy losses were one of the factors which contributed to near mutinies of the French Army during the following month. The only real gain for the allies that spring was the capture of Vimy Ridge in Northern France, by the Canadians, but this was only achieved at the cost of 11,285 lives.[2]

The following letter was written by Second Lieut W. P. Kinneen of the Dublin Fusiliers, to his mother in Eyre Square, Galway. 'Hell Fire Village' mentioned in the letter has been correctly identified as 'Hell Fire Corner':

Connacht Rangers Parade day at Renmore Barracks, some years prior to the Great War. Private Thomas Croke, second row, third from the left, had been a member of the RIC, but resigned having after witnessing some evictions. Lieutenant Colonel Henry Jourdain is seated centrally in the front row. (Courtesy of Don Walsh).

Scottish troops relaxing after training at Dangan.
(Courtesy of the Tom Kenny Collection)

Dog Fish Lane, Claddagh. (Courtesy of the Tom Kenny Collection)

Irish Guards recruiting at Eyre Square, Galway.
(Courtesy of the Tom Kenny Collection)

Captain Wyndham Waithman of Merlin Park, one of the senior recruiting officers for Galway. (Courtesy of Martin Geary and Norbert Sheerin)

Connacht Rangers who served throughout the four years of the war. Patrick Lynskey from the Claddagh is third from the left. It is believed the other soldiers emigrated to Australia and never returned. (Courtesy of Michael Lynskey)

St. Patrick's Band, prior to the Great War. Jack Hoare is third from the left in the first row of boys standing. He joined the Connacht Rangers, as did a number of band members. The band played at many of the recruiting meetings, and accompanied troops to Galway Station as they began their journey to the front. (Courtesy of Ann Walsh)

The Ballinasloe Volunteers, 1914. Most of these men enlisted in the British Army and served at the front. (Courtesy of Eva McHugh)

Irish Rebellion May 1916.
A group of Officers with the captured rebel flag.

A group of British officers with the captured rebel flag at the Parnell Monument, Dublin, following the 1916 Easter Rebellion. (Courtesy of the Frost Collection)

A memorial to the nine men who lost their lives at Inverin on 15 June 1917. The memorial was unveiled in June 1970. (Author's collection)

Girls in the Galway Woollen Mill, where many of the soldier's uniforms were manufactured. (Courtesy of the Tom Kenny Collection)

Wounded soldiers and nursing staff in Almondsbury Subsidiary Hospitsl, England, 1915.
The soldier standing in front of the window is Major Richard Potter, of Furbo House.
(Courtesy of Helen Spelman)

St. Nicholas' Collegiate Church, November 2000, decorated with poppy crosses for
Remembrance Day. (Author's collection)

The Supply Company of the American Peace Commission. Private Michael Donohue (the uncle of Thomas Feeney of Fair Hill, Claddagh, is located in the back row. The photograph was taken in May 1919, outside a Paris Hotel during the Peace Conference. Note the weaponry in the background. (Courtesy of Thomas Feeney)

Loughrea World War I veterans at the British Legion Hall, Piggots Lane, *circa* 1921. Some of the men have not been identified and these are indicated by the dashes. Front row, from left: Puddley Barrett ----- Hynes, Tommy Danniels, Harry Furey, Tommy Shaughnessy, Martin Holleran, Bisey Green, Tom Haverty. Middle row, from left: Martin Kelly, ----- Hynes, Paddy Duffy, Tom Casey, Billy Toole, Michael Caffer-Hynes, Pakin Madden, Jack Kelly, Peter Whelan, Paddy Shaw. Back row, from left: Ned Goonan, ------, John Joe Walsh, ------, Mike Duffy, Paddy Barrett, ------- (Courtesy of Ferdy Wheelan)

Inscribed stone in the Island of Ireland
Peace Park, Messines in Belgium.
It contains the words from one of
Tom Kittles famous poems, 'To My
Daughter Betty.'
(Author's collection)

Irish Guards, 1915, Catterham Barracks, Sussex, just before they were sent to France. Private
Thomas Flaherty is third from the left in the second row. Private Jack Monaghan, St. Patrick's
Avenue is second row, fourth from the left. (Courtesy of Johnny Flaherty)

Crossing the canal. (Courtesy of the Irish Guards)

In the trenches. (Courtesy of the Irish Guards)

Casualty.
(Courtesy of the Irish Guards)

Stretcher bearers return from 'No Mans Land' with their human cargo.
(Courtesy of the Irish Guards)

Soldiers rest on what remains of the banks of the Ypres Canal after an attack.
(Courtesy of the Irish Guards)

Ypres in 1912.
(Courtesy of Associated Newspapers Ltd. & Eamonn McNally Collection)

Ypres after the attack. (Courtesy of the Irish Guards)

View of the battleground at Passchendale. Note the ruined tank stuck in the mire as the bombardment continued. (Courtesy of the Irish Guards)

Troops working away at everyday
duties in between battle.
(Courtesy of the Irish Guards)

Irish Guards resting after the Battle of Neuve Chapelle. (Courtesy of the Irish Guards)

Soldiers of the Royal Field Artillery relaxing between actions. Private James (Jim) Comber is on the extreme left, seated with his back against the shed. (Courtesy of Gerald Comber)

B Company, 2nd Royal Dublin Fusiliers, winner of the 'Inter-Company Bayonet Fighting Shield', 1914. Back row, from left: Private Byrne, Corporal Toole, Private Pallas. Middle row, from left: Private Murray, Private Cullen, Private Black, Company Sergeant Major Sutton, Private Parry, Private Leonard, Private Leonard. Front row, from left: Lieutenant Captain Hughes, Private O'Neill, Sergeant Esmonde, major H.M. Shewan, D.S.O., Lieutenant R.M.W. Massey-Westropp, Sergeant Nix, Private Kirwan, Private James Ruffley. Private Ruffley was one of five brothers from Bohermore, Galway, who fought in the Great War.
(Courtesy of the Ruffley Family)

Renmore Barracks. The white tents were erected to accommodate additional troops.
(Courtesy of the Tom Kenny Collection)

Four British officers in Egypt during the build-up for the assault on Gaza. Victor Smith is first from the left, and Maurice Neligan is third from the left. Victor Smith was the man responsible for the Smith Collection of photographs. he was an enthusiastic photographer and some say that he shot more film than bullets during the war. (Courtesy of the Smith Collection)

Troops of the Royal Field Artillery Regiment pose on the Pyramid of Giza.
(Courtesy of the Smith Collection)

Crossing the Sinai Desert.
(Courtesy of the Smith Collection)

Allied troops preparing for action during the campaign in Palestine.
(Courtesy of the Smith Collection)

Gun crew preparing for the assault on Gaza.
(Courtesy of the Smith Collection)

Photograph believed to be of the Allies entering the Holy City, Jerusalem, December 1917.
(Courtesy of the Smith Collection)

The devastating consequences of an artillery bombardment.
(Courtesy of the Irish Guards)

Allied troops on leave in Paris. Lance Corporal John Partington Casey, Royal Engineers is third from the left, standing. He was a grandfather of the Rabbit family of Forster Street, Galway. He served throughout most of the war, and received the George medal following the battle of Loos in 1915. He was eventually invalided out of the army. His uncle, Thomas Casey also served, but was killed in action. (Courtesy of Peter Rabbitt)

Vice Admiral Sir David Beatty.
(Courtesy of Eamonn McNally)

Troops in a 'dug-out' look out across destroyed tillage fields.
(Courtesy of the Irish Guards)

Private Joseph James Henry, Seaforth Highlanders, was
killed in action around the village of Iwuy during the
Battle of Cambrai on 13 October 1918.
(Author's collection)

Mametz Woods, Somme. The trees were reduced to splinters during a fierce bombardment. (Courtesy of the Irish Guards)

The town of Albert after being shelled. Note the statue of the Madonna leaning over from the steeple of the church, almost ready to plunge to the ground. According to tradition, if the statue fell it would have been a bad omen for the Allies. It did not fall, and is still the focal point of the restored church to this present day. (Courtesy of the Irish Guards)

Bethune before the shells landed, 1916.
(Courtesy of the Irish Guards)

Bethune after the bombardment, totally devastated.
(Courtesy of the Irish Guards)

Guillemont village after the attack.
(Courtesy of the Irish Guards)

Horror on the road to Guillemont.
(Courtesy of the Irish Guards)

The road to Guillemont today, with the Guillemont War Cemetry in view.
(Author's collection)

Ginchy Ridge, an example of the conditions the troops had to overcome during battle.
(Courtesy of the Irish Guards)

Aerial view of the first Battle of Cambrai.
(Courtesy of the Irish Guards)

Tanks brought into action at Flesqviers.
(Courtesy of the Irish Guards)

Allied troops marching across the Hindenburg Line.
(Courtesy of the Irish Guards)

Allied officer informs the troops of the Armistice, 11 November 1918.
(Courtesy of the Irish Guards)

Princess Mary Gift Box.
(Author's collection)

Memorial Plaque to Private Joseph Henry.
(Author's collection)

The Guillemont Ginchy Cross.
(Author's collection)

The Connacht Ranger Memorial
Window in the Cathedral of Our Lady
Assumed into Heaven and Saint Nicholas
(New Cathedral), Galway.
(Author's collection)

The Irish National War Memorial, Island Bridge, Dublin.
(Author's collection)

The Great War Memorial in St Nicholas'
Collegiate Church, Galway. (Author's collection)

The Cenotaph, London
(Author's collection)

The tomb of the Unknown Warrior in Westminister Abbey.
(Courtesy of the Dean & Chapter, Westminister Abbey)

The Round Tower in the Island of Ireland Peace
Park, Messines, Belgium.
(Author's collection)

Menin Gate, Ypres.
(Author's collection)

The Ulster Tower.
(Courtesy of Joe Loughnane)

The Thiepval Monument, Somme, France.

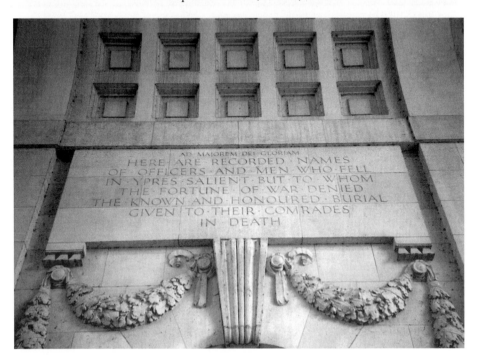

AD MAIOREM DEI GLORIAM
HERE ARE RECORDED NAMES
OF OFFICERS AND MEN WHO FELL
IN YPRES SALIENT BUT TO WHOM
THE FORTUNE OF WAR DENIED
THE KNOWN AND HONOURED BURIAL
GIVEN TO THEIR COMRADES
IN DEATH

Inscription on Menin Gate, Ypres.
(Author's collection)

PEACE PLEDGE

"From the crest of this ridge-which was the scene of horrific carnage in the First World War on which we have built a peace park and Round Tower to commemorate the thousands of young men from all parts of Ireland who fought a common enemy, defended democracy and the rights of all nations, whose graves are in shockingly uncountable numbers and those who have no graves, we condemn war and the futility of war. We repudiate and denounce violence, aggression, intimidation, threats and unfriendly behaviour.

As Protestants and Catholics, we apologise for the terrible deeds we have done to each other and ask forgiveness. From this sacred shrine of remembrance, where soldiers of all nationalities, creeds and political allegiances were united in death, we appeal to all people in Ireland to help build a peaceful and tolerant society. Let us remember the solidarity and trust that developed between Protestant and Catholic Soldiers when they served together in these trenches.

As we jointly mark the armistice of 11 November 1918-when the guns fell silent along this western front-we affirm that a fitting tribute to the principles for which men and women from the Island of Ireland died in both World Wars would be permanent peace."

The Peace Pledge in the Island of Ireland Peace Park, Messines, Belgium.
(Author's collection)

(1) I had one marvellous escape. Returning with a working party one night from the front line, we came under shellfire in 'Hell Fire Village', when two shells burst in front of me, doing us no damage but showing us we better hurry. The next thing I remember is a blinding flash, a hit in the solar plexus, a blast of a thousands winds, deafened, winded, and I was completely taken off my feet. I picked myself up to find the men behind me lying here and there. The shell burst 3ft from me, and though I was between the shell and the men knocked out I did not get a scratch. Another shell burst and I ran into the area where it exploded – with the cloud of dust, falling earth, bricks, etc. – the thought sticking me that another would not burst in the same place. After that I went back and shouted to the men to come on, but no one answered; I shouted again, and a wounded soldier replied – 'I can't, sir, I'm hit.' We lost twenty men all told on that occasion, two being knocked out by the shell that landed at my feet.
(*The Galway Express* 2-6-1917)

These three letters are in connection with Bernie Fahy from Claregalway, who was killed in action in 1917. The first is a letter to his mother. The second are the contents of the telegram announcing his death, and the third is from his commanding officer, to Bernie's mother giving her details of his death:

(2) Falmouth 4th March 1916.

My Dearest Mother,

Your letter reached me safely a few days ago and am sorry to hear that you are suffering from rumatic pains. I know what they are, I had my share of them, you want to take care of yourself and don't do too much work and what ever you do keep out of the rain. I found whenever it was damp that they got real bad but when it rained they eased off again. Thank God they left me and I hope they keep away. Well Mamma we have got no priest with us our company is to small, but where we are going there are some, we are always marched to church every Sunday we have got a nice little church here in Falmouth, I will get a post card of it and send it to you. We have arranged with the priest to receive Holy Communion tomorrow.

(Fahy Family Archives)

(3) Post Office Telegraphs

Southampton OHMS. Of last night 6.37 p.m.

Mr. R. Fahy, Cregboy, Claregalway, Ireland.

Very much regret to inform you of information just received that your son 4/1423 Lance Corporal Bernie Fahy, New Zealand Engineers Tunnelling Company, previously reported died 19th April is now reported killed in action 20th April.

(Fahy Family Archives)

(4) NZE Tunnelling Coy. B.E.F. France. 19-4-17.

Dear Mrs. Fahy,

I deeply regret that it is my painful duty to inform you of the death of your son Lance Corporal B. Fahy, who was killed in action at 5.30 p.m. today while nobly doing his duty. Knowing him for a true and honourable man, I can fully realise what a grievous loss his death will be to his mother. He has proved himself of great service to this company, and has always done his duty bravely and well; and I feel that I have lost a personal friend, for whom I had a great admiration. He will be buried at 10.30 a.m. tomorrow and I have procured a Roman Catholic priest to administer to last sad rites. I will send forthwith his personal effects to you, and if there are any further particulars you wish to know, I shall be glad to furnish them. – P. S. Corlys, Lieut. O.C. No. 3 Section.

(Fahy Family Archives)

The third battle of the Aisne was fought between 27 May and 18 June 1918. The battle began when the German First and Seventh armies broke through allied positions and advanced approximately ten miles towards Chateau-Thierry, thus placing Paris under threat. The ground was bitterly fought over with the British Ninth Army Corps and the French Fifth Army doing their utmost to stop the German advance. By the time of the third battle of the Aisne, the United States had entered the war and the American Third Division were involved in combating the progress of the German troops. However, it was lack of reserves and overstretched supply lines that eventually brought the German advance to a standstill. One of the areas they had occupied was the village of Vaux on the Paris-

Metz road, the Germans then pushed forward to the Belleau Wood area. This became a major battleground for the American marines, who were so close to the enemy, that their own artillery could offer no real support. The marines were ordered back to the southern edge of the woods, and then the full might of the allied artillery was brought to bear on the woods. The greenery was completely reduced to splintered timber and it reeked with the stench of death. While the marines entered the woods in a 'mop-up' operation, the allies turned their attention on the village of Vaux. The Germans had occupied and fortified the village houses. The allied bombardment began at dawn, and an hour later the shelling was lifted towards the slopes beyond the village preventing any German reinforcements from reaching their stricken comrades. The allied infantry were then sent into action and had completed their task by noon.[3]

This letter was written by an officer of the Royal Field Artillery, expressing his condolences to the mother of Pte John Fahy from Portumna, who was killed in action. He was described as 'only a boy' when he volunteered for service in 1914 and survived almost four years of war:

(1) No doubt you have heard of the great loss the war has brought to you in the death of your son, John. I feel I must, however, write to you and sympathize with you in this great sorrow. John has been my man since January, 1917, and all this time has been my friend. I feel his absence both for his friendship and loss of his ever ready capable services. When I left the battery a month ago he came with me in spite of their efforts to keep him. I have seen that all his belongings have been forwarded to you by the ordinary channels. I want to tell you that he died instantly and therefore absolutely without pain. He was not disfigured, being hit in the back of the head. To-day he has been buried in a registered graveyard by the Brigade Padre. I am seeing that a white wooden cross is erected with his name painted on. The poor fellow is more fortunate than many thousands who die out here, and are buried without ceremony in a nameless grave. So you have some comfort in your hour of trial. He was a brave soldier and feared no danger.

(*The Connacht Tribune* 8-6-1918)

Rifleman Thomas Donohoe wrote to his wife just before being sent to France. He died of wounds on 12 June 1917 in London:

(2) Wednesday 10-1-1917

Dear Bridget,

Received your overwelcomed letter today glad to know that you and children are all well as I am in the best of form. Dear B we have very bad cold weather here presently no sign of it changing. .. expect to be leaving here on Friday or Saturday next. I am greatly in doubt that we are going to France or Salonika so I ask you in the honour of God not to be worrying or troubled about me as I will be all right as I have great confidence in God ... can do all so take good care of yourself and the children. Dear B I am not one bit put about so I know I had to go through this as its in Gods hands now whatever he thinks best. I am going to confession on ... tonight so I will be well prepared. I ask you to get another mass said for me, some of the boys would not tell their wives until they were fine but I thought it better to tell you in time so again I ask you not to worry about me but pray fervently and God will bring me back safe to you. I think it won't last much longer we will give it the finishing touch. May God pity the German I will come across oh what a cruel murdering he will get. Dear B tell the boys I can't get any melodeon nor had no time to look for one ... the ... don't trouble me much either. Tell them I was asking for them. I suppose they would be frightened in their skin if they were in my place but I am not nor wont. Dear B you should have my last letter on Friday instead of Sunday what is the cause of it. I was expecting a letter on Monday last and I did not get it until today isn't it too bad the way they are delayed I was sure there was something wrong with you so don't delay the next letters and if you possibly can send me a few shillings & pipe & tobacco as will ... and its the last I will ask again until I go home for good. So I hope its not too much as I know its hard on you but still when its the last I hope its not to much. Curley would parcel them up for you, try to send me a good pipe. We all had to make a will so I willed you all as we will be only getting six pence a day out there all the rest will be saved over for us so if I am turned up you will have the remainder as you know its a old saying its hard to kill the bad thing. Dear B, don't worry anyhow as you will be alright by me also with Gods help. We were sent out new clothing and new hats we are expecting forty-eight hours leave but I think we wont get any if we did I would go home, we are going to be inspected by the King tomorrow 15 thousand of us so it will be a fine sight. So again I ask not to be worrying about me and cheer up as I am in the best of form and do the best you can for yourself and the children and good bye with best love to you and the children x x x x x x one extra for yourself, don't delay letter. – 5188 Rifleman Donohoe P. O. R. Sutton. – Cheer up Bridget. Warminster.

(Jordan Family Archives)

CHAPTER XIII

THE BATTLES OF YPRES

There were four battles of Ypres, the first taking place during October and November of 1914. From the very beginning of the war the Belgian town of Ypres, became vital to both sides, because whoever controlled the town held the key to the channel ports. Before the war, Ypres was a small, quiet, little-known town, with a population of approximately 22,000. However, by the end of the Great War, all of Europe and indeed, the world would remember the name Ypres as a place that witnessed all the horrors of war. It has been stated that there is no battleground in the world more sanctified with soldiers' blood than Ypres, with casualties occurring there at triple the rate of any other sector. The Germans wanted to capture the town and use it as a hub for munitions and supplies because its roads led westwards to the ports.

The British were well aware of the German objective and prepared to resist any attempt by the enemy to occupy the area. Because Ypres could not be defended from trenches, the higher ground to the east of the town became the fortification. This position became known as the Ypres Salient, and over the following four years it became the slaughtering ground for hundreds of thousands of soldiers. The British pushed forward towards the ridges, known as Passchendaele, Broodseinde, Gheluvelt and Messines. Among those who fled the town were the Benedictine Nuns, whose order had been in Ypres for over two hundred years. However, once the German shelling began, they decided to leave, and eventually ended up in Kylemore Abbey, County Galway.[1]

The first battle of Ypres began on 20 October 1914, when the German drive for Ypres began. On 21 October, the Second Connaught Rangers took up positions in fields north of Ypres near the village of St Julien.

They suffered a number of casualties that day and for the following three days bore the brunt of German artillery fire. The Rangers were relieved on 24 October by French troops; however, they had not been resting for very long when the military situation took a turn for the worse. The Germans succeeded in breaking through east of Ypres and the Rangers were immediately deployed to plug the breach. The Rangers suffered severely under a deluge of murderous machine fire that depleted their numbers, causing one witness to describe the battlefield scene as a 'perfect hell on earth'.

The battle raged for ten days, by which time the British lines were almost broken, but a brief lull in the fighting allowed them to regroup and replenish munitions and supplies. The Germans were also reinforced and their next attack began with them charging in mass formation into grouped machine-gun and rifle fire. The town was shelled by enemy howitzers, resulting in its destruction and causing the deaths of many civilians. The gothic cathedral where many of the women had taken refuge was hit, as were the civilian aid stations, and a school where children were at play.

With the town reduced to rubble, many of its inhabitants fled. An allied officer later reported that the only person he saw in the town was an aged Flemish woman, who was attempting to save her house from the flames with buckets of water. Weather conditions during the battle added to the misery, it was bitterly cold and constant downpours of rain caused water logging and mud in the trenches. As time went on, the weather got steadily worse with frost and snow causing even more problems, but still hostilities continued. On 29 October, the Germans launched a massive assault between Messines and Gheluvelt and despite many losses, the British held the trenches. The Germans did manage to break the British line along the Menin Road, but a gallant bayonet charge by the Worcesters 'saved the day'.[2]

On 8 November, the Connaught Rangers pulled back for a well-earned rest in the Polygon Woods. Unfortunately, it was the place chosen by the German Imperial Guard for another assault on Ypres. This began on 11

November, when German artillery pounded the allied positions, forcing the British to abandon their trenches and take shelter in a nearby wood. When that shelling finally stopped, thirteen German divisions attacked across a nine-mile front running from Messines to the Menin road. The action was so intense that every available man, cooks, orderlies, engineers etc were thrown into the defence of Ypres.

Although the Germans had gained about a thousand yards overall, a British counter attack stopped any further advance. The Germans responded by shelling the British lines, and the town with heavy artillery, hitting the sluice and lock gates of the canal, thus flooding the surrounding area. Many of the Irish regiments suffered high casualties under the savage German attacks. Five days later, the remnants of the Second Connaught Rangers were moved to a rest area at Bellewarde Farm. There were so few officers and men left that they could no longer be called a Battalion, thus, it was decided the survivors should be amalgamated with the First Battalion Connaught Rangers. Many of the fatalities were never found, but their names are recorded on the Menin Gate, along with thousands of other missing soldiers. By the time the battle ended in late November, the Germans had taken an estimated 150,000 casualties, with the allies totalling about the same. The first battle of Ypres stripped the British Army of many of its best and bravest officers. Upon seeing the carnage, Sir John French is reputed to have said: 'All that remains for me to do is get killed.'[3]

The following letters and interviews are from various Galway soldiers who fought at Ypres. One of the Galway soldiers killed in action at the first battle of Ypres was Capt. Richard Kinkead. He was attached to the Tenth Hussars, but had formally served with the Royal Army Medical Corps. He was the son of Professor Kinkead of University College Galway and the family lived at Forster House. Just four days before he was killed, he wrote a letter to his family in Galway. It arrived a few hours after the telegram from the war office announcing his death. The following are extracts from the letter, and the second is the contents of a post card from a comrade:

(1) I am fit and well and sound in wind in limbs, except for pains in back and legs from over strain of the muscles, due to lifting men out of the trenches and carrying them back. We have to do it as the trenches are very small, and one or two wounded men fill up a whole trench, so they must be got out unless the fire is too hot. We had a day's rest yesterday, but are in the trenches again to-day; came in last night, and it was a wet, miserable night. We took a lot of prisoners last night. The arm-chair people at home with their cry of 'universal peace' and 'there can never be a European war,' small Army and little Navyites, ought to be out here now, and see the miseries and horrors the peasants here go through, the number of wounded and killed, and a few other sights – villages and farms blazing all over the country. If we had only had a million and a half of an Army of our present standard the Germans would be on the Rhine by now, and the war nearly over.

One sees in a war like this the sort of stuff our officers are made of. They are mostly 'tophole' chaps, worshipped by the men; and if there are shells etc. flying they use this to lead by example. Even when things burst over one's heads, one must not duck or jump – the men would see it. You would be surprised to see how quickly the men follow one's example. I hope after the war Tommy will get the recognition that is due to him, because he is one of the very best. The other day a farm, where I had been sleeping in a barn, was shelled and set on fire. My corporal, thinking I was still asleep, went into the blazing fire to fetch me out, and was not satisfied until he had searched the whole place. Now, this corporal is one of the 10th Hussars, and had only known me since I came to the regiment, just over two months.

(*The Galway Express* 7-11-1914)

(2) Dear Sir – I am writing to thank you for tobacco and cigarettes received on the 5th inst. My comrades also wish to thank you for your generosity; these gifts are most acceptable and are highly approved of by us boys. You will excuse me mentioning Capt. Kinkead of the R.A.M.C., whom I happened to be with on the morning he was killed, whilst attending to the wounded. I have seen several in the papers for the V.C.; if ever a man earned one your namesake should figure amongst them. – Yours sincerely – 6204 W. Rowson First Troop, C Squadron, Tenth Hussars, Eight Cav., Brigade, Third Div., Brit. Expeditionary Force.

(*The Galway Express* 13-3-1915)

The following extract is from an interview given by Pte P. Conneely, a Connaught Ranger from Oughterard:

(3) … they concealed themselves in a trench convenient to a thick wood. After a time they discovered that some Germans were hovering about, probably on a mission similar to their own. The enemy opened fire on the Connaughts, but their aim was inaccurate as the darkness of the early morning prevented them from seeing where they were. The Germans, who far outnumber the British, made an effort to hem in the Connaughts in the trench, but the latter's quick-fire succeeded in making them withdraw, and though they came on again, they were driven back. A German who was retiring fired a rifle shot into the trench, and the bullet struck Pte. Conneely in the back of the neck, inflicting a deep glancing wound. A comrade rendered first aid, the enemy having withdrawn to the wood, after killing one and wounding him, though their (the enemy's) losses must have been heavy, as in their retreat the Connaughts fired several rounds at them. Pte. Conneely and his comrades remained there all night, and in the morning he and a companion, when on observation duty, observed a German sniper behind a hedge. The German fired twice, one shot missing, and the other striking the butt of a tree five yards from him, splinters of which struck Pte. Conneely in the face. The sniper's third shot hit Conneely's comrade in the head. Conneely fired at the German whom he had the satisfaction of seeing 'kicking' and knowing that he had paid that gentleman's passage to eternity he proceeded to do all he could for his wounded comrade, who, however, died in his arms.

Acting on instructions from the Commanding Officer, the remaining eight retired, and it was lucky they did so, for no sooner had they left the trench, than the Germans came out of the woods as plentiful as bees. Having joined their Company, they were engaged all that day in one of the fieriest fights of the whole war, and they drove back the enemy and captured some trenches and prisoners, besides inflicting enormous casualties on them. At last the opportunity came for Pte. Conneely to get his wound dressed properly. He was taken to a roofless old house, where there were fourteen other wounded. As the place was in danger of being shelled they had to walk a mile and a half, and it was with difficulty many of them struggled along. On their way they were fired on from a wood by Germans, and they had to run for it with the doctor, and conceal themselves under a hedge. When they got on the moves again, and crossing an open plain to the dressing station, the enemy fired on them again with rifles and when these could not find their billet with a maxim gun. The handful of wounded 'ran for it,' and succeeded in reaching the temporary hospital, where their wounds were dressed. Pte. Conneely, who is now all right, is going back to his Battalion on Monday.

(*The Galway Express* 5-12-1914)

This is another extract from the interview with Sgt Stephen Shaughnessy, the Irish Guardsman from Tuam:

(4) From that day until the 30th October there was continuous hard fighting, and on the evening of the 30th followed a fiercer shelling of the enemy since the beginning of our advance. The battle continued until the 31st when our troops were forced to yield a slight distance to the enemy. On the same night we recaptured those trenches, on which a terrific bombardment was opened on the following morning by the Germans. After six hours the Prussian Guards advanced, and we were forced to retire with 600 casualties. In this retirement I was accompanied by Private J. C. Cannon and Private Jim Burke, both of Tuam. Only about 150 of the Irish Guards remained, and trench warfare was kept up until 6th November, when, after heavy bombardment, the Germans gained a further advance. At this time the enemy's strength was ten to one. We endeavoured to hold the enemy with machine gun and rifle fire, until they succeeded in penetrating the French line about two or three miles on our right, and managed to come behind our rear line. During the attack Pte Joe Cannon was captured, and while retreating, Captain King-Harman was the only officer I saw alive. He was then standing up and firing his revolver on the Germans, who were only 60 yards away. I, or any one else in our battalion did not see him alive afterwards. At that time our troops were retiring, and the only comrade I found within reasonable distance was Private Bermingham of Clonmel formerly of the R.I.C. We discussed the situation. He got over the trench to fall back to the troops reforming our rear. As I was getting out of the trench a rifle bullet came through my great coat, penetrated my cardigan jacket without touching my body. We formed up again, and were reinforced by the Life Guards Cavalry Regiment, notwithstanding which we were unable to regain our lost territory. When darkness came we were brought back a mile behind the line for a rest and refreshments. The roll was called, and only 47 of the First

Battalion answered. At that time I ascertained that my brother, Patrick, who belonged to No. 4 company, was wounded, and removed to hospital. The remainder of us in the Battalion, along with the fresh troops, dug new trenches within 60 yards of the enemy's line. We remained in them for eleven days during hard fighting, during which the enemy were repulsed in several attacks. On November 21 we passed through the burning town of Ypres, and marched sixteen miles to a town called Metrin, where we had about five weeks rest. While there we were inspected by King George. Previous to the inspection, our battalion was increased to fighting strength by fresh drafts from England.

(*The Connaught Tribune* 6-11-1915)

Lieut Lee of the Royal Field Artillery wrote to his father, J. W. Lee in Newcastle, Galway. His father was a former police inspector and had been 'Mentioned in Dispatches' during his time in the colonial service. When the war began he tried to enlist, but was refused on the grounds that he was to 'advanced' in years. However, he was instead appointed as commander over a German prison compound in England:

(5) I have often intended writing to you, but I have been fearfully busy ever since I came here. I am with a Howitzer Battery, and I have seen action ever since I joined it. It would be useless for me to attempt to describe all the weird things one sees here, and also the thrill of coming under fire for the first time. The unceasing rat-tat of bullets and machine guns, and the boom of big guns, one gets used to it, but the sight of dead and dying is something that cannot soon be forgotten, and always makes one sad and dejected. When I first acted as a forward observing officer, and saw the terrible destruction of our guns; saw houses blown to atoms, men running for their very lives, while others lay dying and wounded, I used to feel quite sorry for our enemies, but then, when I witnessed the melancholy sight of the tiny crosses all around the place, marking the resting-places of our own brave fellows, I used to feel cross with myself for such feelings.

The German artillery has not been effective since I got here; they usually shell unfortunate little villages, and it is usually poor, harmless civilians that fall victims to their fire. I was coming through a little village some days ago that the enemy were shelling, and a shell fell right on the roof of a little cottage. I got my men to see if we could be of any assistance, and we discovered that the only occupant of the house had been a little boy aged six years, who lay dead on the floor, with his poor head bleeding fearfully. Just then his mother returned, and the scene was awful! Her husband and son were in the army; her husband was killed, and her son was wounded, and believed to be a prisoner, and now her only consolation – her little son – lying dead in her wretched home. As we heard this, I noticed one of our huge big gunners, who had gone through absolute hell since early in the war, turn awkwardly and draw his sleeve across his eyes. We were to come back and rest for a bit, but as soon as we got back, we were ordered to go into action again. It is extraordinary how happy the men are. Immediately we came out of action they organised a boxing tournament, and had great sport. I acted as 'time keeper' and quite enjoyed it all. Later in the evening they had a concert, and it was ripping. I never heard so many comic songs in my life! And some of the men sang beautifully.

(*The Connaught Tribune* 6-3-1915)

The second battle of Ypres was fought between April and May of 1915. The attack saw the town of Ypres being shelled again on 20 April. However, after two days of bombardment, there was a respite, with little gunfire in the morning. There was a slight, but pleasant breeze coming from the direction of the enemy lines. During the afternoon, the troops in the trenches could even hear the sound of larks and thrushes singing, and then suddenly, at 5 p.m., this gave way to the sound of heavy artillery. This lasted for about twenty minutes, and it was then that some of the men heard a hissing sound. In the distance there appeared two greenish-yellow clouds, which merged as they floated towards the allied trenches. It covered a five-mile section of the front line, scarcely higher than a man's head. Some of the troops who witnessed it, seemed transfixed by its 'beauty', but as it swept over them, it brought a slow excruciating death. It was chlorine gas, a new and deathly weapon, and it lasted for about fifteen minutes.

One of the unfortunate soldiers to die in this attack was Pte John Condon of Waterford. He was just 13 years and 11 months when he became the youngest combatant to die in the Great War. Although the surprise was complete, the Germans failed to capitalise on it, because many of them feared that if they covered the ground too quickly, they might risk death from their own gas. Some of the allies survived by urinating on their handkerchiefs and shirts and using them as masks. However, most did not fully realise what was actually happening and suffered the consequences. The gas attack resulted in a four and a half mile gap opening up in the allied defences, leaving the Germans only 2,500 yards from the town. Nevertheless, the hesitation on the part of the Germans, gave the British time to close the gap. [4]

On 24 April, the Canadians were forced to relinquish some of the ground at St Julien. Orders were immediately issued that it must be retaken, resulting in various battalions being sent into action. The following morning the First Irish Fusiliers, Second Dublins, Second Seaforth Highlanders, and First Warwickshire were part of the front line attack, supported by the Seventh Argyles. They were attacking in much the same formation as the Prussian Guards had done in the first battle of Ypres, and suffered a similar fate. The first lines were practically wiped out, with terrible losses. The following day the allies sent in another division, which included the First Connaught Rangers. By this time the Germans had established themselves along Pilckem Ridge from Ypres Canal to St Julien about four miles north-east of Ypres. Well-placed German machine guns did serious damage to the attacking troops.

Nevertheless, some managed to reach the German barbed wire fences, only to find them completely intact, as the artillery had failed to breach this obstacle. The Rangers had played a significant role and suffered some thirty five per cent casualties. The Germans again unleashed the gas, as they did repeatedly over the following days. The First Leinsters were sent into action on 11 May and took a lot of punishment. However, they managed to inflict heavy casualties on the enemy, but despite this, the Germans held their ground. The Royal Irish Rifles, Munster Fusiliers, Inniskillings and the Irish Guards were also among the assault troops. The latter lost half their strength within minutes during one of the last attacks of the battle. [5]

The following letter was from Fr M. Browne, Chaplin to the First Irish Guards. The letter was written to Michael and Anne O'Flaherty of 37 St Bridget's Terrace, on the death of their twenty year old son, Pte Arthur O'Flaherty. There are gaps in the letter, as sections of it could not be transcribed due to aged condition of the document:

(1)First Battn Irish Guards, B.E.F. 27-3-15

My Dear Mrs. O'Flaherty,

On behalf of the officers and men of the Battalion, I write to break to you the sad news of Arthur's death. He was killed yesterday, Sunday March 26 by a stray German shell which struck the dug out in which he was asleep. Arthur was killed instantaneously while the other two men, who were with him, survived only a few minutes.

I need not say to you how deeply I sympathise with you and yours in your moment of sorrow. As I read the prayers over his grave last night, I thought of far off Galway and prayed Our dear Lord to strengthen you with his grace to bear this terrible blow. Arthur was a dear good lad and a fine Irish Guardsman. Only a few days ago, before coming into the advanced line I had a chat with him about Galway. In his pocket when he died were the prayers and the photos I enclose. He still preserved the little bit of shamrock that came to him with your letter of the 14th.

He did his duty loyally and manfully and with him lies the Rosary. ...was ever at our evening devotions and I think he was among those who received Holy Communion on Thursday morning when attending Mass before coming into the trenches. You may rest assured therefore that now he is receiving the reward of his generous sacrifice. May Our dear Lord and his Blessed Mother comfort you. I shall not forget you in my Mass. Once more on behalf of the officers and men, I offer you our deepest sympathy.

     – Yours Sincerely, F. M. Browne, Chaplain.

(Burgess Family Archives)

The next letter was written by an unknown Galway officer to his friends at home. It gives some idea of the devastation caused by the bombardments and describes the poignant moment of a burial:

(2) The Germans made a terrible attempt at Ypres to break through our line. They brought a fearful amount of troops up, and used asphyxiating gases. We were hurried to Ypres, and came into action under heavy fire, and for six days and six nights we could not leave our guns for an instant. We never took our clothes off, and scarcely had an hour's sleep at times. The roar of the guns was awful. Our battery suffered badly. At one time in three minutes we had four killed and seven wounded. I was very sorry for the men we lost. The destruction of life was terrible, but we drove them back with heavy losses. I shall have stories about this battle, which they say was the biggest ever heard of. We have left Belgium again and arrived in France last night, (May 2), and are going into action again. I was in that battle of Neuve Chapelle, but it was only a street row compared with Ypres. The Germans used a 17-inch shell, which shook the earth when it burst, and made a hole as big as a house. It came through the air with the sound of an express train. I saw it fall in a wood and pitch huge trees bodily into the air, and cut down others for about forty yards around. The most tragic thing I ever witnessed was the burial of some of our men. A few of our men carried the bodies in blankets and laid them silently on the ground, and then we all took off our caps, and the other officer read the burial service. We could hardly hear his voice, as the guns were sill roaring and rifles cracking. It was awful; to think we were shooting with those men a few minutes before.

(*The Connacht Tribune* 22-5-1915)

The following letter was written by Fr D. McHugh from Ballinasloe, Chaplain, who was at the front from the very beginning of the war. It was addressed to his sister:

(3) My dear – I received your welcomed letter. Will you send this letter to – as I find it difficult in such a horrible place to write to all? Well, we are all in danger here, and more so for the past three days, as our men were in the trenches. I was up at the first medical aid station, which was within a 100 yards of the reserve trenches and 300 or 400 yards from the firing line. Shells screaming over us all day and night, and huge 'coal boxes' dropped around us at times. You could not venture out of doors. The moment you went out you heard the whistle of shells, and you had to retire again. We lived the life of rabbits for three days, going out for a moment and trotting in again.

The house we occupied was practically in ruins, but was fortified with 4ft. thick of sand bags outside and inside the pierced walls. The places around us are littered with huts – not a house standing; smashed to atoms, ruins everywhere; at times only the marks of where a house once stood. It was really awful. Within 500 or 600 yards of us a house was put on fire by incendiary bombs, and the same took place yesterday afternoon. The flames shot up into the heavens and devoured all before them. Bullets which were left behind by the troops were bursting and going off frequently. I need not tell you that there was no human being – civilian, at least – around these places; only military were to be seen. I don't think any soldiers were killed.

On our first night we had one man killed, and about 20 wounded. It was terrible to see them coming in to us at all hours of the night and day. They were upset. I had not to give the last Sacrament to anyone though. We left the trenches last night, and we are now, thank God, 3 miles back, where you only hear only the sounds of the guns, and where you can go out into the open and be at rest. It is an awful war, and we wish most earnestly that it was all over. Of course, we have to face the music again, but by degrees you get accustomed, in a way to the frightful explosions. On last Sunday a shrapnel shell buried itself five yards from my open window, but thank God, the soft clay and a pit of potatoes counteracted the effect and spread of the shrapnel. It put clay all over my bed, and I can assure you I got up in quick double time and cleared out. The whole house was deserted. I went to a dug out, but it was worse there, so I went to the trenches for safety. The reason for the bombardment was that there was a battery of heavy artillery just 15 yards from our place. My address is: 6 Argyle and S.H., 152 Infantry Brigade, 51 Division Expeditionary Force, France. I had not my clothes or my boots off for the past three days. We have pretty rough times. Good-bye, and best love to all.

Please pray for us all. – Your fond brother, D. McHugh.

(*The Connacht Tribune* 26-6-1915)

Pte Patrick Moore of the Second Connaught Rangers from Portumna wrote this letter. There is another letter from him in the next chapter. Pte Moore fought at Mons and was wounded at the first battle of Ypres. He had sufficiently recovered to take part in the second battle of Ypres, where he was severely wounded:

(4) Just a line to let you know I am safely back in dear old England, severely wounded, but still getting along splendidly. I think I have done my share, but still the Huns could not kill me. I had some relics from the battlefield for you, but owing to my wound I could not bring them. I remember nothing after being hit, until I wakened in a hospital some hours later, when all I could feel was wadding and bandages around my chest. However, I had the pleasure of knocking a few Huns out before being hit. If God spares me, I will have my revenge, and even if I never fired another shot, in defence of Britain, I can say as an Irishman I had my revenge seven months ago, and I hope that every Irishman who goes to France has the same to say. We got a great reception after landing here. There were about 500 Irishmen on board, so that dear old Ireland was well represented.

(*The Connacht Tribune* 29-5-1915)

The following two letters were from Pte Chas Gillen of the Second Connaught Rangers who was wounded at Ypres. The letters were addressed to Capt. John Raftery in Kinsale:

(5) Nottingham, 27, May, '15

Sir – I hope you don't think it wrong of me writing to you personally? I got wounded during a charge at Ypres and am in the above address. Will you please have a cap badge and numerals sent to me. I am sure, Sir, you remember me being in Galway Depot when I was serving there. I have been at the front for nearly eight months. I was very sorry for Mr. Irwin; he got killed the same day I was wounded. We had to advance over a mile under terrific machine gun and rifle fire. The Germans also used poisonous shells on us. We had two green flags with us during the charge and we were singing 'God Save Ireland', and cheering. We lost a lot of officers and men. I am very glad I joined the Connaught Rangers. It was no mistake to call them the 'Devil's Own.' I wish to tell you, Sir, about the daring of Capt. Ingham, of the 4th Rangers; he was out in front of a company all the time, and the bullets were cutting the grass beside his feet. He is a very brave man. Hoping the Regiment is going on well at home as regards recruiting, – I remain your obedient servant, Private Chas Gillen.

(*The Galway Express* 12-6-1915)

(6) General Hospital, Nottingham, Second June, 1915.

Sir- I beg to thank you for having the numerals sent to me, which I received in due course. I hope to be able to join my Regiment soon and proceed to the front again. I would not like to soldier at home now on account of things being so glorious at the front.

Thanking you again, Sir, for sending me the numerals, – I remain your obedient servant,

Private C. Gillen.

(*The Galway Express* 12-3-1915)

The following three letters were written by Pte Stephen O'Shaughnessy to friends in Tuam. In the third letter, he describes the death of a comrade, Pte James Burke, who was also from Dublin Road, Tuam:

(7) I am sure you are wondering why I did not write sooner, but we have had a longer spell in the trenches than usual, only returning to billets yesterday. Our position is quite close to a canal, so you may guess where I am. Constant sniping and bomb throwing goes on as usual. We are within 80 yards of each other's trenches, so we have to be a bit careful when looking out or our brains would be soon scattered. We have made no progress on our part of the line since my last letter, but of course there is a lot going on along our front that we hear nothing about. It is next to impossible for either side to advance much nowadays. Machine guns capable of firing 600 rounds a minute and rifle fire has made it impossible to live long exposed. As a soldier can fire 20 rounds per minute without any trouble, it is a regular shower of lead whenever there is rapid fire. There is a lot of mining by both parties in this war, but I don't see how it can end. If it is a fight to a finish, I can see it dragging on for years.

(*The Tuam Herald* 17-4-1915)

(8) We are in the same trenches where Mike O'Leary won his VC. I had a narrow escape a few days ago while arranging a sand-bag on top of the trench in the day light. A sniper's bullet caught the finger of my left hand, cutting it slightly on the side, but not deep enough for hospital – in fact it was only a graze; so I was not for it that day, but still I am very lucky. I could get seven days' leave now any time, but it would not be worth my while. Seven days from the North of France to Tuam and back again,

I would not have two days at home. However, if I live until the 12th August I may go, having then completed twelve dreary, hard and dangerous months in France. –I remain, yours sincerely, Stephen.

(*The Tuam Herald* 17-4-1915)

(9) Of course you knew Jim Burke from the Dublin Road. Well, the poor fellow was killed on the 18th May, while our Battalion (the Irish Guards) were advancing to take a position the Germans were holding. He was almost the first man to fall, although in his joking way, just as he was leaving the trench, he said the Kaiser never got the range of him, nor never would. His troubles are over now, but one thing I can say of him is, he was as good and brave a man as ever joined the Irish Guards. He had gone through the hardest fighting we have had since the beginning of the war. About the tenth of November he was with me in the trench at Ypres, and an attack by the Germans started. We were firing as rapidly as possible when a bullet riddled his cap. Burke only laughed and said 'a bit lower the next time if you want to get me'. He was killed by a fragment of a 'coalbox' shell which caught him right on the back of the head. The shells shrapnel and 'Jack Johnstons' were falling like leaves around us, but still we captured what we started out for. He always said that when the war was over, and if he came safely through, he would go home and see old Tuam again. I suppose his poor father and mother must have heard the sad news by this time.

(*The Tuam Herald* 5-6-1915)

Pte M. J. Hayes, a sniper, serving with the Second Connaught Rangers wrote to Mr J. Wynne of Forster Street, Galway:

(10) The worst of this trench warfare is that when it rains one is up to one's knees in water, which flows into the dug-out, while if we were on the move we would not mind the weather. Another thing is that it is very seldom we can catch the Huns putting their heads out of the trenches. I caught only four last week.

(*The Galway Express* 28-8-1915)

Sgt H. Fallon, a Connaught Ranger who was wounded at Ypres, gave the following interview while recovering in a Manchester hospital:

(11) I consider myself very lucky to have escaped alive at all, for when we made the charge it was a perfect hell on earth. We suffered enormous losses. When I got wounded I was close on the German trenches, but, then, we scarcely had 150 men left out of a thousand. We had to advance over open ground in the charge and our men were mown down by the score. But nothing could stop the Connaughts, and they gallantly kept on, until I am afraid, very few were left. After being wounded I managed to get under a little ditch. My wounds were dressed by a Sergeant of my own regiment. He had to leave me, and I was joined later by a Canadian and a Gurkha, both badly wounded.

We had to remain there, close to the enemy's lines until dark, as to stir in daylight meant certain death. The ground was fairly cut up with German artillery. How I got out of the battlefield I consider a miracle, as shrapnel was bursting on all sides of us, and bullets were flying by the thousand. The ground was covered with dead, but I am sure the Germans suffered much more heavily. I was also at the battle of Neuve Chapelle; but we lost many thousands there, it was only child's play to the battle at Ypres. The town of Ypres is a regular death-trap. The German artillery are always playing on it. Passing through the town the night before the battle we lost several men. The Colonel and Adjutant were also wounded.

(*The Galway Express* 5-6-1915)

Pte P. O'Connor became the first Galwayman serving with the First Connaught Rangers to receive the Distinguished Conduct Medal. He was extremely lucky to have survived and believed that his life was saved when a bullet struck his Princess Mary Gift Box, which he had in his breast pocket at the time. The box, complete with bullet was later placed in the window of *The Galway Express* offices:

(12) D. Coy. First Batt. Connaught Rangers,

India Expeditionary Force. 6 May, 1915.

Dear Sir, – I have the greatest pleasure in letting you know that I have received the Distinguished Conduct Medal for bravery on the field. I now claim to be the first Galway man of the 3rd Connaught Rangers who has received this great honour. Hoping by the help of God to have the pleasure of distinguishing myself again and again, I remain Yours, etc.

– No. 4324 P. O'Connor.

(*The Galway Express* 15-5-1915)

Lance Corp. J. Fisher of the Royal Irish Rifles gave the next interview while recovering from wounds. He sent a 'war trophy' an Iron Cross, to be displayed in the window of *The Galway Express* office:

(13) The engagement at Fromelles on the 9th May was one of the stiffest the R.I.R.'s were in. After the usual artillery bombardment, that regiment, with the Berks and the Lincolns, advanced and, with fixed bayonets, soon had the Germans on the run, capturing their first four lines of trenches, which they held for some hours until the Germans, having brought up vast reinforcements, retook the trenches. In the engagement the R.I.R.'s lost heavily. 18 officers and over 1000 men went forward to the charges; 10 officers were killed and the remaining 8 were wounded, while only 137 men came back. It was a veritable 'Valley of Death.' It was in retirement, after evacuating the trenches, that Lance Corpl. Fisher was knocked over. He received a shrapnel wound in the hand, which blew off his third finger and shattered his second one, and blew the top off the little one; a similar wound in the chin and nose, which were much damaged, and also a wound in the leg. He was able, however, to hobble back to his own lines, where he was temporary dressed before being removed to hospital. And how Lance Corporal Fisher had a revolting story to tell of the manner in which the Germans treated British wounded. They fired a deathly shell, which emitted a burning liquid, and the unfortunate wounded, who lay helpless and unable to stir, were burnt to death. It was horrible he said to hear the shrieks of the helpless victims, and no help could be rendered to them under the terrible fire of the enemy. All who did not meet this fate were bayoneted by the Huns.

How Lance Corporal Fisher got the Iron Cross furnishes an interesting story. In the charge, he got into one of the German trenches, and as he put his head into a dug-out, bang went a couple of revolver shots, which, however, fortunately missed him. He rushed at his assailant and promptly bayoneted him, when he found he was no other then an officer of the Prussian Guards, who was decorated with the Iron Cross, which the victor quickly appropriated. (*The Galway Express* 17-7-1915)

The third battle of Ypres, also known as the battle of Passchendaele, took place between July and November 1917. The allied offensive, which included British, Canadian and Australian troops, was launched under Douglas Haig. It was an attempt to capture the ports along the Belgian coast being held by the Germans. The battle was long and bitter and fought in the appalling conditions of driving rain and waterlogged trenches. Before the battle, the British had tunnelled under the German positions at Messines Ridge and by the end of May; had completed nineteen tunnels, some over a half-mile long. They packed a million pounds of high explosives into these tunnels. On the night of 6 June, all the explosives were primed and ready. The British commander in the field, Gen. Sir Herbert Plummer addressed a press conference, and when asked his opinion on the outcome of the battle, he replied: 'Gentleman, I don't know whether we will make history tomorrow but we will certainly change geography.' The British artillery ceased firing at 2.40 a.m. and there was complete silence for twenty minutes; when the nineteen mines were detonated together, with devastating consequences. The explosion was such, that it was later reported that Lloyd George, working in 10 Downing Street, London heard and felt the quake. More than 20,000 German soldiers were killed or wounded, while those who survived were shocked into a trance like state. The British attacked immediately and by evening had gained their objective.

The fighting continued for several days, but the Germans counter-attacked, inflicting some 25,000 casualties on the British. During the last two weeks of July, the British fired over three million shells at the German lines to 'soften them up', as a major infantry assault was planned for the last day of that month. The night before going 'over the top' the rain came down in torrents, turning the area into its natural state of bogland. Even in this mire the British were ordered to attack and by the end of the day, they had sustained 31,850 casualties. Later when Haig visited Plummer, he was informed of the great success in 'bagging' 5,000 German prisoners.[6]

The thunderstorms continued until mid August giving the troops some reprieve, but the attacks resumed as weather conditions improved.

Plummer's new tactics for this battle was 'bite-and-hold' and involved taking a section of the enemy's position and securing it against counterattack. It was achieved by ensuring that the advance of each division was limited to some 1,600 yards, thus they would remain within reach of their own artillery and machine guns. As the troops moved forward, so did the artillery. On 20 September his troops went over the top protected by a vicious artillery barrage. This attack proved successful and succeeded in its objectives almost everywhere. On 26 September, he delivered another heavy blow to the Germans at Polygon Wood, followed by a third on 4 October at Broodseinde. Luck was on the side of the British that morning, just as the Germans were preparing to launch their own attack, the British artillery rained down on them.

The German forward trenches were crowded with troops awaiting orders to attack, and the carnage which followed, was later described as one of the worst days of the war for the Germans. After this attack, Plummer's tactics failed, not due to German resistance, but because it became extremely difficult for him to move his artillery over a landscape that had been totally destroyed by his own bombardments. On 6 November the allies successfully stormed Passchendaele Ridge, but it cost them 217,000 casualties. However, the Germans did manage to avoid defeat and the fighting continued until 20 November, when ice prevented further madness. By the end of the battle the allies had captured some five miles of bogland, which was of no strategic importance and had taken enormous casualties in doing so.[7]

One of the casualties was Corp. John Walsh of Forster Street. He wrote this letter to his mother just six days before he was killed in action at Ypres:

(1) 25th July 1917

Dear Mother,

Just a few lines hoping you and all at home are well as I am myself. I wrote you a letter yesterday, so I am writing you this letter today as it may be over a week or ten days before I can write to you again. So you can guess the remainder. I hope I'll get a right one this time as it is the only way to get home out here. Tom and myself are going on well so far. Don't forget to tell Bridie I'll write to her shortly, if God spares me. Tom should be shortly getting a pass if all goes well. I have no more to say this time, hoping to here from you shortly. I shall write to you at first opportunity again. – Your Son, xxx John Walsh. (Ward Family Archives)

The following account of the battle was sent by Galway soldier, R. E. Smith, of the Third Seaforth Highlanders. While it is mainly about the Scottish regiments, it is interesting in that he makes reference to the amount of Galwaymen serving with the Irish Guards:

(2) It was a glorious afternoon on the 30th August when the bugle sounded the fall-in, and every man leaped from his bed and at once proceed to don what we term in France 'fighting kit.' Everyone of us knew what lay before us, we were going up to go over the top and drive Fritz from those positions which for nearly three years had been impregnable to the British Armies in France. The Highland Division had been chosen to go over side by side with the Guards, and as one watched them falling in – the setting sun shining on the different tartans, Gordons, Argyles, Seaforths and Blackwatch – it seemed impossible for anything to stand before them. Each man wore a little sprig of heather in the front of his steel helmet, an emblem to remind him of the heather-clad mountains of 'Bonnie Scotland,' to which most of them belonged. Everything was still as each platoon moved off independently, with the exception of one of our heavies which continued to send over with great persistence its 'iron rations' in all probability to somewhere behind the German lines. Occasionally one of our aeroplanes came over our heads keeping a watchful eye on us, and while our aviators are near no German plane dare touch us. As darkness came on the artillery began to show activity, and we could hear the whiz of the shells as they passed over our heads. The enemy also soon replied and sent a lot of high shrapnel over our heads, but seasoned veterans such as the Highlanders did not pay much attention to it, and you could hear one say to the other 'wait until morning, we will pay them back for all this.' In a platoon everyone has their special chums, who always stick together, and on this occasion, knowing that we were going into some fight, as the Yankees say, we laughed and cracked jokes to keep our spirits up. As we neared the Yzer Canal

the artillery had increased to great violence, and we proceeded to cross over to the opposite bank. Just as I reached the centre of the pontoon bridge – whiz over came a shell and I knew it was coming near, most of us threw ourselves flat on the bridge, and the shell landed about five yards from me in the water – a good job too – if it had been on the bridge I would not been able to write this letter, instead would have been in the Express 'Killed in Action.' Once in the communication trenches we felt alright, and slowly wended our way towards the lines where we were to wait for the morning. We arrived in our position without further mishap and lay down to snatch a few hours sleep before the attack commenced.

As daylight began to make its appearance our excitement rose, every man was looking for his rifle and bayonet, rubbing off bits of mud with anything he could lay his hands on. 'Five minutes to go, boys,' I said as my wrestlet watch pointed to quarter to four. That five minutes slowly ticked away, and at ten minutes a great red glare lit up the sky, the very earth seemed to shake and tremble as our mines went up, then the artillery burst forth into a wonderful barrage for which we are so famous, and with a cheer the Highlanders left the trenches and advanced as if on parade towards the German lines. The Germans were sending up S.O.S. signals to their artillery, but he was too late in replying, and by the time he got started we were well on the way. Crossing the first three German lines we encountered very little opposition. The tanks were floundering along in front of us looking for machine gun implacements, and certainly did remarkable good work and saved the infantry a lot. I saw a big shell burst a yard or two in front of a tank, the tank went down in the shell hole out of sight, and the next thing I saw was it climbing up the other side and proceeding on its journey, its machine guns spitting fire with a vengeance. All at once the man at my side gave a shout and fell. I heard the report of a rifle and knew it must have been a sniper. I was not wrong, for a German jumped out of a little concrete dug-out and started for his lines at top speed. We sent a hail of lead after him and down he went. We advanced for about two miles, and every time we saw Germans they turned and ran like hares; the ground was littered with their dead bodies, our shells bursting amongst them with wonderful accuracy and precision.

As we neared our objective the opposition increased, but nothing could withstand the wild rush of the Highlanders, and as at Beaumont Hamel, Roclincourt and Arras, they carried everything before them. That night the Germans launched a stronger counter attack against our newly-won position, but we were not going to capture them to let them fall into enemy's hands again, so we just sailed in and, well, Fritz and his counter attack soon crumbled up. For spite he bombarded us until we were relieved, and I was not sorry to get back again for another rest. One of our boys who had captured six prisoners fell in with an officer of K.R.R., and gave up his prisoners for a drink of rum. He said afterwards – 'That officer may get an M.C. now.' Well, I have been across the top a few times now and I find that now we meet with no opposition whatever. At Beaumont Hamel and other places the Germans did make a fight, but considering the 3rd Prussian Guards were up against us at Ypres, they made a very poor show. I look forward to the war coming to a quick termination. Give us the weather and we will finish the Hun. I met a Corporal of the Guards who hails from Athenry, Jack Cronin, who is known to many Galway people as a well known athlete, and one who has done a great deal on the running track to uphold the famous athletic traditions of the 'Dear old Emerald Isle.' It was like being in Galway again being amongst the Irish Guards, and I spent a very enjoyable night with them. I hope the Galway people had good weather for the Races. I would have liked to have been there, as there can certainly be spent two enjoyable days at the Races, and, well, the Bazaar. Etc., were all right in the evening.

– R. E. Smith, 3rd Seaforths.

(*The Galway Express* 18-8-1917)

The fourth battle of Ypres, also known as the battle of Lys, took place between 9 and 27 April 1918. The allied line had been attacked by mustard gas for two days, before the battle. Following the gas attack, nine German divisions came out of the morning fog and charged towards the allied positions. One of the sectors was being held by four Portuguese brigades, who, upon seeing the German onslaught, dropped their weapons and fled. A British bicycle battalion was rushed up to try and plug the gap, but on the way met the Portuguese, who took the bicycles from the British by force and cycled to Le Havre, where they sat out the remainder of the war. By midday on 10 April, the Germans had gained a great deal of ground including most of Messines Ridge. Over the following days field by field was contested to the bitter end. The remaining positions on Messines Ridge were lost when the allied soldiers were either shot or ran out of ammunition.

The Germans continued their offensive for almost two weeks, gaining some ground, but it cost them dearly. Although the allied front line had broken, they managed to prevent the Germans from reaching Ypres. By 29 April the German commander, Gen. Erich Ludendorff realised that he was losing too many men, in return for such a small success and called off the attack. At the time the allies in this sector did not fully realise the importance of their achievement in holding out against the Germans. However, later Winston Churchill stated that he regarded this action as the decisive struggle for the western front.[8]

CHAPTER XIV

THE BATTLE OF NEUVE CHAPELLE

In October 1914, the Germans took the French village of Neuve Chapelle and from then on, it became an objective for both sides. The village was situated twenty miles south of Ypres. On 10 March 1915 the battle of Neuve Chapelle began with a forty-minute bombardment by the British. The artillery assault took the Germans completely by surprise and was successful in cutting up their barbed wire defences and destroying the front line trenches. The barrage was immediately followed by an infantry attack involving the British Seventh and Eight divisions and two divisions of Indian Corps. They overwhelmed the enemy, but stopped to allow a second artillery barrage, this time directed behind the German lines in order to prevent any reinforcements. The British infantry assault was successful in taking the village and four front line German trenches.

However, due to a communications failure, the British reserve troops failed to arrive on time, which gave the Germans sufficient time to regroup. By the time British reinforcements did arrive, it was too late. The element of surprise was no longer a factor and because the gap created by the initial attack was too small, some nine thousand troops were huddled together in the mud unable to move. One source described them as: 'packed like salmon in the bridge pool at Galway, waiting to go forward'.

There were many Irishmen among them as there were at least four Irish regiments represented in the battle, the First Irish Rifles, Royal Irish, Leinsters and the Connaught Rangers. Because the advance had been held up, the German machine guns and riflemen were in a position to inflict heavy casualties on the British. When orders were given for the reserve British troops to advance, they had to move forward through communication trenches that were packed with wounded soldiers and so were late arriving at their jump-off position. The attack failed, as did the advance on the following day. Although suffering heavy casualties, the German counter attack on 12 March was successful in re-taking their lost trenches and the shattered village of Neuve Chapelle.[1]

It was a remarkably small three-day battle, which marked a change to the vast elaboration of artillery support that signalled the beginning of most of the main battles of the First World War. During the bombardment, the British had exhausted their supply of artillery ammunition. The attack had cost the British some 11,652, killed, wounded and missing soldiers. The British claimed a partial victory at Neuve Chapelle, but better planning on their part would have almost certainly made a huge difference to the outcome of the offensive.

It was neither a defeat nor a victory, but was certainly a 'blood sacrifice for both sides'. It was described as the 'Most Sanguinary Fight Yet', when Sir John French admitted in *The Galway Express* that mistakes had been made, saying there was clearly a breakdown in communications. He defended the loss of life by indicating that the Germans had suffered similar casualties. He also said many valuable lessons had been learnt at Neuve Chapelle and that for future offensives they would require an: 'almost unlimited supply of ammunition.' Given such statements, the human war experiences did not provide any guidelines for them to follow. The appalling loss of life continued and increased on scales unimaginable in warfare up to that time. This was not the fault of the front line soldiers, but the generals, who failed to recognise the reality of trench warfare, which loomed before them after Neuve Chapelle.[2]

Pte Patrick Moore of the Second Connaught Rangers wrote this letter to a friend in Portumna regarding the battle of Neuve Chapelle, again it gives some idea of the day-to-day dangers of sniper fire:

Neuve Chapelle, 14th April, 1915

(1) I take the pleasure of writing to you during a lull in the fighting. I have just returned for a rest after continous fighting since the 14 March. I am sure you read in

the papers about the famous battle of Neuve Chapelle, at which the old Connaughts played so prominent a part. There was a terrible bombardment by our artillery. The Huns got a great hammering that they will never forget. There were 500 guns playing on them, and they were literally blown to fragments. The traces of the awful shell fire can still be seen. Such a sight was never witnessed by mankind. When we dashed on them with the bayonet, they could be seen huddled up in the trenches, pale and dejected wretches. Trench after trench was taken without the Hun making the least resistance. They only put up their hands. They are dirty cowards. They have such a thing as a sniper. He is stuck or hidden in some old crevice, and perhaps you might be going to a stream for water, and an innocent man gets shot. The Munsters are along side us in the trenches, and they have a melodeon, which raises the old Irish hearts during the lull in the fighting. We had Mass in the trenches on Easter Sunday, thanks to our brave Irish priests, who are just as brave as the men.

– Patrick Moore.

(*The Connacht Tribune* 1-5-1915)

Lieut Roderick de Stacpoole of the Royal Field Artillery was killed in action on 11 March 1915 at Neuve Chapelle. He was from Mount Hazel, Woodlawn, County Galway. On 7 May, a solemn requiem mass was held for him at the church of Saint's Peter and Paul in Ballymacward, and it was presided over by Dr Gilmartin, bishop of Clonfert. His older brother, Robert, a Connaught Ranger was killed at the Marne in September 1914. Both are remembered with a memorial plaque in the church. Another brother, Hubert, of the Leinster Regiment, was in hospital recovering from wounds at the time, while a fourth brother, George, was serving with the Connaught Rangers.

The following is an account of Roderick de Stacpoole's death:

(2) The deceased officer who was only 19 years of age, was the youngest of the four sons, at the front, of Duke and Duchess de Stacpoole, Mount Hazel, Ballymacward and was the second of them to give his life for his country. One of his superior officers gives in a few words, a graphic picture of what Lieutenant Roddy de Stacpoole was, and how he died. This officer writing says – 'If you see Humphries tell him how

deeply the whole brigade regret the death of that high-spirited boy, de Stacpoole, in years only a child, with the face of a girl, he had the heart of a hero. He was killed carrying a telephone wire across an open, fire-swept field. Having put his men in safety, he took the post of danger himself.'

(*The Galway Express* 29-5-1915) [3]

CHAPTER XV

DARDANELLES & GALLIPOLI LANDINGS

The Dardanelles is a strait which joins the Aegean Sea with the Sea of Marmara and is part of a waterway that leads from the landlocked Black Sea to the Mediterranean. The strait is approximately thirty-seven miles long, and about two hundred feet in depth. It averages some three to four miles across, and is about one mile at its narrowest point. For hundreds of years it has been the crossing point for invading armies between Europe and Asia. It has a long history of military activity and in 1841, the major powers of Europe, Great Britain, France, Prussia and Austria agreed that Turkey should have control of shipping through the strait. It was a decision that proved regrettable for the British by the beginning of the First World War. In early January 1915, Russia requested military support from the allies in order to relieve the pressure on its troops in Caucasus.

Churchill, who was first lord of the admiralty, persuaded the government to use the navy to force open the Dardanelles so that supplies could be shipped to Russia quickly, and to defend Egypt. His plan also included a bombardment of Constantinople (Istanbul), Turkey. In February 1915, Anglo-French forces shelled some of the outer forts which protected the Dardanelles. Troops also landed unopposed on the Gallipoli Peninsula, but a chance to inflict more damage on the Turks was lost, as the attack was not followed up.

On 18 March, an attempt was made to run warships through the strait, but four were lost to heavy gunfire, while a number of others were damaged by mines, forcing the British fleet to call off the attack. During this attack, the allies lost some 750 soldiers, while Turkish casualties were less than 200 men. The only thing these attacks achieved, was to alert the Turks of an impending assault, which gave them time to fortify their positions and call in reinforcements before the Gallipoli landings.[1]

At dawn on 25 April 1915, the bombardment of Gallipoli began under the command of Sir Ian Hamilton. Shortly afterwards the allies began landing at various points on the peninsula. There were very few places suitable for such a force to land, as much of the area is protected by high cliffs. The allies landed at a number of that they felt they could secure along Cape Helles and named them S, W, X, Y and V beaches. At S, X and Y beaches, the British landed with little or no opposition. Across the water at the Kum Kale, the French also landed unopposed. Many of the Turks fled, while hundreds surrendered before the French withdrew the following day.

However, the story was very different on W and V beaches, where the Dublin, Munster, Hampshire and Lancashire Fusiliers landed in the face of strong opposition. On these two beaches the troops found themselves fighting for their very lives, with heavy Turkish fire causing hundreds of casualties. Even a hundred yards from shore on W beach the Lancashire Fusiliers were struck by hails of bullets. As the troops reached the beach they were confronted by barbed wire at the waters edge, but they managed to struggle through and around the obstacle. Of the 950 troops who landed, over five hundred were killed or wounded.

At V beach the Dublin Fusiliers found themselves in an even worse position, as can be seen from the letters of Sgt J. Colgan, because they were struck by a heavy barrage of rifle and machine-gun fire upon arrival. Although the allied bombardment had been severe, causing one eyewitness to say that the 'very heavens shook', it did not dislodge the Turkish sharpshooters, who were making the allies pay in blood for every inch of ground. *The River Clyde*, a ship carrying the Munster Fusiliers and Hampshire Regiment, had to get as close as possible to land. Doorways had been cut in either side of the bow leading to gang-planks, down which the troops had to rush in order to reach the beaches. As the Turkish machine-guns opened fire, columns of troops tumbled from the gangplanks into the sea.

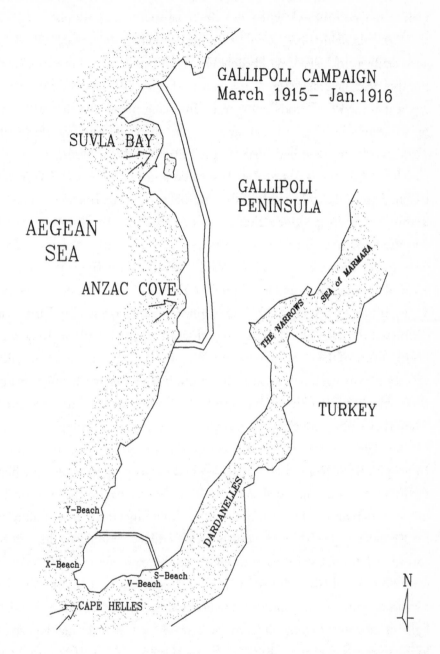

GALLIPOLI CAMPAIGN
March 1915– Jan.1916

SUVLA BAY

GALLIPOLI
PENINSULA

AEGEAN
SEA

ANZAC COVE

SEA of MARMARA

THE NARROWS

TURKEY

Y–Beach

X–Beach

DARDANELLES

S–Beach
V–Beach

CAPE HELLES

N

Note: scale not applicable.

Map of the Gallipoli Peninsula. (Courtesy of Eamonn O'Regan & Michael Conneely)

According to one report the men were simply 'butchered', and the sea turned red with blood, while the air 'boiled with bullets'. Nevertheless, through this hellish fire, some of the troops managed to reach the shore and secure a small section of beach. For some twenty-four hours the small number of survivors sheltered on the beach-head while the allied battleships again pounded the Turkish positions. The slaughter of the British troops on these two beaches was achieved by less than one hundred desperate Turkish soldiers, who had survived the initial naval bombardment.[2]

Meanwhile the boats of the Australian and New Zealand (B) troops touched ground a mile north of the original plan at Ari Burnu, on a beach dominated by steep slopes. The reason for landing at this location, which became known as Anzac Cove, was never satisfactorily explained. They were under the command of Sir William Birdwood. This area took the form of an amphitheatre, dominated on three sides with steep slopes and a succession of ridges. They landed unopposed because the Turks had dismissed the idea of a landing in such an inhospitable place. They were keenly aware of the importance of reaching the high ground quickly, which was about two and a half miles to the summit. They began moving towards their objective immediately, but were only a mile and a half into the climb, when they came under fire from the assembling Turkish troops.

The Turks were under the command of an outstanding officer, Mustapha Kemal, who had force-marched his men upon realising where the ANZACs had landed. The Australians saw Kemal on the crest of the hill at Sari Bair and fired on him, but without any effect. Their failure to hit Kemal and reach the summit in those crucial minutes, could well be considered the most decisive moment of the campaign. The ANZACs were overlooked from almost every quarter and constant enemy fire sent a steady stream of dead and wounded back down to the narrow beach. The fighting continued along all fronts and by 4 May the Turks had lost some fourteen thousand men, while almost ten thousand ANZAC troops were dead. Mustapha Kemal realised that they could not drive the allies back into the sea and ordered his men to dig in, while the allies also prepared for a long hot summer.[3]

The village and castle of Sedd el-Bahr were captured as the allies pushed for more ground. Fighting continued over the following weeks, but the peninsula was not secured. On 7 August, elements of the allied Tenth Division arrived at Suvla Bay. As the sun rose in the morning sky, the Turkish guns opened fire on the approaching boats. In one boat alone, seventeen members of the Dublin Fusiliers were killed or wounded. Two battalions, the Inniskillings and Irish Fusiliers landed and concentrated their efforts around Lala Baba. A new beach was discovered at Suvla point where Galway born, Gen. Sir Bryan Mahon arrived with three other battalions. There were delays caused by orders and counter orders, which had a serious effect on the operations.

Once the beaches were secured, Chocolate Hill and a number of other strategic places became the objectives. The Turkish fire caused many casualties among the Irish regiments, with the battles continuing throughout August. The Fifth Connaught Rangers faced the Turks at Chunk Bair and following this encounter, they were given four days rest on 13 August 1915. Upon returning to the trenches, they prepared for the desperate attack at Suvla on 21 August. A simultaneous attack by the ANZAC troops was also planned and the objective was for both forces to link up and provide a single united front against the Turks. Another objective of the Rangers was to capture two important wells at Kaba Kuyu. After a short encouraging speech by their commanding officer, the Rangers charged through a hail of bullets towards the Turkish trenches. Following a stubborn fight, the Turks gave way and the Rangers captured the coveted wells, but many valuable lives had been lost. The assault was a complete success, although the Rangers roll call indicated twelve officers and over two hundred and fifty men less the following day. On 29 August they were sent to attack another Turkish position, Hill 60. The cohesion of their attack won the admiration of all who were present when they achieved their objective with amazing swiftness.[4]

The record of the Irish Division at Suvla Bay and indeed throughout the Gallipoli campaign is one of heroism and courage. One source commented that the valour of those whose blood has saturated the sands of Suvla Bay should never be forgotten. There were heavy losses among the allies, and although reinforcements were constantly arriving, the campaign at Suvla failed. By the end of September 1915 the Gallipoli offensive was virtually abandoned. Hamilton was relieved of his command in October, and was not appointed to any other post during the war.

Between 28 December 1915 and 8 January 1916, the allies began to ship out. By this time, an estimated 300,000 Turks had been killed, wounded or were missing. There were 265,000 allies dead and of all the troops involved in this horrific fighting, it was the Australians who were most effected by the experience. The Gallipoli Peninsula is now preserved as a national park and Mustapha Kemal had a monument erected there, in memory of all those who suffered on both sides. There are also a number of war cemeteries on the peninsula, with many of the Irish buried at Sedd-el-Bar, a few yards from the water's edge where they fell.[5]

There are a number of letters and interviews included below from men who served in the Gallipoli campaign. The information contained in the first report was given during an interview with Sgt O'Brien, a Connaught Ranger, who was at home recovering from wounds in October 1915:

(1) They left Basingstoke camp on Thursday, July 8th by train for Davonport, and on the following day embarked on the SS Bornio, escorted by two cruisers. They reached Gibraltar at 6.30 p.m. on July 14th, and left a day later arriving Malta on July First [sic]. The contingent marched to Alexandra on July 23rd, where they remained prior to sailing for Lemnos until the 25. Lemnos, which is about 60 miles from the peninsula, was reached on 28th at 5 a.m. The troops disembarked at 9.30 on the following day, and remained on the island a week, during which their time was occupied getting into readiness for action after the voyage. Lemnos was sailed from on August 5th, and a landing made on the peninsula in the vicinity of Anzac. The troops were taken on lighters to the shore at 10.30 p.m. Orders were given to proceed to a place called 'shrapnel gulley,' as they were to be shortly under fire. Their contingent comprised the 29th Brigade and included the Connaughts, Leinsters, Royal Irish Rifles and Hampshires. Their landing on the peninsula was comparatively safe, save a few casualties, unlike the dismemberment of the remainder of the regiments which attempted to enter from Suvla Bay, resulting

in heavy loss of life from the enemy's heavy guns. 'Shrapnel gulley' is about a half mile from the beach at Anzac.

Our landing was unknown to the enemy, and after proceeding for some time on the beach in the direction of the gulley, the guns opened a fierce bombardment, which lasted until 6 a.m. on the following day. Some of their shells reached the gulley, but our only casualties were Private Hall and myself. I heard the whizz of the shrapnel shell, and being unable to shelter, I fell flat on the ground. I could not avoid the danger, and received portions of shrapnel in the chest and back. I was taken to the hospital. In a few days we received instructions to be in readiness to reinforce the Australians. The battalion sheltered under a hill occupied by the Australians. They were not required during the engagement, and orders were given that they should proceed two miles in the vicinity of Walker's Ridge, where the enemy still continued to be held in check without the assistance of the Irish troops. There were one hundred and fifty casualties. For ten days they were engaged in burying the dead, amongst which were some of the Welsh Fusiliers, Gurkas and Turks. Their stretcher bearers performed their work exceedingly well, and under heavy fire went out to remove the dead. On the 20th August they received orders from their Brigadier-General that they had to undertake an arduous task on the following morning before day-break. They were ordered to capture a well, which supplied the Turks with an enormous supply of water. Three battalions, the Brigadier-General said, had already failed to capture the well, and he finally decided that the Connaughts should succeed, and that there should be no retirement. In the early hours of the morning of the 21st they moved towards the Turks position, a distance of one thousand yards without any cover. 'C' and 'D' companies, supported by 'A' and 'B' advanced. The Gurkas formed a second general line, and the Welsh regiment the general reserve. They succeeded in capturing the well, after very severe hand to hand fighting in the trenches. The engagement was fought within four hundred yards of the enemy's position, with a heavy artillery duel on both sides. The Connaughts, who lost a few in the engagement, not content with their success, advanced to another of the enemy's trenches, where they were subjected to heavy machine gun fire on each side of their ranks. The losses, which were heavy in the second encounter, were between two and three hundred. They were subsequently relieved by other troops, and after a brief rest received orders to charge on Anafanta.

The attack commenced on the afternoon of the 27th, and was successful after additional heavy casualties. It was an important point of vantage for the enemy, and as in the case of the attack on the well, it received implicit directions from the General. They received a letter from Major-General Godfrey, Australian Command, complimenting them for their bravery, calling on them to consolidate their position, and to continue doing their duty as they had been doing with the true valour of Irishmen. Copies of the letter, which was read to them by the Colonel, were taken by the troops. It also appeared in the Peninsula Press. In the engagements with the enemy the Connaughts suffered heavily, and owing to the weakness of their strength they were detailed to retire to the beach, about two miles from Anzac, for a rest. Small parties of them were daily engaged in digging communication trenches. Others of them, not employed in this work, kept themselves fit by gymnastic exercises and musketry drill for a short time each day. In the meantime reinforcement came to their aid. On arriving at Anzac in August there were 1,000 Connaughts, of which only 140 remained when he was ordered to return for home service on September 26. After leaving hospital he returned to the fighting line, and endeavoring to capture a height one of his wounds burst, and he was subsequently sent home.

(*The Connacht Tribune* 30-10-1915)

Ernest Egan of the Australian Mounted Troops was wounded in Gallipoli. He wrote the following two letters to his father while convalescing in a Malta hospital. His father had been a former member of the Royal Irish Constabulary in Oughterard:

(2) Imtapa Hospital, Malta, May 1915.

My Dear Father – In action on Saturday, the 8th May, I was wounded in the head and brought here. It was not what could be called serious by any means, but if I had my head raised half an inch higher, I think I would not be here now. Before the landing at the Gallipoli Peninsula all troopships were anchored at Lemnos for some days. We left there on Saturday, 24th April, and the troops on Sunday morning before dawn were landed at different points. The Australian and New Zealand troops were landed at Sairbois, a point not far from the lowest Gulf of Saros. Our chaps fought splendidly; we drove the Turks from position after position. The first day we landed we drove them back close on four miles. I often heard it said that no troops could stand in front of the British bayonets, well as far as the Turks are concerned, it is a fact. After the first two days they never attacked by day, every attack was made by night ... Observing orders we let them come close, then joined in a withering of fire on them. As they came closer, we jumped from our trenches and let them have the bayonet. The first taste of the bayonet was enough. They turned and fled. For the first couple of days they were glad to keep quiet; their night attacking after was half-hearted. It was evident they were being urged forward. They used to come within 30 yards of our trenches and then run back as hard as they could back to their own trenches again.

We captured some German officers dressed in their own uniforms, badge and all complete. They often rushed up to our trenches and shouted: 'For God's sake, don't shoot, men: we are Australians.' Their idea was to get in amongst us, give us orders and learn our strength, but we had been warned against German tricks, and we were not to be taken in. Two German officers who were taken to Alexandria, said that they stood aghast at our bravery, they could not believe that men would have the courage to advance as we did. On the 4th of May the Second Brigade was told that it had made a name for itself, and that it was now fit to take its place with the best soldiers of England or France. On the 5th we left Saivilair, and embarked on minesweepers. We were landed at Cape Helles, and had a day's rest. We then moved further forward and halted for some hours. Next day we moved on; about mid-day we halted, dug trenches, and made ourselves secure against the shrapnel. On Saturday evening about 5.30 we left our dug outs and advanced against the enemy. I shall never forget that advance. The French artillery supported us; their artillery is magnificent. Above the din of all the guns, we all knew the one gun that was playing havoc among the enemy – the H.M.S Queen Elizabeth 15-inch gun. Our objective was a line of trenches about 1,000 yards in front, and about 600 yards behind them a village. We captured both, but it was in this attempt that I was wounded. As all the letters leaving here are censored, I cannot tell you about the part I took in it. The accuracy of our naval guns is marvelous. The first fort at our second landing place had two huge guns mounted on rails. I am sure a good-sized man could get into the breach of either of them. They were fixed on wheels; a large platform was at the back of each gun, to which seven steps led. Those guns were twisted up in every possible way; even the rails under the wheels were smashed; the steps were coiled up like rope – the whole lot only fit for the scrap-heap. It took only two battleships about half an hour to do all that damage. You will excuse the scribble; it is the best I can do just at present. I expect to be here for at least six weeks. I will write you again. Hope you are in the best of health. I don't suffer any pain from my wound. – Love to you all

– Your affectionate son, Ernest.

(*The Connacht Tribune* 26-6-1915)

(3) Imtapa Hospital, Malta, 25, May, 1915

My dear Father – I hope you received my other letter and post card sent from here. My wound has improved splendidly; I suffer no pain at all. At first it was thought it would be serious, but there is no fear of that. I expect to be sent to a convalescent hospital soon, where I will have plenty of time to gather up the lost strength …We have just had the news that Italy has declared war on Austria. The war must soon come to an end now. Austria is well beaten, and the Turks are only half-hearted in the defence of their country. Were it not for the German officers the Turks would lay down their arms. I have seen the German officers urging them on, themselves being always in the rear. The Dublin and Munster Fusiliers fought splendidly at Gallipoli. They were the first regular regiments to land. Their landing was far more difficult than ours, but barbed wire or shrapnel had no terror for them; they jumped into the water, and took everything before them. They were ordered to charge a trench on a height, but before being ordered the officer in charge told them that they had a very difficult job, in fact he said 'It is doubtful if we can take it.' One of the Munsters shouted: 'Let us at them Sir; sure it is as easy a job as we can strike.' They charged the Turks amid tremendous excitement. The sailors on the ship went mad with delight, they cheered for all they were worth, and shouted, 'Bravo Ireland.' They took the trenches with ease, and drove the Turks back 600 yards. I will write soon again. I hope you are in the best of health. Love to all. With best love.

– Your affectionate son, Ernest.

(*The Connacht Tribune* 26-6-1915)

Sgt J. Colgan of the Royal Dublin Fusiliers is responsible for the following accounts. The second letter was written to his sister, a nurse from Palmyra Park. They give graphic accounts of the Gallipoli landings, and record the death of Galway priest, Fr Finn:

(4) On Saturday evening, the 24th April, they left the transport, and got on board a number of mine sweepers which brought them towards the famous straits. They remained on board during the night. On reaching the danger zone before dawn, they left the mine sweepers and got into a number of boats, which were being towed by steam pinnaces, manned by men from the fleet. In the boats were a number of naval seamen whose duty it was to row them ashore when they reached the last stage of the journey. Before they got into the boats they passed the Australians, and the latter gave the Dublin boys a cheer. Leaving the mine sweepers, they were told to get as quickly as possible to the landing place. There were three small boats to each pinnace. After about a quarter of an hour's sailing in the boats they heard the booming of guns, as if it were the rolling of distant thunder. While passing into the straits, some war correspondent – our informant could not find out who he was – told them to sing 'Tipperary', so they made the welkin ring with the popular strains. Sailing along, they passed close to a Russian battleship, which owing to its unpronounceable name, was designated the 'Packet of Fags'. This ship was in the act of bombarding the forts, and it demolished a mill which was full of Turkish snipers.

On board one of the boats was the Rev. Fr Finn, who was the first Catholic chaplain to fall in the war. He was advised by the men to remain on the mine sweeper, but he would not hear of it. He said it was his duty to be with them, no matter where that was. The mine sweeper accompanied the boats to the straits, and when about 200 yards from the shore the officer on the bridge gave the order to wheel to the left, and was immediately after killed. Another officer mounted the bridge and took the wheel, and he fell mortally wounded. Up to this many of the younger soldiers did not know what the ping ping of the bullets in the air meant, but the deaths of these two seamen wakened them to the hard realities of the situation. The heavy rifle fire of the Turks was now directed at the men in the boats, and in the space of a few minutes the boats were filled with dead and dying men. Many of those less seriously wounded attempted to jump overboard, thus presenting fine targets for the Turkish marksmen. One of the men succeeded in getting out of the boat in which the Sergeant was, but when his head appeared above the surface, he was killed instantaneously with a bullet in the brain. Another soldier from Belfast while speaking to our friend was struck by a piece of a shell on the head, which split his skull in two from crown to his chin. It seemed now as if hell was let loose, and there was nothing for it but to be slaughtered like rats in a trap.

All the seamen who were given the task of bringing the troops ashore were killed. The few who were left could not tell exactly what was happening. After weighting the odds, the sergeant decided to try and reach the beach, and was just endeavouring to jump into the sea when a piece of a shell struck him in the back of the hip, after which he fell back and lay in the bottom of the boat. Eventually, himself and another soldier managed to get into the water, and endeavoured to swim ashore. Severely wounded as he was, this proved no easy task. However, after what seemed hours, he reached the beach. Here an officer who had escaped dressed the more serious of his wounds, and in this condition he remained all that night. The few who reached the beach formed themselves into a firing party, and thus kept off the Turks for the time being. Out of the 36 men in the boat, only himself and another lived to tell the tale. Next night they were taken off the beach under cover of darkness, and were conveyed to the battleship 'Cornwallis', where they were attended to. From that they were sent to a hospital ship, and brought to Malta, where they remained until convalescent. We should add here that Father Finn reached the shore, but died there, while in the act of giving absolution. In July they were sent to the peninsula again and the sergeant took part in many battles including Chocolate Hill, from which they had to retire owing to lack of reinforcements. Shortly after this he fell victim to dysentery and fever, and was invalided home, where he is now recuperating preparatory to him taking his place with the colours again.

(*The Connacht Tribune* 30-10-1915)

(5) Just a line, to let you know that I am going on all right. I thank God I was not killed, as there were only six of us left out of a boatload of 32. It was simply awful. It seemed literally to rain bullets and shrapnel. I only got three, one grazing my right shoulder, another across the small of the back, and the last, and worst of all, on the left buttock. This latter came out at the top of my thigh. From this you can form an idea of what it was like. It was a large wound I got, but it is in no way sore now. A large splinter of shrapnel was taken out of it most skilfully, and it is healing very well now. The hospital is packed with wounded. On our boat alone 500 came. There were some awful sights – some blind, others stricken dumb, while there are others without limbs. One could think that there could not be any of us and the Munsters left, as we were the first to try and effect a landing, and we got a thrice warm reception. On the first roll-call only 175 of the battalion answered their names, and we only mustered ten

officers. From this you can imagine what it was like.

(*The Connacht Tribune* 29-5-1915)

The following letter was received by M. Donnelly of Kylemore, Portumna from one of his sons who was wounded in Gallipoli:

(6) I am still in the same hospital and I am getting on well. I was expecting a letter from Patrick every day. I would like to know how he is getting on. I wonder if he had to go under an operation, and whether it was successful. I feel you would like to know how we got knocked out, and what kind of place the peninsula is. Well the scenery is anything except beautiful. There is nothing to be seen but bare sandy hills on which nothing will grow. The level plains are thinly covered with tall course grass, and sometimes a prickly kind of shrub. What strikes one most curious is, no matter where you look you cannot see anybody or anything more, and all the time you know there are thousands of Turks a few yards in front. But one gets used to it, and also finds out it is safest not to be looking about except through a periscope. The heat during the day, and the cold during the night, together with the scarcity of water, are bad enough, but the plague of flies is worse than all. They start to annoy one about half an hour before sunrise, and never leave off until sunset. During mealtimes they are at their worst, especially if there is any jam knocking about. We were drafted from Cape Helles or the Southern part of the peninsula on August 19th, and landed at Cape Suvla, which is called the northern part on the morning of the 20th. We remained on the beach all that day, cooking, bathing and resting. We got the word to fall-in in full marching order just at nightfall. We were also served out with a triangular piece of tin with two holes in it. When we saw that, we know we were in for it, because the regiments that are going to charge are always dished out with pieces of tin, which are tied to their backs so that our artillery know when to lengthen their range.

We marched right across Salt Lake plain, and across Chocolate Hill, a distance of about five miles. The scenery here is not so desolate as in the Achi Baba district. It has been laid out in fields and planted with large trees. Some of the fields appear to have been recently ploughed, and here and there stands a poor-looking house of some Turkish farmer, of course empty. We lay in the open on the morning of the 21st, hidden from the Turks by a hill of shrub. We had orders to advance by two o'clock in the afternoon. So we started to cook our breakfast, which consisted of tea, biscuits and bacon. The next and most important matter was to fill our water bottles, for in an advance, one never knows how long one may have to go without getting another supply, and in the case of getting wounded, the first thing one thinks of is a drink. We started to advance at the appointed time, led by our Company Officer Capt. Eager, and a Sergeant-Major. It was six hundred yards to the first line of Turkish trenches. We were to cover that ground in three rushes. We advanced in single file through the shrub, Eager and the Sergeant-Major in front, and we covered the first two hundred yards without anyone getting hit, but in covering the second 200 we suffered terribly. I got hit just then. The bullet that went through my thighs smashed another man's arm that was lying just a little behind me. There were about 15 of us between dead and wounded in the one spot. Any who were able crawled into the shrub, and there they remained until the shrub took fire. That was the most awful and appalling sight I ever witnessed. Some of the wounded were not able to crawl away from the fire, and were calling piteously for help. Others who were dead caught fire, and their ammunition was exploding and flying in all directions. When we saw that, we took our equipment and spare bandoliers of ammunition off and threw them as far away as our strength allowed us.

The fire had not yet reached us, but was gradually working its way and closing around us in a semicircle. Just then the grass in front of us caught fire and we were then surrounded on all sides by fire, and the only way out was right through the burning grass, across 50 yards of open ground, which was raked by Turkish rifle fire. All who could walk, and had only slight wounds made a dive for the trench 50 yard away. It was only a chance to get there. I shall never forget all my life the splendid courage and bravery of the men who quenched the burning grass with blankets, fully exposed to the terrible Turkish fire. They not only quenched the fire, but went around and pulled the wounded out of the burning shrub. They then pulled the dead away, and took off their equipments, which were on fire owing to the ammunition exploding in the pouches. They then offered to carry us across the open into the trench. At first we would not risk it, but, eventually, they persuaded us to chance it, and I am glad to say, we got over safely. I was able to move along with the help of a man on either side, but Patrick had to be carried. I hope the bravery of these men will not go unrewarded.

We remained in the unused trench until nightfall. Some soldiers passing gave us a box of cigarettes so we did not feel the time passing except those of us who were wounded through the body, and these poor fellows were continually asking for water. We were taken to the dressing station as soon as it got dark and our wounds seen to. I heard the doctor saying to Patrick 'You have got a fracture, lad.' Patrick then asked if he should lose the leg, and the doctor said there was no fear of that. In the morning we were carried down to the ambulance, which took us to the beach. I lost sight of Patrick in the morning, and never saw him again. I made enquiries at the dressing station, where I remained all day. I also enquired on the hospital ship that night, but none of the orderlies remembered seeing the name. I then thought he got hit with shrapnel on the way down. You can imagine how pleased I was when I got your letter saying he was in hospital in Manchester. I met one of the officers belonging to our regiment the other night. He has only just come back from the peninsula. He says we lost more then half our men on the 21st August, and among the officers killed that day was Capt. Eager, who was my Company Officer, and led the charge that day, and as brave a man as ever faced an enemy.

(*The Connacht Tribune* 13-11-1915)

Corp. David Rider of the Connaught Rangers wrote the following letter regarding the death of Pte Tom Quoyle, a former Galway teacher. His father was also a teacher in the Claddagh National School, while his brother, John, taught at the Galway Workhouse, before he too, joined the Connaught Rangers. The letter was addressed to Tom Quoyle's sister:

(7) 5th Connaught Rangers, 29th Brigade, 10th Irish Division, Mediterranean Expeditionary Force, 23rd August 1915.

Dear Miss Quoyle, It is with deepest sorrow and regret that I have to inform you of the death of your brother, Tom. He died nobly in the arms of victory at the very last of the Turkish trenches. I know he is in Heaven, for he was at Confession several times for the last week. He was always a regular Confession goer and a good advisor, and just before the battle he told me that he was free of conscience and placed himself under the protection of God to do with Him what he thought best. A rough wooden cross marks the place of his burial. That, and a fervent prayer, was all we could do under the circumstances.

You will excuse me for the manner in which I write you, but he was my chum, in whom we placed each other's confidence, and I deeply regret his early death. May God rest his soul. Weep not now, but pray, and pray hard. More things are wrought through prayer than this world dreams of. I write you this, knowing that you will break this terrible news gently to your father and mother. I pray they will receive it in a calm manner.

– Yours very truly, CPL. David Rider.

(*The Galway Express* 11-9-1915)

The following letter was written by Pte P. Murray of the Royal Irish Fusiliers:

(8) The spirits of the men while on board were splendid, and one would not think they were going on such a deathly errand, and that many of them would never see their native shores again. There was one officer on board Lieutenant Costello, son of Mr. T. A. Costello, Galway; and the last time I saw him alive was when he was leading his Company against the Turks; he was killed a few days after I was wounded and I was very sorry to hear of his death ... disembarkation of the troops in the launches was accomplished in an orderly manner under the supervision of Colonel Jourdain, whose good work and thoughtfulness brought us to shore without many casualties. Under shelter of the cliffs we took a short rest and then advanced up the cliffs and into 'Deathly Shrapnel Gully'. All was peace and quietness, until the Australians started to advance, when there commenced one of the most terrific bombardments and rifle and machine gun fire that was ever witnessed on the peninsula before, and then our casualties started but they were very slight. Every shell passed over where we were lying, but thanks to Colonel Jourdain's judgment we were in a place of comparative safety. For about eight hours or more the bombardment lasted, and it was about the most terrific ever was seen in the war. There were about 18 or more battleships playing on it along with our land artillery.

About midnight on the next night we were served out with white armlets for identification purposes, and in a few hours word came for us to move up to the firing line, and then we began to see some sights of our comrades, hundreds of them passed us wounded, some of the awfullest wounds one could see. But that was not all, there were about twice as many killed and every time we would look around we could see nothing but dying and dead. However, it had not much effect on the Connaughts for they were as jolly as if they were in camp in England, and mind you we had lost a few men ourselves. All went well with us until the 10th August, when we marched the night before away from where we were, and word came that the rest of our Division, R.I.R., Leinsters, the 10th Hants., were after making an advance on our left wing and that they were being driven back, so our Regiment were sent for and after a few hours march we arrived at the scene of action, and just in the nick of time, when we arrived there, it knocked us out to see all the casualties among our Division; two thirds of it was cut up.

While we were resting Captain R. B. Cooper A Company, stood up and told us that there was a breastwork near the enemy's line, that some of our comrades were up there holding out and that there was no chance for them, so he told us that he promised the General, that we (A Company) would get to the breastwork and hold it till not a man remained. At our Colonel's word we advanced away from the hill and up towards the breastwork. Considering the size of the action we had very few casualties. There were a lot wounded, but none killed and all the time we were very short of water. A and B Companies advanced together and D and C Companies remained behind for supports. I was acting as observer to Captain Cooper, and in company with a signaller, Private Gilligan, when about at the crest of a hill, Gilligan was ordered to send a message back, and no sooner did he raise his hand than he received two gunshot wounds that knocked him out of action. A few minutes later I was ordered to take the range of where our enemy was lying, and I had just set to work in the open when I was knocked out myself, passing my instruments to the next man, Private Marples who was killed shortly afterwards, and I was taken down to the beach and had my wounds dressed, and was sent on board a hospital ship bound for Egypt.

(*The Galway Express* 24-3-1917)

Pte Shaughnessy of the Royal Munster Fusiliers, from Ballinasloe, was a member of the landing party at Suvia Bay, and wrote the following account:

(9) I got wounded on the 15th August. We landed on the 6th. It is too terrible for words to describe. We had to jump into the water – a lot got drowned. The shellfire was so heavy we could not stick in the boats any longer. The Turks were entrenched

a few yards in on the shore; so we were exposed to the fire of rifle and quick firing guns. Anyone would think that it was impossible for a human soul to land, but as I often said, the Irishmen could do anything they took in hand. It was the 10th Irish Division, composed on Connaught Rangers, Munster's, Dublin's, Royal Irish Fusiliers, Royal Irish Rifles, 18th Royal Regiment, Lenisters, Inniskilling Fusiliers. When we landed on the shore land mines started to blow up by the dozen and as we were advancing along, the legs and arms of our comrades were falling amongst us, blown into the air by these mines.

We were exposed all the time to a murderous fire, but we went along yard by yard until we got up to them. That was at Chocolate Hill. The Connaught Rangers were first to attack. Nobody ever witnessed such a sight. Although the Turks were about 10 to 1, the gallant Rangers tackled them like lions with butt end of rifles and the steel and after a desperate fight, lasting about an hour at least, we managed to put them on the run and then we let them have it. For four days we were in the open, without food or water and under fire all the time. We had three days supply, but it got wet with the seawater and soaked in blood but that didn't dishearten the sons of Erin. I don't care what anybody says, when it comes to hand-to-hand fighting, there is none in the British Army to compare with the Irish. God save Ireland. We lost 700 men and 19 officers in five days. (*The Galway Express* 25-9-1915)

Sgt J. Naughton of the Fifth Connaught Rangers wrote to his friend, Martin Moloney, of Lombard Street:

(10) Just another few lines to let you know that we are still strong and hearty in our little 'dug-out in the East.' I really forget now how long ago it is since I sent you my last, and first letter, but as I have a spare half-hour before dark – the sun is well on its way to the western horizon – I thought I might profitably employ it in dropping you a line, because I have not forgotten that you were always an interested and sympathetic listener to any of my old yarns. Our artillery are practicing in solo for the Turco's benefit, and but for that, one might imagine there was no war at all so infrequent is a rifle shot. Our men are walking about the slope of our particular little hill where our dug-outs are and along our little valley as cool and unconcerned as if they were at home. We are still in the same place as when I wrote you last, though great changes have occurred since, so

great, I believe, that another month or so may see an end to the Dardanelles operations. The weather has turned a bit colder at night, and we were served with our great-coats a few days after I last wrote, and three days ago we were given two army blankets apiece. Up to that we had been lying on the ground, but we felt no hardships. I am still lost in wondering admiration at the excellent administration affairs, which leaves practically none of our necessities unprovoided for. Today we had a new shirt apiece granted, and oh! the delicious sense of personal cleanliness the mere feel of it brought. One wants to be dirty, though, thank God, we are far from that, to thoroughly appreciate being clean again. I want for practically nothing now but a clean pair of socks and a smoke of real Irish twist, though I have a tin with a quarter-pound of light English mixture. Tomorrow promises to be a gala day as regards culinary affairs, fresh bread and fresh beef having materialised. I omitted to mention before that we very frequently obtain fresh bread.

The days are still very warm, and the fly pests remain unabated, worse, if anything. But, thank goodness, we are not visited at night, as I have not heard even one mosquito, and there are neither sand flies, bugs, nor fleas. To one acquainted, to some extent, with Eastern lands, there is something to be thankful for. I don't know too much of how they are going on either here or in France, any news we get being rather stale, though a War Department telegram is posted up on a notice-board in our valley every morning, giving the latest in bare outline. The mail is eagerly waited for, and newspapers pounced upon with avidity. I suppose you have seen by now our casualties in the papers in the two soirees we had with the Turks? Our first real one, though we had an odd skirmish or so before, was on the afternoon of the 21st Aug. It was a grand sight to see our fellows (I speak of my own battalion, as, of course, there were no other troops attacking on that particular afternoon), and the bayonet charge simply swarmed the enemy, though we all agree in saying that the Turk, as we know him, is a brave and honourable foe, and apart from the usual tricks and subterfuges of war, is a decent fighter, totally unlike his ally, the Hun.

We gained our objective in a few minutes, and the Turkish position we desired was ours, but at a heavy cost, as the enemy fought stubbornly, with bullet, bayonet, and bomb, and even remained to argue the point when he was beaten to the winds. There were many gallant deeds performed by the 5th Rangers that afternoon, two privates being promoted corporals on the field of gallantry and one Sergeant of my own company (B) a Ballina man named Nealon being recommended for distinction.

The poor fellow was forced to go to hospital ten days later as his eyes, though the doctor here provided him with smoked spectacles, steadily became worse, owing to the powder fumes which entered them as he stood over the bombs to extinguish them. Bombs are a great feature in this trench warfare, and so is what is known as the 'counter-attack' – that is when an enemy captures a trench, or portion of one, he at once sets about consolidating it; that is he puts earth up the enemy side of the trench, or else sand-bags to mininise the effect of the enemy's rifle fire as much as possible, and to create a cover from which to repel the counter-attack if the enemy feels strong enough to attempt one. Fresh troops are generally employed for this purpose, and on this particular evening, the Turks did not disappoint us, delivering the counter-stroke promptly and gallantly. So fierce, indeed, it was, that more experienced troops might well be pardoned for failing to hold on to their ground, and I honestly believe it was owing, in a great measure in conjunction with the cool bravery and steady discipline of the remainder of the men, to the ready recourse and bravery of Sergt. Nealon, that the position remained in our hands all through the night. In the most critical moment of the attack, when the gallant Turk, disdainful of life and limb, was literally raining hand bombs on our lines, Sergt. Nealon seized a dead Turk's great coat, and at the imminent risk of his life, ran from bomb to bomb and, rolling them in the great coat, succeeded in putting out the fuse in each case. This, I believe he continued for an indefinite period.

Clouds conceal the slopes from about half-way up, leaving the summit on the island quite visible, however. You have read, no doubt, about the gallant deeds of the Munsters and the Dublins, who are in the 10th Division (Irish), to which we also belong, and, no doubt, you were proud of them as we all are. The 10th Division consisted of the 29th and 30th Brigades; the 29th having four battalions, the Sixth Leinsters, 5th Connaught Rangers, Sixth Royal Irish Rifles, and 10th Hampshires; the 30th Brigade consisting of the Sixth and 7th Royal Dublin Fusiliers and the Sixth and 7th Royal Munster Fusiliers. Unfortunately the 29th and 30th Brigades were separated on landing, and the 29th Brigade has since been operating with the Australian and New Zealand forces, fine fighters both, but naturally we would rather be with our own Division. Our Brigadier-General (Cooper) was dangerously wounded and all of his staff killed almost at the moment of landing, so we fell under the command of General Godley, of the Australians, who is, I hear, an Irishman himself. He gave us great praise for our conduct during the charge of the 21st and the following night, and expressed himself sorry in not having more battalions like us. Our part in these operations will, I don't doubt, be described under the heading of the Australian operations, as distinct from the operations of the 30th Brigade (10th Division), who were under the command of their own Brigadier and General of Division.

The men of our battalion who were wounded obtained great praise from the doctors and nurses for making light of their sufferings, being cheerful and uncomplaining, and only anxious to see a wounded comrade attended to before themselves. One story which has trickled back from hospital may illustrate this, and is well worth re-telling. One chap, pretty severely wounded in the head, was having it bandaged on the hospital ship, when the nurse involuntarily exclaimed, 'Oh poor fellow, what a bad wound.' When the patient looked up at her with a smile, and then with an assumption of roughness, said, 'Arrah, nonsense, Miss; don't make me blush. Sure me grandfather often got more at a fair.' The sufferings of some of our fellows must have been awful, yet the majority kept asking: 'How did the battle go? Did we win? Were our commanders and officers pleased?' One poor fellow of our company – on second thoughts, I will not tell you of that. It is too sad and horrible, though brave too. I hope to have the pleasure of telling you of our second battle in my next, which though just as bravely attempted was not so successful.

(*The Connacht Tribune* 9-10-1915)

This account of the death of Second Lieut Gabriel Costello of the Royal Engineers (formally of the Tuam Volunteers) was published in *The Tuam Herald*:

(11) In the full flush of youth – he was barely twenty-five – gifted with good looks and a fine physique, his tragic end arouses a keen sense of pathos, combined with a forceful realisation of the grim ruthlessness of war. But, after all, there is gladness in the thought that this gallant young fellow died at the post of duty and added another Irish name to the long bead-role of honour. His heroic end is at once a cause for lament and inspiration. Thus let it be; and while we pay homage to his memory, let us hope that others will emulate his example. He and thousands who have similarly yielded up their lives would have wished for no nobler epitaph.

(*The Tuam Herald* 28-8-1915)

The following extract was taken from a letter by Norman Browne, a former student of University College Galway:

(12) We left – on the 16th August. Early next morning at about 3 o'clock, we neared the Gallipoli Peninsula. We could hear the heavy booming of our 15-inch naval guns, which were shelling the Turkish positions on the hills. A thundering crash from the ship followed by a thick column of smoke as she let go her broadside, and few seconds later, in the dim light of early morning, the shell bursting about ten miles away on the distant hills, creating a sudden flame of light, a crash, and then dense clouds of smoke and dust, gradually rising upwards. The enemy replied, and as we came nearer to that part of the coast where we were about to take part in effecting a new landing, a few shells burst around our ship. They created no panic, only interest. The order to land was given. 'Lightest' and little boats were manned, and we made for the shore. Two of our boats were hit by shells, and before the whole battalion had disembarked wounded were being carried back on board on stretchers.

We formed up under cover of a hill, and then the orders were given to advance. We carried our full kit: pack, a blanket, a waterproof sheet, two days' iron rations, a water bottle, respirators and rations in haversacks, a rifle and 220 rounds of ammunition – a heavy weight to carry in the heat. Advancing by short rushes, we went on for about two miles, all the time under heavy shrapnel fire, and then took a rest under cover, and took off our packs. Then on we went, with our haversacks strapped to our backs in lieu of the pack, over hills, and then along a sandy beach. Horrible sights we passed; men dead and mangled, wounded, groaning piteously, men lying dead as they fell in the charge, rifle and bayonet fixed in their hands. The enemy had the range of the beach to a 'nicety', and the men were falling all around. Our men were splendid, and worthily upheld the best traditions of the regular British Army, advancing coolly without a sign of fear. I didn't feel nervous and shaky, as I had expected to be. Here at last was some definite result of our eleven months' training.

Our chief worry was where to get the next rest under cover, and a smoke. Absolute cover from shell fire there is nowhere on the peninsula. Shrapnel especially is very treacherous. It bursts in the air, and sends a hail of lead and iron bullets, wire, glass, nails, pieces of iron girders, etc., in all directions. We had advanced about four miles inland.

We were lying flat on our stomachs in extended formation, after a rush on an open plain, when a shrapnel shell burst over me. I felt a sudden blow, as if from a heavy stone, followed by a numbness, but no pain, and, of course, my arm was useless. I got my field dressing put on, and, carefully avoiding advancing troops where most of the shells burst, I made my way back to the field dressing station. Before nightfall I found myself on board a hospital ship, and on 12th inst., I arrived in hospital here. I expect to have a few weeks convalescence here, and then be sent back to rejoin my regiment.

Our toll in officers was very heavy the first day. So far as I can ascertain from others of my battalion who were wounded on the evening of the 7th and on the 8th, Edward Weatherill (since killed) was all right up till then. We made a very big advance and gained an important position. The new landing is expected to lead to decisive events in the war. When I go back it may not be half so bad, as our men will have had time to entrench themselves. Our advance was in the open, along the beach, and over a large plain, under heavy and accurate shell fire. On the left of the plain were groves of mulberry trees, and here, right in the midst of us, a few snipers were hidden, who did a lot of damage before they were spotted.

(*The Galway Express* 4-9-1915)

CHAPTER XVI

MESOPOTAMIA, PALESTINE & SALONIKA

In 1914, Mesopotamia was an area bounded by the Rivers Tigris and Euphrates. It is now the country of Iraq, but at the time it was part of the Turkish empire. Allied operations against the Turks in this area began with the landing of an Anglo-Indian force at the mouth of the Shatt al-Arab in November 1914, but they suffered a humiliating defeat by the Turks. Nevertheless, by June 1915, they had successfully forced the Turks to relinquish Basra, Shaiba and Amara. The allies established a security cordon around the Basra oil-fields, which was one of their main objectives. They were also successful at the battle of Nasiriya in July 1915. The town of Kut-al-Imara was the next target. It is situated on the River Tigris, and was at the time a grain market and carpet-manufacturing town. The Expeditionary Force was under the command of Gen. Townshend.

In September 1915, he launched the attack after successfully mounting a southern diversionary action, with the real assault coming from the north of the town. After a sharp encounter, the allies successfully routed the Turkish troops. The allies pushed on up the River Tigris towards Baghdad, but met with serious opposition at Ctesiphon and were forced to fall back to Kut al-Imara. They immediately fortified their positions and repulsed the first Turkish attack, but the enemy surrounded the town and in December 1915, the siege of Kut-al-Imara began. Although the British relief columns tried to reach the town, they were driven back, leaving Townshend with only one option, surrender. The First Connaught Rangers had been sent forward to support the allies under siege at Kut-Al-Imara. Although they distinguished themselves in action at Abu Roman, where they took the main Turkish trenches, they were unable to help at

Kut-al-Imara. On 29 April 1916, with no hope of the reinforcements breaking through, Townshend surrendered his force of some 3,000 British and 6,000 Indian troops. According to reports, the treatment they received from the Turks was barbaric, and left two-thirds of the British and half of the Indian troops dead during a forced march to captivity of some 1,200 miles. On 23 February 1917, the British under Gen. Maude recaptured the town and it remained in allied hands until the war ended. On 11 March 1917, the allies captured Baghdad and this was followed by a victory at the battle of Ramadi in September. By November 1918, Mosul and Kirkuk were also under allied control.[1]

Operations in Palestine, which was also under Turkish control at the time, began in February 1915, with the Turks making an unsuccessful attack on the Suez Canal. The Turkish governor of Syria launched the attack from Palestine, across the Sinai Desert. The British became so alarmed by the offensive that they began maintaining a large garrison in Egypt. They constructed lines of defence in the Sinai, built railways and laid a water pipeline. The Turks made a second attack on the Suez Canal in March, which was also repulsed. In response to these attacks the British mounted an invasion of the Sinai Peninsula towards the end of 1915. There was a lull in the fighting until April 1916, when the Turks suddenly attacked, slowing the progress of the British.

By December, the allies had taken El Arish, and by January 1917, they had forced a complete Turkish withdrawal from the Sinai. In March 1917, the large allied force assembled in Egypt began their push into Palestine and prepared for an assault on Gaza. The first two attacks on Gaza failed, with a result of 7,000 British casualties, despite having the support of tanks. The British commander was relieved of his command, and Gen. Allenby replaced him. Allenby spent several months preparing for another offensive, however, this allowed the Turks time to fortify their position and strengthen a line from Gaza to Beersheba.

In October 1917, the bombardment of Gaza began, at the same time Beersheba was attacked. The latter fell on 31 October 1917 and the allies, which included ANZAC troops, then turned their full attention on Gaza.

Although the Turks fought well, Gaza was under British control by 7 November. The allies then marched up the coast taking Jaffa along the way and then turned to attack Jerusalem. They entered the 'Holy City' on 9 December 1917. Because of the German spring offensive on the western front, there were no fresh troops available to continue operations in Palestine and they had to delay any additional advances until September 1918. When the British did renew their attack they forced the Turks northwards, destroying two Turkish armies in the process and inflicted severe casualties on a third. The Turks were also under pressure from the Arab armies of Abdullah and Feisal, to whom 'Lawrence of Arabia' was attached. By the end of September the British had crossed the border into Syria and were advancing towards Damascus. With the aid of Arab allies, the British defeated the Turks at Damascus and entered the city on 1 October 1918.[2]

An officer of the Royal Engineers wrote to John and Honor Cunniffe of Addergoolemore, Dunmore about their son Michael, who was killed in the closing weeks of the war:

(1) On active service with the Mediterranean Expeditionary Force. Dec 8/18 G.H.G Leiu. E.C.H. Palestine.

Dear Mr. and Mrs. Cunniffe,

Just a few lines to let you know a few things in connection with your dear son. Well as you know that poor Mic's time has gone and only too sorry to say so, as he was one of the best and a jolly good mate to us, we were all surprised to hear of his death as we could not believe it, he was one who could have put up with anything and always had enjoyed the best of life and its hard times. I think that he had beared out here with us all for nearly four years and in the finish of the war he had to leave us, but we are all sorry but things will happen in a war life. Well the other week I and another young fellow who used to work in Bradford with Michael and I worked in Leeds not far from Bradford, we went to a place called Haifa were he is buried. I got a cross made for him such a nice one too and we went and put it on his grave and also took a photo of it so that when we get it done I will send you one or two of it but I think that Mic was put away quite nice and careful. But I or some of us would have liked to have been there when he was put

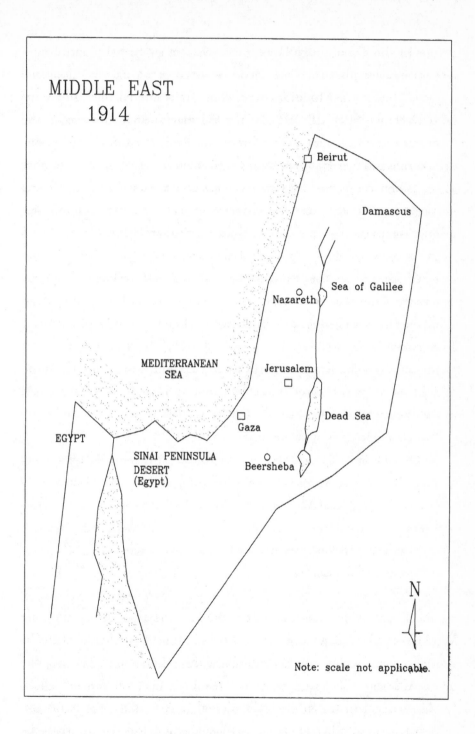

MIDDLE EAST
1914

Beirut

Damascus

Sea of Galilee

Nazareth

MEDITERRANEAN
SEA

Jerusalem

Dead Sea

EGYPT

Gaza

SINAI PENINSULA
DESERT
(Egypt)

Beersheba

N

Note: scale not applicable.

Map of the Middle East 1914 - 1918.

(Courtesy of Eamonn O'Regan & Michael Conneely)

away but unfortunately we could not get in reach of the grave, I had to go 70 miles or more to put his cross up so I think you can understand but Mr. and Mrs. Cunniffe you can rest some that he is buried in a nice cemetery and we have done all in our power to see that he was looked after. Well Mr. Cunniffe I want to ask you a few things. I got a collection up amongst the lads of the Coy of which Michael belongs to and all we want to know is would you if you care to do it at home, the money that we have got there's been a suggestion that we should forward the money on to you and if you would be kind enough to get a memorial tablet made at home and put it in the church that he belongs to at home and we thought it would be a good idea if you would do it, that's if you think its best, as we thought of doing it and then sending it home for the church so if you would suggest the best thing and let us know we should be awfully pleased. I should have written before now but we have been awaiting for your address. I got it from a person that lives in Bradford so you must excuse me for not writing you before this and I will give you the full particulars of what I know, he died on the 11/10/18 and was buried on the same day he lies in Haifa Military Cemetery number 5 grave, so that is all I know and I will send you a Photo of it when I get them done. So I will close now and we send our sympathy to you from the bottom of our hearts as follows: – These are his fellow pals he worked within the Coy and will be affected.

Second Corp Gill G.Second Corp Thompson,Sapper Hoperoft W,Sapper Sosery, Sapper Rourke C,Sapper Ben H,Sapper Boyden A,Sapper Hull I,Sapper Phipps,Sapper Marshell,Sapper Ninnio A,Sapper Sing G, Sapper Mcfitley H,Sapper Hutton, Sapper Lenords.

I remain yours faithfully Second Corp G Gill.

(O'Connor Family Archives)

Salonika became an important Greek port for the allies during the First World War. On 6 September 1915, Bulgaria signed an alliance with the central powers, which effectively brought them into the war against the allies. Although there were other reasons, their decision was influenced by the dual stalemates on the Gallipoli and Italian fronts. The terms also included financial gain and the future transfer of territory to Bulgaria at the expense of Serbia. Bulgaria agreed to go to war against Serbia within thirty days and with the support of Germany and Austria, it was hoped to achieve an immediate and decisive victory over the Serbian Army.

The Greeks immediately became fearful of being attacked by Bulgaria, and requested support from the allies. The Greek prime minister, Eleutherios Venizelos had advised the British and French governments that if they sent 150,000 troops to Salonika, he was confident he could bring his country into the war on their side. However, King Constantine being a brother-in-law of the Kaiser, and believing that his best option was to remain neutral, dismissed Venizelos. Nevertheless, the allies took matters into their own hands and began landing their forces at Salonika on 3 October 1915, in spite of the king.

Over the following weeks more troops began arriving, among them were soldiers who had just returned from Gallipoli. By the end of October there were about 40,000 troops assembled in Salonika. On 11 October Bulgarian troops invaded Serbia. They were supported in their attack by German and Austrian forces. Although totally outnumbered, the Serbs proved a formidable enemy. Three times the Central Powers forces seemed to trap the Serbs, but they always managed to disengage and successfully retreat. Their route took them through the mountains of Montenegro and into Albania and by sea to Corfu. The allies had advanced in a bid to connect with the Serbian Army, but being outnumbered by the Bulgarians, were forced to retreat in early December. Although their military objective failed, it was decided to maintain three French and five British divisions in Salonika. In the summer of 1916, they were joined by 100,000 Serbians and elements of the Russian and Italian armies. In July, they began their advance up the Struma Vally, but were forced to withdraw when the Bulgarians attacked the allied centre. It has been said that among all of the allied nations, the Serbs stood out as the supreme warrior race: 'tough, wily and apparently indefatigable.' Gen. Franchet d'Esperey took command of the allies and a carefully planned offensive began in September 1918, which led to Bulgaria surrendering unconditionally within two weeks. Following the surrender, the allies forced all German and Austrian troops out of the Balkans.[3]

This letter was written by Fr William Mullins, a well-known priest in Galway, and chaplain to the British forces connected with the expeditions

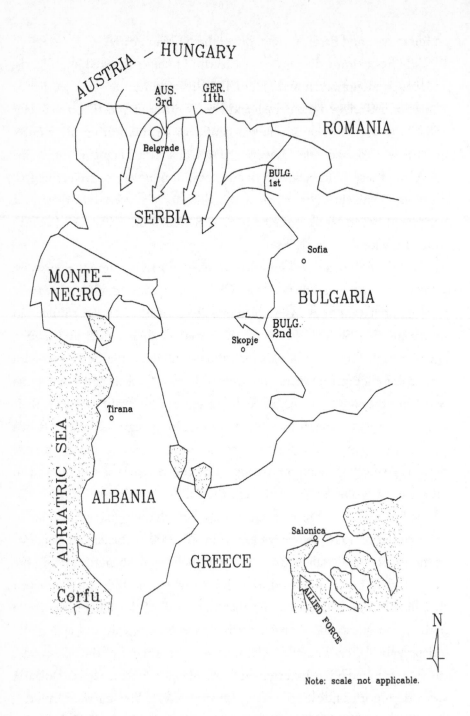

Map of the Salonika Campaign.

(Courtesy of Eamonn O'Regan & Michael Conneely)

in Egypt and Salonika. He starts his letter by criticising the 1916 Easter Rebellion:

(1) First, let me say I am really sorry for the Irish business. You, or any other Irish person, do not know what we Irish people, and especially we Irish priests, have to put up with here; not that there is anything said directly, that we should be able to refute, but the amount of talk that goes on indirectly is what we have to put up with. Though all sensible Irishmen deplore and condemn the Irish Rising; one never hears about the big coal strike or such thing in England and Wales, which, to my mind, equally endangers the war as the Irish flash-in-the-pan.

Let me leave the subject. This is an awful country. Heat is no name for it, I can assure you, this is real active service. I am now practically three months between Egypt and Greece, and a bed I have never seen since. Sometimes we are in dug-outs, and again in a bivouac on the other side of the mountain. The latter consists of a thin waterproof held over you with sticks about the size and length of a walking stick. We have had very little rain here for the past two months, but on two occasions we had it pretty bad for a few hours. Of course, we have our meals in the open and on the ground, though if we are staying in a place for any length of time, we rig up a kind of table, consisting of portions of timber or wagon, with sand bags for feet. We try to manage to get a piece of a box to sit on. We have to rough it. Bully beef, etc. Sometimes a change to better things, but very seldom, as we are miles away from 'anywhere'.

No doubt you have heard of the hooks found in the bully beef, which is packed in the U.S.A. by a firm named Reed – I think that is the name. Well, in that bully beef we found some hooks, one of which I enclose. The sight of it may put some Sinn Feiners thinking. On no account let the hook out of your possession, though you may keep it till I ask you to send it to me. One of our officers got it and says he wants it back. Send me the paper. I am writing this on my knee, so you must not blame me if you can't read it.

… St Paul's journeys were nothing to mine since I came to Macedonia. I have suffered more in three months than I did since I was born, or, I hope, ever will again. We had night marches from place to place. At the end of five or six hours' marching we came to our camp at any time between 11 p.m. and 2 a.m. I need not tell you we had no beds; we lay on the ground with nothing over us but the canopy of Heaven. It is a funny life if one could shut ones' eyes and ears to the inconveniences. As I write (12 o'clock noon) lying on the plains of Macedonia – can't say where – the Allied, British, French and Serbian guns are going like lightning, and so since 5.15 a.m., and no sign of them ceasing. We have got to work at long last. Though the enemy's position is strong, almost impregnable, they are going to have a shot at it. The Serbs who seem to be good soldiers, are thrusting to avenge their defeat in the earlier period of the war, and the Russians, who are here, are a fine body of soldiers. This is a fine country, if developed, as it will be later on by – In parts, it reminds one forcibly of Connemara, especially the part called the Twelve Pins. Tis lovely listening to the roar of the guns as long as they do not throw a few shells into us, and give us a hot time. The weather is still fairly hot, but not as bad as it has been, and I can tell you when your body is under a bivouac there is not much protection from the sun. With all the inconveniences of sun, trekking, hunger, etc., I am glad I am out to do my bit. I have had only two deaths for the last six weeks, though I fear, I shall have more before very long.

(*The Connacht Tribune* 2-9-1916)

This interview was given by Lance Corp. John Leahy of the Third Connaught Rangers, while he was at home on sick leave from Salonika:

(2) Prior to the outbreak of war he was a member of the printing staff of the 'Evening Mail'. Last September he was sent with a detachment to fill up the gaps in the 5th Battalion at the Dardanelles. When the transport left Malta a submarine was sighted. The ship was immediately put about and kept out of danger until nightfall, when she was enabled to resume the voyage. During the period when the risk was imminent the soldiers were paraded on deck with full marching equipment including pack and 200 rounds of ammunition. Over this each man had a lifebelt. 'Except you had a knife to cut loose you were bound to go to Davy Jones', remarked Lance Corporal Leahy. The voyage was completed in safety and Leahy spent a month assisting the Australians at Anzac, where sapping operations were the chief occupation. Then he was transferred to the Tenth Division at Salonika. The conditions there in the early part of the Balkan campaign were far from ideal. The men slept 20 in a tent, and when a regiment was landed there was frequently no accommodation for the first night. In the absence of regular payments some regiments, including the Connaughts, had to do without candles or soap. These are regarded as extras, and are not served out. There was plenty of cigarettes and 'tons of food' but soap was not to be obtained without cash. Leahy occasionally was

glad to use his shaving lather to get the luxury of a wash. 'The mud is very gluey at Salonika,' he says, 'unless your boots are tightly laced you'll leave them behind at the first step from the tent.'

(*The Galway Express* 15-1-1916)

CHAPTER XVII

THE BATTLE OF LOOS

The battle of Loos began on 25 September 1915. It was an attempt by the British and French forces to regain the mining district around the towns of Loos and Len, and to possibly capture Lille. Among the British forces, were a number of battalions that were going into action for the first time. In one section the Forty-seventh London Division were led over the top by the London Irish kicking their regimental football before them. The battle of Loos was preceded by the usual heavy artillery bombardment, signalling an imminent infantry attack. It was the first battle in which the British used gas as a weapon.

However, the wind shifted and it started to blow back on their-own lines, resulting in the cylinders being quickly shut off. The British were stopped by continuous machine gun fire during the initial advance, but resumed their attack the following day. The 15,000 strong infantry formed into ten columns, each consisting of over a thousand men, and began marching towards the enemy lines as if they were marching across a parade ground.

The German troops were astonished at the sight of the entire front covered with British troops. They even stood up on the parapets of their trenches and fired almost triumphantly the masses of men advancing towards them across the open ground. The German machine guns also opened fire with devastating effect; the British were falling literally in hundreds. Nevertheless, they continued to march forward in good order, until they reached the first German position, which was protected by impenetrable barbed wire. Only then did they turn in retreat, leaving a field of corpses which even nauseated the Germans. So great was the feeling of compassion and mercy on the German side, that some withheld fire as the British retreated. The British lost over 8,000 men either killed or wounded in the senseless attack.[1]

There were, however, temporary successes in some sections at Loos. The London Division reached the German lines and secured them after a fierce bayonet engagement. They then moved on to a second line of trenches, which they also cleared. The Scots were also successful and captured the defences at Loos and then pushed beyond the village. Over the following week the allies persisted and did manage to drive back the Germans lines. On 8 October the Munster Fusiliers, and Irish Guards gave an excellent account of themselves near the Chalk Pit Wood sector.

However, their reserves were badly organised and were not employed quickly enough to help stop a German counter-attack, which resulted in the allies being forced back to their original line of fire. Loos gained little strategically, approximately 3,500 yards south of the Hohernzollern redoubt had been penetrated, but had resulted in about 60,000 British casualties overall, including three generals.

It was following this battle that Sir John French was more or less forced to resign because of his differences with Sir Douglas Haig. During a royal visit to France in October 1915, Haig told King George V that Sir John French was a source of great weakness to the army and said that he had lost the confidence of all concerned. The Secretary of State for War, Earl Kitchener, and the King promoted Haig as the replacement for Sir John French, and the latter was gone by the end of the year. Unfortunately for the front line troops, they were placed under a commander who was 'cold' and 'unsympathetic' towards them.[2]

The following letter was written by Pte Arthur Kersaw Peters of the 78th Field Company RE. He was a former building trades instructor in the Galway Technical School, but enlisted in the army when the war began. The recipient of the letter was Mr Webb, principal of the school:

(1) In the ordinary course of events, I should be back in Galway with my classes, but I am afraid this session must pass before I see Galway again. I hope you will have a muster of students and a successful session, and the building classes are as good and

better than in the past. I have been out now for nearly three months. The time has passed quickly, and considering the circumstances, the life is not bad. At present our section is working on a light wooden railway, which is to be used to convey rations and materials to the trenches. I work at present in the open, and can see the German front line trench three quarters of a mile away, and often a bullet will whiz past, which, of course we don't mind. It is the ones that find a billet we dread. Our camp is at present in a wood in the rear of the trenches, and often shells burst near us. One day 28 came over in a half hour, and the holes they made would almost take a decent sized cottage. I was very nearly hit last week by a small shell during our dinner time. Fortunately the weather has been fine for us. A few odd days we have had downpours, and then the conditions are wretched, the roads muddy, while the trenches are full of water and mud. Notwithstanding all discomforts, our solders are splendid, a little grumbling, of course, as a soldier is born so. I see we have been having a small success lately, and I hope it will continue. We are about 1½ miles from a village where we can purchase a few extras. The army rations get a little monotonous. It is wonderful how a few families have stuck to their homes even when a stray shell may at any time demolish them. Kindly remember me to all the staff.

(*The Connacht Tribune* 9-10-1915)

In October 1915, Lance Corp. P. Walsh of the Argyll and Southerland Highlanders wrote the following account of the battle to his mother in Woodquay. The letter was written while he was recovering from wounds in the Northern General Hospital, Lincoln:

(2) I am glad to say that I am all right now, and am lying in hospital here. I don't suppose I shall be fit for discharge for a few months or so, and then I shall get home for about a month. I got wounded at the battle of Hill 70, with a piece of shrapnel, which struck me in the head, and penetrated the brain. I was operated on at Staples, in France, and the shrapnel was removed. My head is healing now, and everything will be all right (D.V.) except that my eyes fell a bit weak, as the optic nerve was affected in some way. I can walk about, but am not allowed to get up as yet. I shall tell you about the great battle when I get home.

The charge took place at 6.15 a.m. on Saturday, 25th September, and we all got over the parapet with only a few causalities. I had to laugh at one Seaforth Highlander, who was lying wounded on the battlefield, with a lighted cigarette in his mouth. He smiled as we passed him and said, 'Go on Argylls'. We did go on, and took all the ground for about three miles, when the enemy began to get serious. Then we satisfied ourselves by holding on to what we had got until midnight, when we got relieved or something. On Sunday morning we could only count 19 men out of our company. After that we were again shoved into the thick of it, and I came out all right. On Monday evening I collected as many Argylls as I could (about 14), and brought them up to the firing line, as I was the only N.C.O. among them. Suddenly we heard rapid rifle fire from the enemy, so we manned the first parapet. It was then I got struck. I have omitted the exciting parts till next letter. I hope you are all in the pink.

(*The Connacht Tribune* 9-10-1915)

The two letters which follow were written by Pte Patrick Larkin of the Irish Guards who was wounded twice, once at Ypres and later at Loos. He was later killed at the Somme. Patrick was from Woodford and wrote a number of letters while at war:

(3) Warlay Bks, Brentwood, Essex, 20-1-16

Dear Father

Just a line hoping it may find you all in good health. I was at the front in France from July 20th until Oct 10th when I was wounded at Loos in the right shoulder and right leg. It was not serious my shoulder was stiff for quite a while. This is my second time to be wounded. I was at home on leave for a month I had a very good time. Grandmother and John are living good. I was in hospital for two months in Scotland and a forthnight in France after being wounded. I underwent three operations to get the shrapnel taken out of my shoulder. There was a very big fight at Loos our regiment alone lost eight hundred men. I hope mother and Jimmie and sister Alice are all well. I would like very very much if sister Alice or Jammie would write to me. I won't be going to France again for about two months. I hope you wont delay in writing to me. I wrote to ye from France on two occasions and I never got an answer. We have some Americans fighting with us and the Canadians. It is a terrible cruel war, I was lying for eight hours in a trench after being wounded before I was brought away. All Guard Regiments and Splendid

Regiments. I have no more to say at present.

> – Remaining Your, Loyal son P. Larkin.

(Larkin Family Archives)

(4) Warlay Bks, Essex, England, 19-2-16

Dear Father,

Received your letter today. Glad to hear you are all well. I am very sorry I did not receive any of you previous letters. My wounds are perfectly healed now. But I have not been returned to duty yet. I enlisted November 1914, went to France March 1915 was wounded 18 May at Ypres and went out again in July and was wounded in October at Loos, I was only slightly wounded 18 May. It is a terrible war. I got Aunt Alice's letter today also. Isn't she very friendly and to write to me. Very glad to hear Jimmie is doing so well. I expect to see you all when the war is over, we had a mild winter but it was very bad in France the troops suffered severely from wet and cold. I suppose the war hasn't affected the American people very much. Where I am stationed is only sixteen miles from London we were stationed in London about nine months ago. I will send my photo first appropriately, write when if is convenient to you.

> – From Your Soldier Son, P. Larkin.

(Larkin Family Archives)

While this report was not written about the main battle of Loos, it is included in this section as the action took place at Loos. It is also significant regarding the Easter Rebellion, but as with other letters and interviews published by the media, one must be careful of its content. If one is to believe in its authenticity, then the Germans were aware of the rebellion in Dublin almost as fast as the rebels in Galway. The interview was given by a Galway officer, who fought in this section:

(5) While Irishmen at home were insanely destroying life and property our countrymen in the trenches were earning fresh laurels in the fight against the common enemy. The bravery of the 16th Irish Division at Loos recently has now received official recognition, and some particulars of the manner in which they fought were supplied during the week to an Express representative by a young Galway officer home on

furlough, Sec.-Lieut. J. F. Roland, Royal Irish Rifles. The Irish regiments engaged included the Connaught Rangers, Enniskillings, Dublin's, Munster's, Rifles and Fusiliers. On the 24th April, at four o'clock, a.m., the Germans delivered a gas attack and made a furious assault on the Division's lines in the vicinity of Loos, on the Hulloch and Hohenzollern fronts. Though the attack was somewhat in the nature of a surprise the Division met it very successfully, and repulsed it with heavy losses to the enemy. The Germans essayed another gas attack afterwards and were successful in taking the first line of trenches, as many of the men in it were gassed. However, a counter-attack was ordered, the trench retaken and the German offensive eventually broken up after sanguinary fighting by the Irish Division, which took a large number of prisoners. That the Germans knew of the contemplated rising in Ireland was evident from the fact that on the afternoon of Easter Monday they ran up cardboard notices opposite the Irishmen's trenches saying English soldiers were slaughtering their women and children in Ireland, that the country was in open revolt etc. etc., and asking the Irishmen in the trenches to lay down their arms. Needless to state this had not the desired effect, except that the Irish soldiers indulged in some 'strafing' at the expense of the Germans. Several Galway officers and men were in the recent fighting, including Captain S. Gwynn, M.P., Lieut. Seymour, Lieut. Jack Kneafsey, Lieut. Semple etc.

(*The Galway Express* 13-5-1916)

CHAPTER XVIII

THE BATTLE OF JUTLAND

In August 1914 the German High Seas Fleet, under the command of Admiral Reinhard Von Scheer an experienced sailor, began sorties into the Heligoland Blight. He attempted the same at the Dogger Bank in January 1915, but was repulsed on both occasions. In the first five months of 1916, Scheer made a number of sorties, which resulted in German battleships arriving off the English coast and bombarding Lowestoft. Towards the end of May, the British admiralty became aware that the German fleet had put to sea once more. At the time, the British Grand Fleet was commanded by Admiral Sir John Jelliceo and was situated at Scapa Flow, an expanse of sea enclosed by the Orkney Islands, Scotland. Urgent messages were immediately sent to Admiral Jelliceo and Vice-Admiral Sir David Beatty commanding the battle cruisers fleet at Rosyth, on the Firth of Forth. On 30 May, both fleets were put to sea to conduct a sweep of the coastline. They were unaware of the German fleet's position, which was steaming towards the Skagerrak, the waterway separating Norway and Denmark's Jutland Peninsula. The British fleet consisted of twenty-eight battleships, nine battle cruisers, eight armoured cruisers, twenty-six light cruisers, and seventy-eight destroyers. Admiral Von Scheer had under his command twenty-two battleships, five battle cruisers, eleven light cruisers and sixty-one destroyers. Both fleets were on a collision course, and the first the British knew of the actual enemy location, was when one of their ships signalled that she had sighted two enemy vessels, whose crew were engaged in boarding a neutral merchant ship. Beatty's battle cruiser fleet went to investigate and on 31 May, Jutland, the biggest sea battle of the First World War began.[1]

The German 'scouting' battleships that Beatty encountered were under the command of Admiral Von Hipper. At precisely 3.48 p.m. the firing began with Beatty opening hostilities. The Germans returned fire and Beatty's flagship *Lion* was hit by four shells from the *Lutzow*. The German attack continued and their next victim was the *Indefatigable* which was destroyed, sinking within thirty minutes, losing all but two crewmen. *The Queen Mary* suffered the same watery fate, going down with a loss of 1,266 men. *The Tiger* and *Princess Royal* were also hit. At this point, Beatty decided that his best plan of action was to disengage and locate Jelliceo and the Grand Fleet.

However, his course was leading him directly into the path of the main German fleet and as dusk arrived, Betty turned and pulled away steaming towards the Grand Fleet. He was followed closely by the German ships and the engagement then turned into a running battle. During this phase of the battle, four German ships were hit, the *Von der Tann*, *Seydlitz*, *Lutzow* and *Deffinger*. As they closed on the British ships, the Germans soon became aware of the huge British fleet now steaming towards them. At a range of about 8,600 yards, the British formed a single line and engaged the enemy. There is much confusion about the combat which followed and some of the action still remains unclear. What is certain is that the British suffered more casualties when the *Black Prince* was sunk, taking with it all its crew. *The Defence* was also blown apart and rapidly disappeared beneath the waves. The Invincible was also lost. *The Warrior* and *Warspite* were forced out of action after being hit by enemy fire. The German fleet also lost additional warships among them the *Elbing*, *Frauenlob* and the *Pommern*.[2]

Admiral Von Scheer's fleet was taking a pounding and he decided to turn for home, leaving a number of battle cruisers to cover his retreat. It was about 8 p.m. when the British fleet disengaged and pulled away, heading for their home base. The remaining German warships continued to harass the British with the result that the fighting continued until well after midnight, with further damage being inflicted by both sides. It was a brutal sea battle and one in which both sides claimed victory, but there is no doubt that the British had taken the worst of the hammering. After the battle, a total of 117,025 tons of British warships and 61,180 tons of German warships lay at the bottom of the sea, along with thousands of unfortunate sailors from both sides.

The British casualty list included 343 officers and 6,104 sailors having lost their lives, with 564 of all ranks wounded. The German casualties included 172 officers and 2,414 sailors dead, with 90 of all ranks wounded. Although the British lost more ships, they had the advantage of a larger navy and managed to secure control of the seas. With the exception of an encounter between German dreadnoughts and British battleships near Heligoland in November 1917, the Germans did not venture outside their base for the remainder of the war. Earlier that year, Admiral Beatty had stated that the only way to defeat an enemy was through blockade, he believed that advancing on the battlefield, killing the 'Huns' in thousands was not the way to win the war, but rather to cut off their supplies.[3]

CHAPTER XIX

THE BATTLES OF THE SOMME
THE BIG PUSH

The 'Big Push' or the battle of the Somme as it became known was initially planned as a co-ordinated offensive by the French and British armies. However, the Germans attacked Verdun in February 1916 inflicting enormous casualties on the French. By April 1916, most of Europe knew the British were organising a major offensive and that the Germans would feel the results of it somewhere 'soon'. By the summer of 1916 the French troops were still occupied fighting off the attack at Verdun and because of this, the battle of the Somme would have to be primarily a British effort. The attack would take place over approximately a twenty-five mile front. During the week before the battle the British bombarded the well-entrenched Germans, firing over a million shells at their defences. The bombardment had little effect on German positions other than to serve as a warning of an impending infantry attack. Consequently, the Germans were able to strengthen their defences before the assault. Many of the shells failed to explode and many more were simply shrapnel shells, which had little effect on the barbed wire and earthworks.

Although some of the experienced British soldiers suspected that the bombardment did not have the desired effect, the attack still went ahead. The battle plan was crude in the extreme and was based on the assumption that the first line of attack almost always failed, while the second line of attack generally failed, but sometimes got through. The third line of attack nearly always got through, but sometimes failed, while the fourth line of attack almost always succeeded. When the German commander at Verdun, Gen. Erich Von Falkenhayn, was informed by Gen. Von Below that such an attack was imminent on the Somme, he was delighted, but said that he couldn't imagine that the allies would be 'equally stupid.'[1]

At 6.35 a.m. on 1 July 1916, the guns, which had been firing incessantly all week, roared out in a crescendo for the final bombardment. At 7.28 a.m. the supreme moment came when the officers sounded their whistles and the allied troops climbed out of their trenches carrying over 60lbs. of equipment, and began walking towards the German lines. There had been a slight drizzle earlier, but it had cleared into a sun filled morning. Within minutes of the allies leaving their trenches, the German artillery began to rain down on them with a devastating effect. For those who survived the artillery barrage, the machine guns were waiting and as they closed on the German lines, these guns opened fire inflicting horrendous casualties.

Despite these losses, wave after wave of troops were sent into the firing line, adding to the carnage, and this was repeated on a lesser scale throughout the day. Of the four battalions of Northumberland Fusiliers 'Tyneside Irish' consisting of 3,000 men, most became casualties. They were not the worst hit; the First Newfoundland regiment had ceased to exist. A little over thirty minutes after the battle had begun, Haig recorded in his diary that reports were 'most' satisfactory and that his troops had crossed the German front line trenches. One wonders from which position he was watching the battle, as it was catastrophic along most of the front with his soldiers being killed in their thousands. At Beaumont-Hamel the Dublin Fusiliers were one of the leading battalions to sacrifice themselves to the deadly hurricane of fire.

The most successful troops on the Somme that day were the French, and the Thirty-sixth Ulster Division, consisting of the Royal Irish Rifles, Inniskillings and Royal Irish Fusiliers, who were situated close to the centre of the attack. The Ulstermen advanced together, and many of them were hit even as they were preparing to advance. Nevertheless, the whole line moved forward through clouds of smoke as German machine guns swept across the battlefront. Eventually, they reached and took the first line trenches while the second and third fell in turn. Because none of the other units had reached this position, the Ulstermen found themselves alone, with no company to link up with. Moreover they were reduced to

'Over the Top, 1 July 1916.' (Coutesy of Eamonn O'Regan)

half their strength, with no reserves or ammunition for support, thus, they had to relinquish some of their hard earned ground. Their commander, Gen. Nugent later stated that: 'None but troops of best quality could have faced the fire which was brought to bear on them, or losses suffered during the advance.'[2]

By the end of the day, the losses were staggering with over 60,000 British casualties strewn across the battle zone. Douglas Haig had the large-scale battle he had wished for, but at an appalling cost in human lives. The battle of the Somme proved to be the worst and most tragic battle in British military history. Very little ground had been captured; only some sections of the German forward defence zone had been shallowly penetrated. For those who survived the day's battle, the evening brought its own torment, as they had to endure the 'eerie demonic' sounding cries and screeches of the wounded and dying in the killing fields of no-mans-land which lasted throughout the night. The burden had proven far too great for the stretcher-bearers and thousands were left to suffer alone in the open.

The poet, Siegfried Sassoon, who witnessed the carnage, wrote: 'I am staring at a sunlit picture of Hell.' The tragedy of the Somme had far reaching effects felt right across the United Kingdom and Ireland. Many families in Galway became extremely worried as telegrams and newspapers reports arrived. *The Connacht Tribune* of 15 July reported that the present 'great push' by the allies was taking its inevitable toll of life. It went on to say, that homes in every part of Ireland had been plunged into mourning and that: 'Galway has given many men to the war and many more of them are now facing death in the present offensive.' The report stated that the casualties included 'rank and file' from almost every town in the west of Ireland. Despite these appalling losses, Haig continued the attack over the following months, and it deteriorated into a total blood-bath which rivalled Verdun.[3]

On Sunday 3 September, the Sixteenth Irish Division, were called up to be included in a huge assault on the villages of Guillemont and Ginchy. It was an attack that would be remembered as one of the most glorious chapters in the history of the Irish Brigade and would not be forgotten in France. These two villages were important strategic positions held by the Germans and knowing of an impending attack, they had made serious defensive preparations. The Irish Division included the Royal Irish Fusiliers, Royal Munster Fusiliers, Royal Dublin Fusiliers and the Connaught Rangers. At noon, the British opened the attack with a tremendous bombardment, followed by a creeping barrage of 18-pounders, behind which a storm of battalions were preparing to advance.

The German barrage began, but did not impede the men of the Irish Division as they went over the top in perfect order. Their reckless bravery undoubtedly saved lives as they reached the German lines in good time and prevented the enemy from using their machine guns. By evening their victory was complete with Guillemont being secured for the allies. An observer later described the attack as the: 'charge of the Irish Brigade' adding that the Irish Division had added another chapter to the history of Irish valour. The following day, Fr William Doyle of the Sixteenth Division recorded the terrible scenes in the aftermath of the battle. The concentration of death was almost unbelievable with 'half rotten corpses' trodden underfoot and pulverised. Many lay 'stiff and stark', with open staring eyes where they had fallen. He had tried to prepare himself for the worst, but all he had read or 'pictured' in his mind did not spare him from the reality of the horrors he 'now' faced. A number of days later, the Irish Brigade went into action again, this time at Ginchy. The capture of Ginchy on 9 September was the only success on the entire front that day. The British War Correspondent, Philip Gibbs, reporting on the attack, stated:

> The splendid success of the Irish Brigade from a military point of view is their success of taking a hostile front of 900 yards and to depth of nearly a mile with no supporting troops on either flank … From a non-military, untechnical human point of view the greatness of the capture of Ginchy is just in the valour of those Irish boys who were not cowed by the sight of death very close to them and all about them and who went straight on to the winning post like Irish race horses. The men who were ordered to stay in the village almost went into a rage because they could not join the next assault.[4]

It was mid-November before the battle finally ended, and this was mainly because the ground had frozen over, forcing an end to the carnage. The total allied gain in territory was at most, eight miles in depth in some areas, over about twenty-miles of front. The battle of the Somme was possibly the most horrifying battle in the history of human conflict, costing the lives of some 615,000 allies, with German fatalities reaching an estimated 500,000.[5]

The following are accounts of the battle are from various Galway sources. The first is a report on the death of Alexander Young, VC, killed in action at the Somme:

(1) Mr. Joseph S. Young, J.P., U.D.C., Corrib House, Galway, yesterday (Thursday) morning received an official communication from the South African War Department, London, notifying him that his brother, Lieut. Alexander Young, V.C., of the South African Scottish, had just been killed in action. Accompanying the commutation were the usual letters of sympathy from the King and Queen. The news has been received with the deepest regret in the City, for, although Lieut. Young had been in the Colonies for many years, he had many friends in Galway, and when on a visit to his brother last November, a few weeks before he left for the front, he gained the popularity of all classes. The Galway Urban Council yesterday adjourned without transacting any business as a mark of respect. In June last Lieut. Young was wounded in the left arm at 'the Devil's Wood', as it is known amongst the men, and rejoined his famous colonial regiment only three weeks ago, and went into action almost immediately in the 'great push' on the Somme. In 1890 the deceased officer joined the Queen's Bay's and since then he has been in no fewer than four campaigns. His decorations included two South African Medals, a medal for the native rebellion of 1906, and the much-coveted V.C. It was while defending the line of communications in South Africa that he won the latter. He had served for a considerable period in the Cape Mounted Police, and had a farm in Natal.

(*The Connacht Tribune* 28-10-1916)

The following report concerns three Galway City brothers, Matt, Pat and Joseph Melia. Matt was killed at the Somme:

(2) It is only by degrees that the truth about the heavy toll exacted from Galway in the present big Allied advance in France is leaking out. On Tuesday of this week, Mr. Martin Melia, of Mainguard-st., Galway had intimation from the War Office, that his step-son, Mr. Matt Melia had been killed in action in north France on the 4th September. His mother, Mrs. Egan, who is prostrate and inconsolable at the terrible intelligence, has had the usual messages of condolence from the King and Queen, bearing a facsimile of the signature of the Secretary of State for War, Mr. Lloyd George. The deceased was attached to the 8th Batt. of the Munster Fusiliers. He has another brother, Pat Melia in the First Batt. Connaught Rangers, who is now in hospital suffering from wounds recently received. A third brother, Joseph Melia, is in Egypt. He joined the Munster Fusiliers at the outbreak of the war, but is now attached to the Royal Irish Regiment. He was wounded immediately after the landing at the Dardanelles, but quickly recovered and is still on active service. Three brothers with the colours is something of a record even for a Galway family, and is a significant fact at a time when the Die-Hards are clamouring for conscription for Ireland. Much sympathy is felt for the parent and foster-parent of the deceased young soldier in a form of bereavement which is now shared by all classes in the land, high and low. (*The Connacht Tribune* 7-10-1916)

The next report records the death of Pte Martin Geary of Long Walk. A letter follows this from his commanding officer to Pte Geary's mother:

(3) Amongst the many gallant Irishmen who laid down their lives in the present big advance on the Somme, is one of the finest specimens which Galway sent to the front. Pte. Martin Geary, of Long Walk, who fell at Poziers on the 3rd September. Intimation of his death has just been conveyed to his parents, who are amongst the most respectable and respected, people of the district to which they belong. Naturally, the bereavement has left them almost inconsolable, especially the mother. The deceased belonged to the Australian Imperial Force. On the invitation of his sister he went out to the great island Continent just a year before the war broke out, and he enlisted this October 12 months. He was only 22 years of age, and had been a life long teetotaller. He is still favourably remembered in the city of his birth, where his many aimable

[sic] qualities had secured for him hosts of friends before his emigration.
(*The Connacht Tribune* 7-10-1916)

(4) Dear Mrs. Geary – I wish to convey to you the deep sympathy of myself and of the men left in my platoon on the death of your son, Martin, one of Number Seven. He was a good soldier, always ready for work, as strong as they make them, and never in trouble. My men have lost a good comrade, and I have lost a soldier than whom I wish to lead none better. Your son, Mick, as his mates knew him, was killed on the morning of September 3rd last, when the First Prussian Guard Reserve Regiment was cut to pieces by the Queenslanders of the 49th Batt., your son's regiment. It was outside Poziers on the road to the famous Mouquet Farm. We ran right through, but had to pay the price. We hope that your son's and your sacrifice may end in the securing of the lasting peace for which we are striving. The officer commanding my company and my fellow officers, join with me in this letter of condolence – I remain Dear Mrs. Geary, yours sincerely, R. Tambling.
(*The Connacht Tribune* 7-10-1916)

The following letter was written by the commanding officer of Pte Henry Spain of the Thirteenth Canadians, who was killed in action near the Somme. He was one of five brothers at war, the others being Joseph, Michael, Patrick and Christopher. They were all sons of Michael Spain from Portumna, who also had four nephews and two grandsons at the front. His son-in-law, Patrick Monaghan, was in a German prisoner of war camp. Henry Spain's death brought to eleven, the number of Portumna men killed at the time. His father received the letter during Christmas 1916:

(5) France, December, 1916.

Dear Sir – No doubt you have already heard of the death in action of your son of this battalion. He belonged to my section, and I thought perhaps that you would like to know the circumstances of his death. You will feel proud to know that he was killed on duty in the front line. The enemy were giving us a pretty hard bombardment, a direct hit on our trenches killed Pte. Spain and one other. He was hit in the head and killed instantly, not disfigured. He was as fine a soldier as ever faced the enemy, and I feel proud that I had him in my section. He was carried back by his comrades, and lies buried in a large well-kept military cemetery just behind the line. Beside him lie two others of the grenade section, who were killed about the same time. Although we miss him terribly, we cannot help feeling pride for one who died as your son did, and I have no doubt that you, knowing that your son died while on duty, serving his King and Country to the very end, it will help to console you and the other relatives of the deceased. I trust that this may help to bring comfort to you all in your sad bereavement.

– Yours very Sincerely, D. Brush Donald.

(*The Connacht Tribune* 30-12-1916)

Mr. T. Keane of Shop Street received three letters regarding the death of his son, William Keane, who was killed in action at the Somme:

(6) It is my painful duty to have to tell you of the death of your son, Lieut. W. Keane, who was shot this morning at 6.30 a.m. by a sniper. He was at the time trying to engage this sniper who had been giving a lot of trouble. Your son was an ideal officer and gentleman. Nobody could have come into contact with him for even a few minutes without realising what an able boy he was. He died a noble death. We buried him this afternoon in the cemetery close by here. I have arranged to have a cross put over his grave, which will be permanently marked.

– Lieutenant Colonel Weldon.

(*The Connacht Tribune* 18-11-1916)

(7) His energy was extraordinary. He was working day and night, and was always very cheerful, no matter how trying the conditions, and they were very trying at times. He had recently been selected as Sniping Officer to the Battalion in which he took a great interest. The more I saw of him the more I liked him and the more I valued him as a brave, reliable officer. You have every reason to be proud of your son.

– Captain Hornadge.

(*The Connacht Tribune* 18-11-1916)

(8) I cannot tell you how much I feel the loss of your dear boy. I was fond of him above all because he was such a splendid Catholic, and did a world of good among the men by his example. Last Sunday, the day before he went into the trenches, he received absolution and Holy Communion and came again in the evening to Benediction, as he always did. He had on many occasions given proof that he was not only an officer, but an Irish Catholic as well. Death was instantaneous and I buried him in a little cemetery here with a cross marking his grave. He died a glorious death, and I have no doubt, he is now enjoying the reward in heaven of his noble sacrifice.

– Chaplin, Fr W. J. Doyle.

(*The Connacht Tribune* 18-11-1916)

This letter was written by Pte P. J. Bowler from Prospect Hill, who was wounded at the Somme:

(9) The Guards' Division (which includes the Irish Guards, Scotch, Grenadier and Coldstreams) attacked at dawn on the 15th September last, getting out of shell holes, etc. As we advanced towards the German lines we met with a terrific fire from the German machine guns, which knocked out a lot of our men. We still kept advancing, capturing their first line, and a large number of prisoners. We were all along pressing very hard against the enemy, and we captured all their trenches and supports, driving the enemy in front of us a distance of three miles, and that ground has been firmly held since by our troops. On the evening of the 15th our advance was checked owing to some cause or other, and we dug ourselves in. The next morning at the same hour we again attacked and encountered the same terrific fire from German machine guns and artillery. We punished the Huns severely, as I noticed by the number of dead that the enemy lost ten to our one. On the second morning of the attack I was knocked out myself by shrapnel, and so was my Captain and Officer, Lieut. Purcell, a Co. Cork gentleman, one of the kindest and bravest officers with the British Expeditionary Force. He visited Galway on a recruiting tour with the Guards' Band. I was through the battle of Loos on last September twelve-months, where the Guards did very good work. After I was wounded I was conveyed to the base and put on board a hospital ship, which left me in Bristol, where I was put into a military hospital.

(*The Galway Express* 10-3-1917)

Mrs Macken of Eyre Street received this letter explaining the circumstances in which her son John had been wounded. John was serving with the Royal Irish Fusiliers when he was injured. There are letters from his brother, Walter, included below. This letter was written by John's commanding officer, Lieut Dawson:

(10) He with several comrades volunteered to raid the German line, with Lieut. D. F. Heath in command. Hiding near the Bosche wire, they, at a signal, sprang forward to enter the enemy trenches. Unexpectedly they found Fritz prepared for them. Seeing it was impossible to carry out the original plan the party commenced to storm the Bosche defenses for all they were worth with bombs. Your son, after throwing all his bombs, turned about to carry back Lieut. Heath (who was wounded in the leg), when he caught sight of one of the enemy about to throw a bomb at both of them. Instantly he threw an axe he was carrying into the Germans face, when suddenly an enemy bomb exploded three yards away wounding him in the leg. His wounds were so severe he was unable to walk back to our lines, when young Greenhaugh (a boy of 19) picked him up and carried him to safety. Pte. J. J. Macken whose acquaintance I first made when joining 'B' Company, was, without doubt, one of my best men, and I always looked upon him more as a comrade than a man of the Company. Every officer and man of the Company recognise they have lost a comrade and a man in him. No man could do more than your son did – that is to volunteer to perform such dangerous work in the face of certain death.

(*The Galway Express* 28-10-1916)

The following two letters were written by Pte Walter Macken, 18092, Sixth Royal Irish Fusiliers. They are examples of the many letters he wrote to his wife, Agnes. He refers to his brother John, who was an orderly in a battalion quite near his location. Another brother, Michael, served with the Canadian Armed Forces and later in the war, a forth brother, Tom, was recruited into the British Army. Both John and Tom survived but Walter was killed in action at St Eloi on 27 March 1916. Walter Macken and his wife Agnes had three children, and the youngest, Walter, became the world-renowned novelist and wrote about his father's experiences in the historical novel, *The Scorching Wind*. The second letter gives some idea of mud filled trenches and the ever-present danger from snipers:

(11) 25th December 1915.

My dearest Agg,

A few lines to wish yourself and my darlings all the blessings of the season. I felt very lonely all this week. I had not a letter from one belonging to me. Did you answer my last letter? If so I have not received it. In any case I cannot blame anyone in particular. I did not give sufficient address. I thought when I got to Rouen, I would be sent up to the firing line a few days or at least a week after. But I am still here and although I was sent out to join the 4th Battallion. I believe we are to be sent to a different Battalion, so I am afraid if any of you wrote to me. It will be some time perhaps I may never get it. If you have not written before this, do not do so until you hear from me again. I expect to be in the trenches in about three days time. You will be glad to know I'm sure that I was at Confession and Holy Communion this morning. We had Midnight Mass here last night. I lay awake all night thinking of yourself and the mites. I tell you I prayed more then I ever did in my life that God would bring me back to you all again, yes, the longing to see you was very strong. Please God I'll see you all again.

So in about three or four days you can start your prayers in earnest as I shall be having my first tussle with those dogs of Germans. But for God's sake Agg, my love don't worry yourself, it will do neither yourself or our darlings any good. How is Mrs C and all at the Racquet Court. I hope they are all well. Did poor Ursula come out of hospital yet. How is she? Remember me to them all. I have not written or heard from John since I came out. I don't want to write to him yet as I'm not sure what part of the line I shall be sent too. And now Agg, I have no more to say at present-until I get to my destination when I shall write to you immediately. Give my love to all at home. Kiss my little pets for me. Goodbye for the present. God bless and keep yourself and darlings safe until I return. Goodbye.

– Your devoted husband, Walter.

P. S. If you did not as yet get my photo, write to Mrs. Baldwin, 19 Lawn Road, Dover.

(Macken Family Archives)

(12) Sunday 13th February 1916

A line to let you know I am still alright. I had a letter from Ivy while I was in the trenches. I will answer it by this post, if I can, it is so good of her to think of writing to me. I thought I might have had a letter from you, I need not tell you how it would have helped to cheer me up, however Agg, I am not vexed at you. I thought you might be waiting to send those photos. I hope that I will have one from you before going in again. Well Agg, I have had my first real dose of trench work. I know it was hard and heard a lot about it but no one realises what it was like until he had had a taste of it. I have had mine. The Germans did not give us very much trouble where we were, but the weather I never experienced anything like it. It started to snow one morning at six o'clock and did not leave off for even five minutes until ten o'clock the next day, then it started to freeze and next day it came on to snow, this went on for four days at least. The trenches we were in had been lately taken from the enemy, they were in a terrible state, in some places above our knees in mud, but we had rubber boots up to our thighs, we prayed a few times that the Germans might make an attack so that we could warm ourselves, we could not light any fires and it was sure and sudden death to put your head over the parapet, their snipers are certainly splendid shots, we were just beginning to have our own back with our snipers though when we were relieved. I am sending you some souvenirs I found on a German that I had to bury. I found an illuminated watch, a purse of German notes, a penknife and a wallet with photographs and some letters and a diary. I gave up the wallet with the exception of one photo, the chap whom I buried is sitting, I have him marked. I believe the officer and some of the rest are prisoners of war. I want you Agg to keep those things for me. I think if you ask Arthur Clarke, he would frame the photos and notes all in the one frame, the photo in the centre, he will know best, he will do it if you tell him I asked. I will register the watch. I was offered a pound for it but refused, let me know immediately when you get this. Did John get his leave yet, I have not heard from him for ever so long. I wonder why he does not write, when I was going up to the trenches, I passed within a short distance of the hospital where he is stationed but could not get to see him unfortunately. How is Mrs. O'C and all the Racquet People getting on remember me to them. Are the pictures doing well? I wish the war was over and me back home again, however I think it will not last many months longer, some thing will have to break shortly. I think we have the better of the Germans now, but the devils will make a terrible fight of it, I'm afraid before they give up, you should hear our artillery when they start at them, it would do your heart good to see the wire fences and parapets going up in the air. The beggars begin to roar and squeal like rabbits, they get into an awful state. I pity them when our fellows start a general bombardment. Well Agg, I will conclude, how are the children, I sincerely trust the little darlings are not catching colds. God protect you all and bring me back safe to you. Goodbye, write immediately when you get this.

> – Your affectionate husband, Walter.

Remember me to K. Griffin and also Mrs. Byrne.

(Macken Family Archives)

The second battle of the Somme began on 21 March 1918. It is sometimes called the Saint-Quentin Offensive or Operation Michael. The battle was the first act of the German Spring Offensive. It was intended to capture Amiens and split the French and British armies. The battle began with German guns opening fire at 4.50 a.m. and for two hours they bombarded the British lines. However, the British quickly replied with heavy artillery fire. At 9.40 a.m. the German infantry attack began under the cover of a heavy fog. The circumstances were for the most part in favour of the Germans, although some of them did lose their way because of the fog. By noon the British commander, Sir Hubert Gough, had very little idea as to how the battle was going, but by then eight or nine of his twenty forward battalions had been virtually sacrificed. His tanks and heavy guns in the forward zone had also been hampered by the weather conditions, as they required 1,000 yards of visibility, but had only about twenty. As night approached the Germans were in possession of the forward zone and dug-in over most of the battle area. Gough then withdrew his right wing by about seven miles. The following morning the Germans moved across the open country northwest of Saint-Quentin. On 24 March, the allies were forced to fall back across the cratered ground, which had been so hard won almost two years earlier. The attack forced the Fifth British Army to retreat, which in turn forced the flanking British and Third French armies to fall back also. The German army advanced as far as Montdidier and were within a few miles of Arras before they were finally halted. It seems that the Germans had moved too far and too fast and in doing so had exhausted their troops and severely stretched their supply lines. They had over-run approximately 1,250 square miles and, thus, forced their own front lines up by about fifty miles.[6]

The following two dispatches were sent by Second Lieut A. McPeake of the Connaught Rangers, while under fire, his second letter written from a crater:

(1) To OC 5th C.R. Le Cateau 7.45 pm

C. Coy took village except one part where they got scattered. Party under Mr. Shanley I think got through to open country, their fate is unknown.

Remainder under myself Mr. McPeake took two Germans who had I think left their machine guns which we took.

Heard party of Germans on Railway trying to reorganise.

Came back to Market Square where we met Mr. Lacey with D Coy + Coy H.Q. who have gone to try to take machine guns at top of town.

Met a few Manchesters.

A McPeake Second Lt

By RunnerC Coy.

(Renmore Barracks Museum Archives)

(2) To OC 5th C.R. Post in Crater

We are being shelled heavily + shells are falling on parapet + road in rear. Fire is being drawn by small parties of the Manchesters who are going up + down road to village. Could we have some counter battery work?

The ground is too soft to give good cover and if a shell falls a few yards near we may all get hit.

A Y McPeake Second Lt

By RunnerOC Post in Crater.

(Renmore Barracks Museum Archives)

CHAPTER XX

THE BATTLES OF CAMBRAI & FINAL PUSH

There were two battles of Cambrai, the first was fought towards the end of November 1917. The target was one sector of the formidable Hindenburg Line, which consisted of well built trenches, concrete shelters and pillboxes, all protected by strong barbed wire obstacles. It had been constructed by the forced labour of thousands of Russian prisoners of war. This was the first battle in which tanks were used in large numbers, with over three hundred of them being employed. The Tank Corps were commanded by Brig. Gen. H. Elles, who had been seeking an opportunity to use them in a surprise attack throughout the summer of that year.

On 20 November 1917, at precisely 6.20 a.m. the allies opened with a surprise artillery barrage. The Germans were totally unprepared for the shells that descended upon them, and the appearance of massed tanks that were rolling towards their lines, followed by infantry. This certainly unnerved many of the German soldiers and some 10,000 of them surrendered, which at that time was a record for the number of prisoners taken by the allies in a single day. The tanks had advanced to a depth of four miles in some places, without suffering too many casualties.

However, in the centre it was a different story, where German gunners engaged the tanks, and knocked them out one by one. One German sergeant, single-handedly destroyed five tanks before he was killed. Thirty-nine tanks were destroyed before the allied infantry could engage the German gun crews properly. Both the left and right German positions had broken, leaving a bulged salient in the centre. Although the tanks were mainly responsible for the initial success, after two days they had reached their limit. One mistake the allies made was that they did not have their reserves sufficiently positioned to exploit the early success.

On 30 November the Germans again demonstrated their ability to mount a formidable counter-attack. They delivered a short hurricane bombardment of mixed explosives, gas and smoke on the British. This was followed by an infantry assault, seeking out weak areas in the British defences, once located, they were followed up by infantry in strength. The Germans began to sweep over the British trenches, before they had time to realise what was happening. Although some of the British troops held their ground, they were ordered to retire within a few days. When the battle was over, the British found they were back to more or less the same position as when it had started. Both sides had suffered over 40,000 casualties.[1]

The second battle of Cambrai took place between September and October 1918. The British preparations for the assault on Cambrai were pre-empted by a German withdrawal from certain areas, which resulted in some objectives being gained without conflict. However, other areas did not prove so easy. Among the Irish regiments involved in the fighting were the Royal Irish and the Munster Fusiliers, the latter having succeeded in capturing a position near Cantaing. By midday on 29 September, the allied Fifty-seventh Division had cleared the Marconing line from the Bapaume-Cambrai road to the Schelde Canal.

In a final attack towards the southern suburbs, the Munster Fusiliers, supported by the Eight King's Liverpool Regiment, surrounded and captured Proville. The Fifteenth Division was also employed in the combat, and included the Royal Irish, Inniskilling, Munster and Dublin Fusiliers. The Connaught Rangers formed part of the Sixty-sixth Division, which was also taking part in the offensive. On 8 October, the allies encircled Cambrai on the southern side and the massed British guns opened up with a strong artillery barrage. Ten minutes into the bombardment the Royal Irish, supported by a tank, advanced behind the barrage. The enemy's resistance diminished and all the battalion's objectives were reached in good time. Numerous prisoners were taken as well as some guns being captured.

The following morning a battalion of Munster Fusiliers penetrated the town, but found that the Germans had deserted Cambrai.[2]

The allies' main objective, the Hindenburg Line, was later broken despite the best efforts of its machine gunners. The hastily re-built defences were repeatedly smashed by the British, and the Germans did not make a determined stand as they had done in the past. This began the allied advance to ultimate victory. Hostilities were to cease on all fronts at 11 a.m. on 11 November 1918, after the Armistice had been signed. The Irish battalions, Connaught Rangers, Royal Irish, the Munster and Inniskillings were told that the fighting would stop at the appointed time.

In their sector, the German machine guns continued to fire all that morning until about three minutes to eleven Then silence, but only for a minute, as a lone German machine gunner fired off a complete belt without a pause. According to one source, he then stood up beside his weapon, faced the allies, took off his helmet and bowed. He then turned and walked away slowly to the rear as silence replaced the roar of the guns. The Armistice had been signed at 5.10 a.m. (officially 5 a.m.), but sadly between that time and the cessation of hostilities, soldiers were killed at a rate of 500 an hour.

As the dejected German army marched back to their homeland, many of them claimed that they had not been defeated on the battlefield, but were 'stabbed in the back', by the navy and elements of the German government. The war had ended for the German navy earlier after Admiral Von Hipper ordered an attack on the British Grand Fleet, which was by this period supported by the American navy. Some of the sailors deemed this a suicidal plan and refused to follow orders. The insubordination escalated, resulting in the sailors leaving the ships and moving inland where they formulated a rebellion, leaving the army as the last line of defence. Regardless, the German troops carried on until they were ordered to lay down their arms. They arrived home to a grand welcome by the German people, who were glad the war was finally over.

By Christmas 1918, four selected allied divisions occupied part of Germany. The Irish Guards crossed the frontier to the sound of their pipers playing 'St Patrick's Day'. The pipers of the Leinster Regiment played 'Come Back To Erin'. Another Irish tune that rang out as the allies crossed the Rhine was 'Paddy Maginty's Goat'. The priority for the soldiers at this point was to remember those who had fallen, and so began the construction of various monuments and cemeteries. A temporary cenotaph was constructed in London for the first anniversary of the Armistice and the corpse of an unknown warrior was taken to Westminster Abbey for burial. The war cemeteries were to be walled and would resemble a classic English country garden, giving an air of peace and tranquillity. A Cross of Sacrifice would act as a focal point in the cemeteries and a symbolic altar would bear Rudyard Kipling's famous inscription: 'Their Name Liveth For Evermore'.[3]

APPENDIX

MONUMENTS, MEMORIALS, MEMENTOS

The Princess Mary Gift Box

In November 1914, Princess Mary, the seventeen year old daughter of King George V and Queen Mary was instrumental in having an advertisement placed in the national newspapers inviting people to make financial contributions to a Sailors & Soldiers Christmas Fund. The purpose of the fund was to provide everyone serving in the armed forces overseas with a Christmas gift from the nation. Following an overwhelming response, a special gift was decided upon and it would take the shape of an embossed brass box, based on a design by Adshead & Ramsey. The gift box was five inches in length, just over three inches in width and over one inch deep, with a hinged lid. An image of Princess Mary is located centrally on the lid and is surrounded by a laurel wreath and flanked on each side by the 'M' monogram.

At the top a decorative cartouche contains the words 'Imperium Britannicum', with a sword being drawn from its scabbard on either side. Beneath the head of Princess Mary another cartouche contains the words 'Christmas 1914', which is flanked on either side with the bow of a battleship forging through heavy waves. On each corner, small cartouches display the names of the allied forces: Belgium, Japan, Montenegro and Serbia. France and Russia are contained in two roundels on the edge of the box, both superimposed on three furled flags or standards.

The contents of the gift box varied considerably. The officers and men on active service at sea or at the front, and who were smokers received a pipe, lighter, 1oz of tobacco and twenty cigarettes in a distinctive yellow monogrammed wrapper. For non-smokers, the gift box contained a sterling silver pencil in the shape of a bullet and a packet of sweets. Indian troops received sweets and spices, while nurses were treated to chocolates. Some items were dispatched separately because of the size of the box. All gift boxes contained a Christmas greeting card and a photograph of the princess.

All of those that were not delivered until after Christmas were accompanied by a card wishing the recipient a 'Victorious New Year'. The wounded, on leave, and the widows and parents of those killed were also entitled to the gift. Prisoners of war had theirs reserved for them until they were repatriated. There was a huge demand made on the postal service and an immense effort was made to distribute the gifts in time for Christmas 1914, and although over 355,000 were delivered by the deadline, many more were late. A shortage of brass also caused problems and some troops did not receive their gift until the summer of 1916. As the war progressed the quality of the brass suffered and the later ones were produced with an inferior alloy. In January 1919, reports indicated that some soldiers still had not been issued with their gift boxes. When the fund finally closed in 1920, almost £200,000 had been donated and over two and a half million gift boxes had been distributed.[1]

Memorial Plaque

In 1916 the British government decided that it was the nations duty to create some type of memento in recognition for the bereaved families of those who had paid the supreme sacrifice in the Great War. To meet this moral obligation, a special committee was set up with David Lloyd George as chairperson. They were to decide on a design for the most appropriate type of memorial.

It was August 1917, before the committee finally decided that the memorial should be a round bronze plaque, four and three quarter inches in diameter. The words 'He / She Died For Freedom and Honour' were to be included together with the name of the deceased. The actual design was decided upon by a competition, of which there were over 800 entries, with a prize of £250 for the winner. The successful design was submitted by Edward Preston, a medallist from Liverpool and it was approved by King George V.

The plaque composition prominently displays Britannia in a standing pose, reverently looking towards the name of the deceased. In her right hand she holds a trident and her left arm is extended holding a wreath of palm leaves, symbolic of triumph, over the name of the deceased. The British Lion is also depicted on the plaque poised in his stride with his head positioned so that the panel containing the deceased's name occurs between this and the wreath above. Two dolphins are well placed to balance the voids in the field of the plaque, these creatures are a symbol of social love. The exergue appears to contain a lion defeating evil, represented in bird form.

The memorial plaques first went into manufacture in a special foundry located at Acton in London, called 'The Memorial Plaque Factory', but production at this location proved disappointing. The work was then transferred to a number of established munitions factories, notably the Woolwich Arsenal. The qualifying criteria was agreed upon, the plaques would be issued to the families of: 'members of His Majesty's forces who had fallen between 4 August 1914 and 10 January 1920.' However, this was extended to 30 April 1920. Memorial scrolls and medals were also issued to the families of the deceased. These Memorial Plaques are often referred to as 'Death Plaques', 'Widow's Penny' and 'Dead Man's Penny'.[2]

The Guillemont – Ginchy Cross

In February 1917, Gen. Sir William Hickie, commander of the Irish Division, had a thirteen foot wooden Celtic cross erected between the battlefields of Guillemont and Ginchy. The cross was erected in memory of the men of the Sixteenth Irish Division, who lost their lives in the attacks on Guillemont and Ginchy in September 1916 during the Somme offensive. Although the Germans over-ran the area in March 1918, the cross was not damaged. It remained there until 1926, when it was replaced by a similar cross.

The new Guillemont Ginchy Cross which is made of Irish Granite was unveiled by Marechal Joffre and blessed by the Bishop of Amiens in May 1926. There was a large attendance of both Irish men and women at the ceremony, which was closed by buglers of the Irish Guards sounding the Last Post. The original cross was taken back to Ireland and from 1926 until 1939 it was erected annually in the grounds of the Phoenix Park, where it acted as a Cenotaph. It is presently housed in the North East House of the Irish National War Memorial in Islandbridge, Dublin.[3]

The Irish National War Memorial

On 17 July 1919, a meeting was held in Dublin to discuss the idea of commemorating the Irishmen who lost their lives in the Great War. Representatives from all over Ireland attended the meeting and it was decided to have a permanent memorial erected in Dublin. A committee was formed and the first location chosen was at Merrion Square. The location was rejected by the Irish Legislature and following this decision every avenue was explored to find a suitable location for the memorial. While this was being pursued, finance from the trust was used to erect memorials to the Irish soldiers on the actual battlefields.

In addition to this a complete record, consisting of eight volumes containing the names of the Irish soldiers who fell in the Great War, was collected and published. It seems that at the time all political parties were supportive of the scheme and a second site was chosen on the southern slopes of the River Liffey, opposite the Magazine Fort in the Phoenix Park. Work on the project began in December 1931. The development of the park was undertaken first and this took two years to complete. The project began with a few workers, but eventually employed a labour force of over three hundred. The work force consisted of British ex-servicemen and the ex-servicemen of the Irish National Army, and all worked amicably together. Large quantities of earth had to be moved and although mechanical excavators could have been used, the policy of the Board of Works for this project was to give as much employment as possible to ex-soldiers, resulting in most of the work being carried out by manual labour.

The granite used, came from Ballyknockan, County Wicklow, and Barnaculla, County Dublin. The War Stone in the centre of the lawn weighs seven and a half tons. A number of the stones in the cross weigh as much as eight tons. The lifting equipment used to move these stones into position, consisted of hand winches, pulley-blocks, telegraph poles and a few hundred yards of flexible steel rope. Sir Edwin Lutyens designed the memorial as a garden of simple dignity. The central 'compartment' consists of a lawn enclosed by a limestone wall with granite piers. The bookrooms at either end are constructed of granite, and house the memorial books. One can exit from either side of the central lawn into sunken gardens. These have central lily ponds and are encircled by yew hedges. The water supply to the fountains and the lily ponds was pumped up from the River Liffey by a hydrostat operated by waterpower. The Memorial Garden was completed in 1938, and although many refer to it as a park, it is in reality a 'Garden of Remembrance' situated in the centre of a large park comprising 150 acres, stretching for a mile and a half from Island Bridge to Chapelizod.[4]

The Cenotaph

In November 1919, a temporary cenotaph, meaning 'empty tomb', was constructed in London for the first anniversary of the Armistice. The original cenotaph was constructed of wood and plaster, but such was the reaction from the people at its unveiling, that it was decided to have a permanent memorial erected. The prime minister, Lloyd George, requested that Sir Edwin Lutyens design the memorial. It was unveiled in 1920, and was constructed from Portland stone, and the inscription simply reads 'The Glorious Dead'. On the closest Sunday to 11 November each year a remembrance service is held at the Cenotaph. The service has changed very little since 1921, hymns are sung, prayers recited and two minutes of silence is observed. The monarch, religious leaders, politicians, state representatives and members of the armed forces gather to pay their respects to those who have lost their lives in conflict. Official wreaths are laid on the steps of the cenotaph and the ceremony ends with a march-past of war veterans. Other types of cenotaphs were also erected throughout Britain and the Commonwealth nations.[5]

Two Minutes Silence

In a letter published in the *London Evening News* on 8 May 1919, an Australian journalist, Edward George Honey, proposed that a respectful five-minute silence be observed to remember those who had given their lives in the First World War. Honey was born in St Kilda, Melbourne, in 1885 and died of consumption in England in 1922. He had served briefly in the war with an English regiment before being discharged due to ill health. He made his appeal for the 'silence' under the pen name of Warren Foster, and hoped that it would be observed amid the joy of celebrating the first anniversary of the Armistice. His request for five minutes of silence was for national remembrance and: 'Communion with the Glorious Dead who won us peace.'

Although a 'silence' had been observed prior to this time, the originality of Honey's suggestion was based on the fact that this was the first time in history that a victory had been celebrated as a tribute to those who sacrificed their lives and health, to make it possible. No official action was taken on the idea until October 1919, when Sir Percy Fitzpatrick made a similar suggestion. A friend of his, Lord Milner, forwarded the idea to the king's private secretary, Lord Stamfordham. The letter requested that a period of silence be observed in all countries of the British empire on Armistice day. Sir Percy wrote: 'When we are gone it may help bring home to those who will come after us, the meaning, the nobility and the unselfishness of the great sacrifice by which their freedom was assured.' King George V was evidently very moved by the idea and took action immediately. Incidentally there is no record to suggest that Honey's letter in the *London Evening News* prompted or influenced Sir Percy. Nevertheless, the king, along with Honey and Sir Percy attended a rehearsal for a five-minute silence involving the Grenadier Guards at Buckingham Palace. Five minutes proved too long and the two-minute silence was decided upon. On 7 November 1919 the King issued a proclamation requesting that on the anniversary of the Armistice, a suspension of all normal activities would take place and that two minutes of silence would be observed: 'All locomotion should cease, so that in perfect stillness, the thoughts of everyone may be concentrated on reverent remembrance of the glorious dead.'[6]

Unknown Warrior (Tomb)

It was while serving on the western front that Reverend David Railton came up with the idea of having the body of one unknown serviceman transported back to England and buried with full military honors. While expressing the reasons he felt that this was so important, Reverend Railton recalled an incident near Armentieres, where he came across a grave with a rough wooden cross inscribed: 'An unknown British soldier, of the Black Watch'. He wrote:

> How that grave caused me to think! But, who was he, and who were they [his folk]? Was he just a laddie? There was no answer to those questions, nor has there ever been yet. So I thought and thought and wrestled in thought. What can I do to ease the pain of father, mother, brother, sister, sweetheart, wife and friend? Quietly and gradually there came out of the mist of thought this answer clear and strong, Let this body – this symbol of him – be carried reverently over the sea to his native land. And I was happy for about five or ten minutes.

Initially, the idea was not given much support, however, after veterans and families of soldiers killed in the war lobbied for action, the government reacted, and the selection of an unknown soldier for burial took place.

Although many other countries have since taken up the idea, Great Britain became the first country to honour their war dead in such a manner.

On Armistice Day 11 November 1920, the Unknown Warrior was laid to rest in Westminster Abbey during an impressive ceremony. The body, borne on a gun carriage was covered with a Union Jack, on which were laid a steel helmet, a khaki belt and a crusader's sword. At the memorial service held in the Abbey, the coffin was presided over by a guard of honour comprising Victoria Cross winners. The King scattered soil over the coffin, which had been specially brought from Flanders. The first inscription is from the coffin and the second is inscribed on the memorial stone:

A BRITISH WARRIOR
WHO FELL IN THE GREAT WAR
1914-1918
FOR KING AND COUNTRY

BENEATH THIS STONE RESTS THE BODY
OF A BRITISH WARRIOR
UNKNOWN BY NAME OR RANK
BROUGHT FROM FRANCE TO LIE AMONG
THE MOST ILLUSTRIOUS OF THE LAND
AND BUIRED HERE ON ARMISTICE DAY
11 NOV: 1920. IN THE PRESENCE OF
HIS MAJESTY KING GEORGE V
HIS MINISTERS OF STATE
THE CHIEFS OF HIS FORCES
AND A VAST CONCOURSE OF THE NATION

THUS ARE COMMEMORATED THE MANY
MULTITUDES WHO DURING THE GREAT
WAR OF 1914 – 1918 GAVE THE MOST THAT
MAN CAN GIVE LIFE ITSELF
FOR GOD

FOR KING AND COUNTRY
FOR LOVED ONES HOME AND EMPIRE
FOR THE SACRED CAUSE OF JUSTICE AND
THE FREEDOM OF THE WORLD

THEY BUIRED HIM AMONG THE KINGS BECAUSE HE
HAD DONE GOOD TOWARDS GOD AND TOWARDS HIS HOUSE[7]

Great War Memorial (Galway)

The dedication of the Great War Memorial in St Nicholas' Collegiate Church took place on Tuesday, 21 February 1920. The Bishop of Meath performed the ceremony before a military guard of honour and a company of boy scouts. The bishop was assisted by a number of clergymen including Canon Fleetwood Berry, rector of Galway, the dean of Tuam, and Canon McCormick, archdeacon of Clonfert. The memorial Celtic Cross containing the names of fifteen soldiers killed in the Great War was unveiled by a soldier and a sailor. The ten-foot cross was carved out of beer stone and contains designs from the Book of Kells. The inscription around the top of the carved plinth reads as follows: 'In memory of the glorious dead from this parish who fell in the Great War' while the base contains the words: 'Pass not this shrine in sorrow but in pride'. During the ceremony a green ensign was flown at half-mast from the tower of the church.

It was an impressive service, which included special prayers and benediction. Canon Berry paid tribute to the men who had lost their lives in the war. He then spoke individually about each of the fifteen men commemorated on the monument and outlined how each one of them had met their deaths, including his own son, Capt. Edward Fleetwood Berry. The service concluded with an effective fanfare played by the band of the Connaught Rangers after which the *Last Post* was sounded. Family and friends of the fallen men then placed wreaths around the monument. The following is an extract from the tribute:

We are together here to-day, to do all the honour we can to the memory of the brave and glorious dead from this parish who fell in the great war, and to dedicate a very beautiful memorial. But, however stately and grand it might be, its chiefest loveliness will always consist, not in any artistic charm or beauty it may possess, but in the silent testimony that it will bear, the story that it will tell of the beautiful lives and noble sacrifice of fifteen splendid and illustrious heroes of whom we are, to-day, so justly proud. It is my privilege and melancholy gratification to pay this brief and feeble tribute to a gallant and noble band of men as ever went forth from any parish at the call of duty to do great deeds, and then to die in the cause of right and the cause of God. No one knew them and loved them as I did – some of them I carried in my arms long ago at that old font and baptized.[8]

The Ulster Tower

The tower near Thiepval Wood was raised as a memorial to the soldiers of the Ulster Division, who fought in the Great War. It was built mainly by public subscription, and was officially opened on 19 November 1921 – almost five years to the day after the official end of the battle of the Somme. It is similar to Helen's Tower which stands in the grounds of the Clandeboye Estate, located near the seaside town of Bangor.

Many of the men who fought in the Ulster Division were trained in this estate before going overseas. The men of the Ulster Division were renowned for their courage and will always be remembered for their valour at the battle of the Somme. On the morning of 1 July 1916 dawn broke early across the battlefield of the Somme. The arrival of the first pale glimmerings of light brought with it drizzly rain. However, this soon passed, and the battle of this long tragic, harrowing day would be fought under a blue, cloudless sky, and a hot pitiless sun. Initially, all went well for the Ulstermen, the German wire had been cut in many places along their sector. In their eagerness, the soldiers forgot their orders to attack in ordered waves, but instead rushed up the hill to the first line of enemy trenches which they took after a short, fierce struggle.

Fired with success they rushed on towards the formidable Schwaben Redoubt – a heavily fortified area on top of a hill criss-crossed with wire, trenches, and underground dug-outs. The leading battalions fought furiously to capture the Redoubt, but then things began to go wrong. The Thirty-second Division to their right had been unable to capture Thiepval village and the German machine guns which should have been silenced, began to fire into the attacking Ulstermen.

At the same time the German artillery also started raining down on them, but despite all of this, they were actually ahead of schedule. This was not achieved in any other sector of the battlefield that day. Nevertheless, they were forced to fall-back with extremely heavy losses. Of the nine Victoria Crosses awarded for the battle, four of them were won by men of the Ulster Division.[9]

Laying-Up The Colours

On 12 June 1922, six Irish regiments of the British Army were disbanded at Windsor Castle. The 'Laying-Up' of the colours as it was called took place in St George's Hall before King George V. These regiments included the Royal Irish Regiment, Connaught Rangers, South Irish Horse, Prince of Wales Leinster, Royal Munster Fusiliers and Royal Dublin Fusiliers. Detachments from the six regiments marched from Windsor Railway Station under military escort. The escort was made up of one hundred members of all ranks of the Third Grenadier Guards, headed by their regimental band.

The Irish regiments were met at Windsor Castle by the king, accompanied by Field Marshal His Royal Highness the Duke of Connacht, the honorary colonel of the South Irish Horse and the colonel-in-chief of the Royal Dublin Fusiliers. At 11.30 a.m. the detachment marched into St George's Hall and faced the king. A royal salute was given and the colours were lowered. The King then inspected the troops and accepted an engraving from the South Irish Horse.

On conclusion, King George V addressed the regiments and his words give some idea of the high esteem in which the Irish regiments were held: 'I pledge my word that within these ancient and historic walls, your Colours will be treasured, honoured and protected as hallowed memorials of the glorious deeds of brave and loyal regiments.' A ceremony to commemorate the eightieth anniversary of the event was held on 12 June 2002 and was attended by 150 members of the Combined Irish Regiments Association.[10]

The Menin Gate

On 24 July 1927 the Menin Gate was unveiled. This huge arch is located in the Belgian town of Ypres and was opened as a gateway through the ramparts leading east onto the Menin Road. Literally every soldier who served in the salient during the Great War marched through this gap in order to reach the western front. On the gateway are recorded the names of 55,000 missing allied troops, whose remains were never found. It was hoped to include the names of all the missing allies on the arch, but they simply ran out of space. A further 34,927 names of missing men are recorded on the memorial at Tyne Cot Cemetery, to the north of Ypres.

At 8 p.m. each night the Menin Gate is shut off while members of the local fire brigade sound the 'Last Post' on the roadway beneath the Memorial Arch. This ceremony was suspended between 20 May 1940 and 6 September 1944, during the German occupation of the Second World War. It is a touching and poignant ceremony, particularly for those who have family members recorded on the arch. It concludes with a member of the *Last Post* committee reciting a verse from Laurence Binyon's poem, 'For the Fallen'. This verse has now become known as 'The Exhortation':

> They shall not grow old, as we that are left to grow old:
> Age shall not weary them, nor years condem.
> At the going down of the sun and in the morning
> We will remember them.[11]

The Thiepval Monument

This monument was erected in memory of the allied soldiers who lost their lives on the Somme. It is 44.2 metres high and was constructed as a series of arches in the general form of a pyramid. The Thiepval Monument was designed by Edwin Lutyens, and work on the monument began in 1928. It was unveiled on 31 July 1932 by the Prince of Wales. The Portland stone panels contain the names of 72,000 servicemen who lost their lives on the Somme, and whose bodies were never found. The monument also serves as a memorial to all those who fought in the battle of the Somme. It is easily visible from kilometres away, sitting as it does, high on the ridge at Thiepval.[12]

The Connaught Ranger Memorial Window

The Connaught Ranger Memorial Window is located in the cathedral of Our Lady Assumed into Heaven and Saint Nicholas, Galway (New Cathedral). The window is in the south wall of the west transept of the cathedral, but unfortunately is very high up, making the inscription difficult to read. It depicts David and Goliath by Manus Walsh. The elephant and sphinx emblems and the numbers 88 and 94 are also included on the window. The window is a touching tribute to the memory of this great regiment.

It was Capt. Russell Maguire who came up with the initial idea, and he collected £600 from survivors and family members of Connaught Rangers to support the project. In the 1967 edition of *The Ranger*, 350 hand painted copies were sent out to members who were unable to visit Galway. However, over the following years, many survivors of the regiment did make the pilgrimage to Galway to view the Memorial Window.[13]

The Island of Ireland Peace Park

In 1996, Paddy Harte, a Deputy in Dáil Éireann, paid a visit to the Somme. During the visit, he became aware that as many as 250,000 Irishmen may have enlisted to fight in the Great War. On his return to Ireland he wrote a newspaper article giving an account of his visit and highlighted the sheer numbers of Irish names inscribed on headstones and monuments scattered throughout France. Many people read the article with great interest, one of whom was Glen Barr and the two men agreed to meet and discuss their views. The result of the meeting was an organised coach tour of the Somme by people from various parts of Ireland. It was immediately clear to both men that many people were of the same opinion as themselves, that something more should be done to remember Irishmen from across the political divide who had died in the Great War.

As a gesture of reconciliation, Glen Barr suggested that young people from both communities should be involved in the project. Paddy Harte felt that a round tower would be the most appropriate type of monument, and his idea was then adopted. The next problem was finance for the project and both the British and Irish governments were successfully approached for funds. Banks, building societies and insurance companies were also targeted. They also required the expertise and support of auctioneers to purchase the site, architects to draft the plans, a company to sponsor the materials, and a road transport and shipping company to ensure that the material reached the location.

The site chosen was located at Messine in Belgium where the combined Irish Divisions fought together in August 1917. Skilled volunteer workers were also required and with the help of FÁS and T & EA trainees the work was completed in two years. On 11 November 1998, the Island of Ireland Peace park was officially opened by the president of Ireland, Mary McAleese, accompanied by Queen Elizabeth II of England and King Albert of Belgium. The writings of various Irish Great War poets are captured in stone and form part of this wonderful memorial to the Irishmen who lost their lives in the First World War.[14]

NOTES

CHAPTER I

1. Cassells, L, *The Archduke and the Assassin: Sarajevo, June 28th 1914* (1985).

   Ferguson, N, 'Germany and the Origins of the Great War: New perspectives', Historical *Journal, Vol. 35, 1992, pp. 725-752.*

   Ferguson, N, 'Public Finance and National Security: The Domestic Origins of the First World War Revisited', Past & Present (Vol. 142, 1994, pp. 141-168).

   Godsey, R. D, *Aristoctratic Redoubt: The Austro-Hungarian Foreign Office on the Eve of the Great War* (1999).

   Gordon, M. R, 'Domestic Conflict and the Origins of the First World War: The British and German Cases' (Journal of Modern History, Vol.46, 1974, pp. 191-216).

   Hamilton, R. F, *The Origins of the Great War* (2003).

   Joll, J, *The Origins of the First World War* (2000).

   Kaiser, D. E, 'Germany and the Origins of the First World War' (Journal of Modern History, Vol. 55, 1983, pp. 442-474).

   Keiger, J. V. F, *France and the Origins of the First World War, 1983.*

   Koch, W. H, *The Origins of the First World War: Great Power Rivalry and German War Aims, 1984.*

   Lieven, D. C. B, *Russia and the Origins of the First World War* (1983).

   Mombauer, A, *The Origins of the First World War: Controversies and Consensus* (2002).

   Steiner, Z.S, *Britain and the Origins of the First World War* (1977).

   Williamson, S.R, *Austria-Hungary and the Origins of the First World War* (1991).

2. Lyon, J. M. B, *"A Peasant Mob": The Serbian Army on the Eve of the Great War',* Journal of Military History, Vol. 61, 1997, pp. 481–502.

   Seligmann, M. S, *"A Barometer of National Confidence": A British Assessment of the Role of Insecurity in the formulation of German Military Policy Before the First World War'* (English Historical Studies, Vol. 117, 2002, pp. 333 – 355).

3. Lieven, D. C. B, *Russia and the Origins of the First World War* (1983).

   Mombauer, A, *Helmuth von Moltke and the Origins of the First World War* (2001).

   Seligmann, M. S, *"A Barometer of National Confidence": A British Assessment of the Role of Insecurity in the formulation of German Military Policy Before the First World*

War' (English Historical Studies, Vol. 117, 2002, pp. 333 – 355).

4. Bartlett, T. and Jeffery, K, (ed), A Military History of Ireland (1996).

Fitzpatrick, D, *'The Logic of the Collective Sacrifice: Ireland and the British Army, 1914–1918', Historical Journal, Vol. 38, 1995, pp. 1017 – 1030.*

Fitzpatrick, D, *The Two Irelands, 1912 – 1939* (1998).

Fitzpatrick, D, *Ireland and the First World War* (1986).

Bartlett, T., Jeffery, K., (ed), Fitzpatrick, D, *'Militarism in Ireland, 1900 – 1922', A Military History of Ireland* (1996).

Jeffery, K, *Ireland and the Great War* (2000).

McCarthy, M, *'Historico-Geographical Explorations of Ireland's heritages: Towards a Critical Understanding of the Nature of Memory and Identity', in M McCarthy* (ed) (Ireland's Heritages: Critical Perspectives on Memory and Identity, 2005, pp. 3-54).

Morrissey, J, 'A Lost Heritage: The Connaught Rangers and Mutlivocal Irishness', in M McCarthy (ed), *Ireland's Heritages: Critical Perspectives on Memory and Identity* (2005, pp. 71-88).

5. Henry, W, *Supreme Sacrifice The Story of Eamonn Ceannt 1881 –1916* (2005, p. 35).

6. Documentary (Videotape) 'The Battle of the Somme – The Bloodiest Battle of World War I'.

Hogg, I. V, *Dictionary of World War I* (1997, p. viii).

Keegan, J, *The First World War an Illustrated History* (2002, p. 43).

World Book Encyclopaedia, 'World War I' (pp. 365, *368, 372, 377).*

7. Blake, J, 'Field-Marshal Sir John French' *Journal of the Galway Archaeological & Historical Society* (Vol. 8, No 4, 1913 – 1914, p. 247).

Glover, M, *Warfare From Waterloo To Mons* (1980, pp. 243, 244, 245).

8. Documentary (Videotape) 'The Battle of the Somme – The Bloodiest Battle of World War I'.

Glover, M, *Warfare From Waterloo To Mons* (1980, pp. 243, 244, 245).

Marshall, S, *The American Heritage History of World War I* (1964, p. 34).

World Book Encyclopaedia, 'World War I' (pp. 364, *365).*

CHAPTER II

1. *Galway Advertiser*: 'The Connaught Rangers go to war', 19-11-1998.
   Sheerin, N, *On Your Doorstep* (1977, pp. 20, 21).
   The Galway Express: 'Austria And Serbia' (1-8-1914).

2. *Galway Advertiser*: 'The Forgotten Heros of the Great War' (13-10-2005).
   Interview: Noel Heaney, 8-8-2004.
   Sheerin, N, *On Your Doorstep* (1977, p. 21).
   The Connacht Tribune: 'Seven Nations At War' (8-8-1914).

3. *The Connacht Tribune*: 'Troops of Western Command – Reviewed in Galway by Man who stopped first German Onrush' (21-7-1917).
   The Galway Express: 'Duration of the War', 9-1-1915; 'Galway Ranger Writes to the "Express" (5-12-1914); 'Local War Items' (17-10-1914; 9-1-1915; 23-1-1915; 13-2-1915); 'For The Front – Galway RIC Volunteers' (2-1-1915); 'War – Battle in the Streets of Galway' (17-10-1914).

4. O'Flaherty, M, *The Claddagh Boy* (1963, pp. 16-21).
   The Connacht Tribune: 'Troops of Western Command – Reviewed in Galway by Man who stopped first German Onrush' (21-7-1917).
   The Galway Express: 'Answering the Call – Claddagh's Magnificent Response' (24-4-1915); 'Duration of the War' (9-1-1915); 'Galway Ranger Writes to the Express' (5-12-1914); 'Local War Items' (17-10-1914; 9-1-1915; 23-1-1915; 13-2-1915); 'For The Front – Galway RIC Volunteers' (2-1-1915); 'War – Battle in the Streets of Galway,' (17-10-1914).

5. *The Galway Express*: 'Ireland's Manpower – Remarkable Official Figures – 161,000 Men Still Available' (18-11-1916); 'John Redmond's Interesting Figures and Deductions' (12-12-1914).
   The Tuam Herald: 'Ireland and Conscription' (8-1-1916).

6. *East Galway Democrat*: 'Men Of Ballinasloe – Irish Brigade' (21-9-1918)
   Keegan, J, *The First World War an Illustrated History* (2002, p. 330).
   The Connacht Tribune: 'More that half a Million Irish Catholics have Enlisted in U.S.A.' (13-7-1918).
   The Galway Express: 'New Irish Regiment in South Africa' (23-1-1915).
   The Irish Independent: 'A Battle in Mexico' (15-4-1916).
   World Book Encyclopaedia, 'World War I' (pp. 364).

CHAPTER III

1. *The Connacht Tribune*: 'Famous Irish V.C. For Galway' (30-10-1915); 'Great Recruiting Demonstration at Clifden' (15-1-1916).
   The Galway Express: 'Call of the Drum', 24-4-1915; 'Field Marshal French – Visits Galway' (21-7-1917).

2. Interview: Gerry Crane (16-10-2005).
   The Galway Express: 'Irish Guards Visit – Galway's Enthusiastic Reception of the Band' (1-5-1915).

3. *The Connacht Tribune*: 'Important Proceedings at the Quarterly Meeting – Recruiting Question – The Chairman's Appeal For Men' (22-5-1915).
   The Galway Express: 'Some Not Wanted in Galway' (15-5-1915).
   The Tuam Herald: 'The Irish Brigade – Recruiting Meeting in Tuam' (15-5-1915).

4. *The Connacht Tribune*: ' The Recruiting Committee' (3-7-1915).

5. *The Connacht Tribune*: 'Recruiting Gatherings at Tuam and Clifden' (3-7-1915); 'Recruiting Meeting' (3-7-1915); 'War Meetings' (3-7-1915).

6. *The Connacht Tribune*: 'Clifden Meeting' (3-7-1915); 'Recruiting Gatherings at Tuam and Clifden' (3-7-1915); 'Recruiting Meeting' (3-7-1915).

7. *The Connacht Tribune*: 'Munitions, Money and Men – Loughrea at War', (10-7-1915); 'Recruiting Meeting at Loughrea' (10-7-1915).

8. *The Connacht Tribune*: 'Munitions, Money and Men – Loughrea at War' (10-7-1915); 'Recruiting Meeting at Loughrea' (10-7-1915); 'Recruiting Meeting At Loughrea' (10-7-1915).

9. *The Connacht Tribune*: 'Recruiting Meeting at Loughrea' (10-7-1915).
   The Galway Express: 'Great Recruiting Meeting at Oughterard' (22-1-1916).

10. *The Connacht Tribune*: 'The Recruiting Campaign' (17-7-1915).

11. *The Connacht Tribune*: 'Recruiting Rally' (9-10-1915).

12. *The Connacht Tribune*: 'Recruiting Rally' (9-10-1915).

13. *The Connacht Tribune*: 'Recruiting Rally' (9-10-1915).

14. *The Connacht Tribune*: 'Recruiting Rally' (9-10-1915).
    The Tuam Herald: 'Recruiting at Williamstown' (4-9-1915).

15. Harris, H.E.D., *The Irish Regiments in the First World War, 1968, p12)*.
    The Connacht Tribune: 'Women's Recruiting League' (15-1-1916).
    The Galway Express: 'Galway Women's Recruiting League' (15-1-1916).
    The Tuam Herald: 'Brevities' (22-4-1916).

16. *The Galway Express*: 'The Voice of Connaught – Great Recruiting Conference in Galway' (5-2-1916).

17. *The Connacht Tribune*: 'Connacht and the Fight For Freedom' (4-12-1915; Recruiting in Ireland' (19-8-1916; 'Recruiting – The Battalion for Commercial Man and Farmers' (1-4-1916; 'Why Not Enlist' (25-12-1915).
The Connacht: 'Voluntary Enlistment – Appeal For More Men' (3-4-1915).

18. *The Connacht Tribune*: 'Aggressive Politics' – 'Striking Pronouncement By Bishop of Clonfert' (15-6-1915; 'Irish Bishops and the War' (11-3-1916).
The Galway Express: 'Conceived By Satan – Matured In Hell' (15-5-1915).

19. *The Connacht Tribune*: 'Come With Me' (3-8-1917).
The Tuam Herald: 'Recruiting at Williamstown' (4-9-1915).

20. *The Connacht Tribune*: 'Co. Galway Farms Mapped out in Berlin' (8-4-1916)

21. *The Connacht Tribune*: 'Life on the Ocean Wave' (18-4-1916; 'Naval Recruiting' (23-11-1917).

22. *The Connacht Tribune*: 'Come With Me' (3-8-1917).
The Galway Express: 'England's Hypocrisy' (10-8-1918).

23. Crealey, A.H. An Irish Almanac (1993, p. 36*)*.
The Connacht Tribune: 'Bishop's Court, St. Augustine St., Galway' (21-9-1918); 'Capt. Alston' (28-9-1918); 'Galway and Recruiting' (16-11-1918); 'It is a Lie' (20-7-1918); 'Men Of Galway' (21-9-1918); 'Men Wanted' (5-7-1919); 'Recruiting Returns' (28-9-1918); 'Remounts and Horse Transport' (21-9-1918); 'The Military and the Galway Town Hall' (14-6-1918).
The Galway Express: 'The New Leader and the Old Policy' (23-3-1918).

CHAPTER IV

1. Henry, W, *Supreme Sacrifice The Story of Eamonn Ceannt 1881–1916* (2005, p. 42).
The Connacht Tribune: 'The Cry for Conscription' (15-12-1917).
The Galway Express: 'The Position of the National Volunteers' (13-3-1915).
The Tuam Herald: 'Ireland and Conscription' (8-1-1916).

2. *The Connacht Tribune*: 'Ireland And Conscription' (23-10-1915); 'The Irish Party and Conscription' (15-1-1916).

3. *The Galway Express*: 'The Position of the National Volunteers' (13-3-1915).
The Tuam Herald: 'Ireland and Conscription' (8-1-1916).

4. *The Connacht Tribune*: 'Conscription – How Ireland was saved from it by the Irish Party' (6-10-1917); 'The Two Policies' – The Practical and the Impracticable' (16-6-1917); 'Recruit Or – ?' (20-7-1918); 'Right Road – Home Rule within a Few Months' (6-4-1918).

5. *East Galway Democrat*: 'New Rallying Song For Carson' (4-5-1918).

The Connacht Tribune: 'Conscription – How Ireland was saved from it by the Irish Party' (6-10-1917); 'The Two Policies' – The Practical and the Impracticable' (16-6-1917); 'Right Road – Home Rule within a Few Months' (6-4-1918).

6. *East Galway Democrat*: 'New Rallying Song For Carson' (4-5-1918).
   The Galway Express: 'Gwynn, Lynch and Sullivan in Galway' (3-8-1918); 'Stephen Gwynn' (25-5-1918).
   The Tuam Herald: 'From Our Own Correspondent' (28-4-1917); 'Sir Edward Carson' (7-4-1917).

7. *East Galway Democrat*: 'Mr Devlin and Irish Conscription' (18-5-1918).
   The Connacht Tribune: 'Irish Nationalists And Recruiting' (10-8-1918); 'Irishmen in the United States Army' (10-8-1918); 'Notes & News' (5-4-1918); 'Notes & News' (1-6-1918); 'Right Road – Home Rule Within A Few Months' (6-4-1918).
   The Galway Express: 'Another Galway Protest – Against Conscription' 27-4-1918); 'Ireland's Appeal to America' (3-7-1918).

8. *The Connacht Tribune*: 'Irish Nationalists And Recruiting' (10-8-1918); 'Irishmen in the United States Army' (10-8-1918).
   The Galway Express: 'Priests and People' (26-4-1919).

CHAPTER V

1. *The Connacht Tribune*: 'The Volunteers' (1-5-1915).
   The Galway Express: 'Galway Harbour Board' (17-10-1914); 'Local War Items' (10-10-1914); 'Riot Sequel – The Carter Appeal Case – Fighting in Galway Streets Described – Soldiers' Stories of Assault with Wooden Guns – Decision of Magistrates Altered' (30-1-1915); 'The Firing Line – At Home' (17-10-1914).

2. *The Connacht Tribune*: 'Severe Sentences' (12-6-1915).
   The Galway Express: 'Local War Items' (10-10-1914); 24-10-1914.
   Henry, W, *Battlefield of the Somme; St. Patrick Parish Magazine: Part V* (2004).

3. *The Connacht Tribune*: 'Galway Civilians and the Sherwood Foresters' (8-7-1916); 'God Bless Germany' (19-7-1915).
   The Galway Express: 'Departure of the Sherwood Foresters' (9-12-1916); 'Galway Volunteers – "Manifesto" by The Sinn Feiners' (24-10-1914).

4. *East Galway Democrat*: 'Ireland's Chance' (28-4-1917).
   Henry, W, *Supreme Sacrifice The Story of Eamonn Ceannt 1881 –1916* (2005, pp. 91,92,93).
   The Connacht Tribune: 'Gallant Gentleman' (20-6-1017); 'Galway Civilians and the Sherwood Foresters' (8-7-1916); 'God Bless Germany' (19-7-1915); Up The

Kaiser' 3-2-1917).

5. *The Connacht Tribune*: 'Republican Flags – Sunday Morning Decorations in Galway' (12-5-1917); 'Troops of the Western Command' (21-7-1917).
The Galway Express: 'Anti-British Dog Sentenced to Death' (25-11-1917).

6. *The Connacht Tribune*: 'Capt. Alston Royal Air Force Will Lecture' (28-9-1918); 'Uproar And Batons' (5-10-1918); 'Recruit Or – ?' (20-7-1918).

7. Interview: Valera Raftery, (27-11-2004).

CHAPTER VI

1. *The Galway Express*: 'Local Items of the War' (15-8-1914); 'Local War Items' (29-8-1914); 19-9-1914).

2. *The Connacht Tribune*: 'Galway As A Naval Base' (23-1-1915).
The Galway Express: 'Galway Naval Basis' (23-1-1915); 'Heavy Gun Firing Heard Near Galway' (7-11-1914); 'Local War Items' (29-8-1914); 30-1-1915); 'Zeppelin Raid on London – Ninety Bombs Dropped' (5-6-1915,

3. Collins, T, *'The Helga/Muirchu: Her Contribution To Galway Maritime History'*, *Journal of the Galway Archaeological and Historical Society* (Vol. 54, 2002, pp. 150, 152, 153).
The Connacht Tribune: 'Galway As A Naval Base' (23-1-1915).
The Galway Express: 'Naval Base' (13-2-1915).
The Tuam Herald: 'Galway Notes' (27-3-1915).

4. *The Galway Express*: 'Spreading False Reports' (13-2-1915).

5. *The Connacht Tribune*: 'Latest War News' (6-2-1915).
The Galway Express: 'Galway A Naval Basis' (23-1-1915); 'Submarines – Off the West Coast – Pirate Craft's Second Visit – Mines Laid in the Bay' (3-4-1915).

6. *The Galway Express*: '8,000 Germans In Clifden! – How County Boys are Misled' (20-5-1916).
The Tuam Herald: 'Defence of the Realm (Consolidation) Regulations, 1914' (16-10-1915); 'Ireland and the Navy' (11-3-1916); 'From Our Own Correspondent' (28-4-1917).

7. *The Connacht Tribune*: 'Food Production in Ireland, 1917' – 'Farmers to the Rescue' (27-1-1917); 'War Rations' (10-3-1917); 'Compulsory Rationing' (10-11-1917).

8. *The Connacht Tribune*: 'Garden Allotments' (24-3-1917).

CHAPTER VII

1. *The Connacht Tribune*: 'Submarine Off Galway' (20-3-1915); 'Two Ships Sunk' (17-3-1917).
   The Galway Express: 'German Submarines On The West Coast' (8-5-1915); 'Presentation at Seamen's Home, Galway' (19-2-1916); 'The Submarine Blockade' (10-4-1915).
2. Marshall, S, *The American Heritage History of World War I, 1964, p. 142).*
   The Connacht Tribune: 'Lusitania Victim' (3-7-1915); 'Lusitania Victims' (3-7-1915).
   The Galway Express: 'Galway Port Project and the Lusitania Tragedy' (15-5-1915).
   The Tuam Herald: 'Galway to the Front Again – Why not Galway Bay, 16-12-1916); 'Tuam Girl on Ill-Fated Lusitania' (15-5-1915).
3. *The Connacht Tribune*: 'An Awful Sight – A Swim of Nearly Three Hours' (18-9-1915).
4. *The Galway Express*: 'At The Ocean's Mercy – Fate of Two Torpedoed Vessels' (17-3-1917); 'Fight For Life – Galway Sailors Rescued in North Sea' (1-4-1916).
5. *The Connacht Tribune*: 'Irish Fishing Boats' (2-6-1917); 'Memorial Unveiling in Inverin' (19-6-1970).
   The Galway Express: 'Blown to Pieces – Tragedy of a Stray Mine' (23-6-1917).
6. Henry, W, *St. Patrick Parish Magazine*, 'The Neptune Disaster' (2002).
   The Connacht Tribune: 'Blown to Atoms – Fate of Galway Trawler and Four Men' (29-12-1917); 'Galway Bay Mine Disaster Fund' (2-3-1918); 'Irish Fishing Boats' (2-6-1917).
7. *The Connacht Tribune*: 'Left To Die' – 'Dying Sailor's Last Letters' (22-6-1918).
8. *The Connacht Tribune*: 'A Fiendish Crime – U-Boat Crew's Inhumanity To Galway Fishermen' (15-6-1918); 'Submarine Victims' (22-6-1918); 'Still Mounting Up' (20-7-1918).
9. *The Connacht Tribune*: 'The Little Grey Home' (19-10-1918).
   The Tuam Herald: 'Local War Items' (8-4-1916).
10. *The Connacht Tribune*: 'A Soldier Journalist', October 1918); 'Men of Galway' (12-10-1918); 'Posthumous Award to Gallant Officer' (7-12-1918); 'The Brand of Cain' (12-10-1918); 'The Mansion House "Leinster" Fund' (7-10-1918).
11. *Galway Advertiser*: 'The sinking of the LE Leinster October 10 1918' (16-10-2003).
    The Connacht Tribune: 'Posthumous Award to Gallant Officer' (7-12-1918); 'The Brand of Cain' (12-10-1918); 'The Mansion House "Leinster" Fund' (7-10-1918).

CHAPTER VIII

1. *Galway Advertiser*: 'The Woollen Mills' (7-5-1987).

   The Connacht Tribune: 'War Fund – What Renmore Fete Achieved for the Connaughts – Result of the Competitions' (18-9-1915).

   The Galway Express: '15 Per Cent – Thriving Condition of Galway Woollen Mills' (2-3-1918); 'Galway Woollen Industry' (20-2-1915); 'Order for Galway Woollen Factory' (19-9-1914); 'Women and the War' (2-10-1915).

   The Tuam Herald: 'Galway Notes' (27-3-1915).

2. *The Connacht Tribune*: 'Galway Munition Factory' (7-8-1916); 'Munitions Factory' (25-3-1917); 'Munitions Factory – Interesting Interview with Captain Downie' (3-2-1917); 'Munitions Making In Galway' (1-4-1916); 'Shell Factory' (6-1-1917); 'Where was Galway' (18-3-1916).

3. *The Connacht Tribune*: 'Munitions Factory – Interesting Interview with Captain Downie' (3-2-1917); 'Shell Factory' (6-1-1917);

4. Interview: James Casserly, 18-11-2005).

   O'Hara, B, *Regional Technical College Galway, The First 21 Years* (1993, p. 28).

   The Connacht Tribune: 'Galway Electric Co., Limited – Notice' (21-9-1918); 'Galway Shell Factory' (14-7-1917); 'Harbour Board – Excellent Work of Galway Munitions Factory' (20-6-1917); 'Munitions Factory – Interesting Interview with Captain Downie' (3-2-1917); 'Munition Making In Galway' (1-4-1916); 'Shell Factory' (6-1-1917).

5. *The Connacht Tribune*: 'Galway Nurse Honoured' (27-10-1917); 'Irish War Hospital Depot' (28-10-1916); 'Voluntary Aid Nursing' (30-10-1916); 'War Funds' (29-6-1919); 'War Hospital Supply Depot' (3-3-1917).

   The Galway Express: 'Distinction for Galway Nurse' (6-1-1917); 'The Committee of the Galway War Fund' (8-1-1916).

6. *The Connacht Tribune*: 'Irish Aviation Station' (22-12-1917).

7. *The Connacht Tribune*: 'War Savings' – 'Executive Committee Formed For Co. Galway' (6-7-1918).

CHAPTER IX

1. *The Galway Express*: 'Connaught Rangers Comfort Fund' (12-9-1914); 'The Connaught Rangers – An Appeal' (15-8-1914); 'Tommy's Thanks', 'Cigarettes For The Connaught Rangers', *'Comforts In The Trenches'* (28-11-1914).

2. *The Galway Express*: 'Co. Galway Motor Ambulance at the Front' (13-3-1915); 'County of Galway Red Cross Flag Week' (2-1-1915); 'Local War Items' (12-12-1914); 'Motor Ambulance' (28-11-1914); 'Red Cross Flag Day' (28-11-1914).

3. *The Connacht Tribune*: 'Irishmen!' (6-11-1915).
   The Galway Express: 'Local War Items' (9-1-1915); The Women of Galway – A Deserved Tribute' (28-11-1914); 'What the Soldier's Wife Will Get' (19-9-1914).

4. *The Galway Express*: 'Canada's Clothing for Galway' (9-1-1915); 'Christmas Gifts from the United States' (12-12-1914); 'Comforts For Our Fighters – Concert and Operatic Performance in Galway' (12-12-1914); 'Connaught Rangers Comfort Fund' (12-9-1914); 'Galway Children Entertained' (24-4-1915); 'Local War Items' (26-12-1914); 'No German Toys' (5-12-1914); 'Presents for Soldiers Friends' (21-11-1914); 'Soldiers' And Sailors' Families Association' (5-9-1914); 'To The Friends of the Rangers' (21-11-1914); 'Xmas Puddings For The Forces' (21-11-1914).

5. *The Galway Express*: 'Belgian Refugees' (17-10-1914); 'For "Belgian Soldiers" Comforts' (27-2-1915); 'Local War Items' (17-10-1914); 12-12-1914).

6. *East Galway Democrat*: 'Ballinasloe War Needlework Guild' (3-3-1917).
   The Connacht Tribune: 'Footwear for the Men at the Front' (23-1-1915); 'Roll Of Honour' (8-2-1915).
   The Galway Express: 'Concert at Soldiers and Sailors' Club' (12-2-1916); 'For Belgian Soldiers' Comforts' (27-2-1915); 'Galway Soldiers' and Sailors' Club' (13-3-1915); 'Local War Items' (16-1-1915); 27-2-1915); 13-3-1915); 'Lady Clancarty's Concert' (30-1-1915); 'Looking after our Fighters – Reading Room for Soldiers and Sailors Opened in Galway' (27-2-1915); 'Reading and Recreation Room in Galway for Sailors and Soldiers' (30-1-1915); 'Soldiers' and Sailors' Reading Room' (27-2-1915).

7. *The Galway Express*: 'National Society for the Prevention of Cruelty to Children', April 1915); 'N.S.P.C.C. – Children's Day in Galway' (8-5-1915); 'War and Child Neglect' (29-5-1915).

8. O'Farrell Family Archives.
   The Connacht Tribune: 'Notes & News – Wounded Soldiers for Galway' (29-5-1915).

The Galway Express: 'Tommy's Thanks', 'Cigarettes for the Connaught Rangers', '*Comforts in the Trenches*' (28-11-1914).

9. *The Galway Express*: 'Connaught Rangers Fund' (13-3-1915); 'Comforts for Connaught Rangers – Prisoners in Germany – Novel Entertainment in Galway' (24-4-1915); 'Help! Help! – Connaught Rangers Prisoner's Strong Appeal' (6-3-1915); 'Prisoner's Thanks' (12-6-1915); 'Tobacco and Cigarettes for the Connaught Rangers' (5-9-1914).

10. *The Connacht Tribune*: 'War Fund'–'Annual Meeting Of The Galway Association – Comforts for Soldiers and Prisoners' (3-6-1916).

    The Galway Express: 'Blackberries for Soldiers' (11-9-1915); 'Comforts for Connaught Rangers – Prisoners in Germany – Novel Entertainment in Galway' (24-4-1915); 'Help! Help! – Connaught Rangers Prisoner's Strong Appeal' (6-3-1915).

    The Tuam Herald: 'An Ambulance For Galway' (17-7-1815); 'Galway War Fund Association' (5-8-1916).

11. *The Connacht Tribune*: 'War Fund, – What Renmore Fete Achieved for the Connaughts, *Result of the Competitions*' (18-9-1915).

    The Galway Express: 'Renmore Fete – In Aid of Prisoners of War Fund – Successful Function' (11-9-1915).

12. *The Connacht Tribune*: 'War Fund – Annual Meeting of the Galway Association – Comforts for Soldiers and Prisoners' (3-6-1916); 'Women's War' (2-6-1917).

    The Galway Express: 'Further Help For The Connaughts' (15-7-1916); 'Great Galway Carnival' (29-7-1916); 'Mesopotamia Day' (14-4-1917).

    The Tuam Herald: 'Books For Soldiers' (29-4-1916).

13. *The Connacht Tribune*: 'An Hitherto Unpublished Story of the Connaught Rangers' Gallantry' (1-6-1918); 'Prisoners of War Entertainment' (19-1-1918); 'Soldiers and Sailors' Comforts' (6-4-1918); 'War Funds – Over £12,000 Subscribed By Co. Galway' (20-6-1919); 'Women's War' (2-6-1917).

    The Galway Express: 'Galway Prisoners of War Fund – Appeal for a Co. Galway War Plate' (4-9-1915).

    The Tuam Herald: 'The County of Galway Naval and Military War Fund' (4-9-1915).

CHAPTER X

1. *The Connacht Tribune*: 'War's Grim Trial' (5-10-1918).
2. *East Galway Democrat*: 'Peace At Last' (16-11-1918).
   Marshall, S. The American Heritage History of World War I, *1964, p. 355).*
   The Connacht Tribune: 'Victory' (16-11-1918).
   World Book Encyclopaedia: 'World War I' (pp. 376, 377).
3. *East Galway Democrat*: 'Peace At Last' (16-11-1918).
   Interview: James Casserly, (18-11-2005).
   The Connacht Tribune: 'City Paper Seized – "Galway Express" Offices Taken by Military' (14-12-1918); 'Government Pounce' (25-5-1918); 'Peace Celebrations in Galway' (28-11-1918); 'Recruiting Ceased' (16-11-1918).
4. O'Dowd, P, *Galway City* (1998, p. 29).
   The Connacht Tribune: 'Fighting Fishermen' (1-3-1919); 'Pier For Salthill', 'Ministry of Reconstruction and Galway', *1919); 'The Rebuilding of the Claddagh'* (9-8-1919).
5. O'Dowd, P, *Down By The Claddagh* (1993, pp. 19, 29).
   The Connacht Tribune: *The Connacht Tribune*: 'Fighting Fishermen' (1-3-1919); 'Pier For Salthill', 'Ministry of Reconstruction and Galway', *1919); Galway', 1919); 'The Rebuilding of the Claddagh'* (9-8-1919).
6. *The Connacht Tribune*: 'The Unredeemed Sacrifice' (15-3-1919).
7. *The Connacht Tribune*: 'Grammar School War Memorial' (14-6-1919. 'The Unredeemed Sacrifice' (15-3-1919).
9. Interview: Paddy O'Neill, 13-11-2005).

CHAPTER XI

1. Glover, M, *Warfare From Waterloo To Mons* (1980, pp. 246, 247).
   Hogg, I. V, *Dictionary of World War I* (1997, p. 156)
   'The Irish in the Great War' (Tony Finnerty Archives).
2. Glover, M, *Warfare From Waterloo To Mons* (1980, pp. 248, 249).
   Hogg, I. V, *Dictionary of World War I* (1997, pp. 116, 156)
   Johnson, T, *Orange, Green and Khaki, The Story of the Irish Regiments in the Great War, 1914-18* (1992, p. 2).
3. Bowman, T, *The Irish regiments in the Great War Discipline and morale* (2003, pp. 49, 50).
   Harris, H. E. D, *The Irish Regiments in the First World War* (1968, pp. 35, 36).
   Hogg, I. V, *Dictionary of World War I* (1997, pp. 146, 156).
   Johnson, T, *Orange, Green and Khaki, The Story of the Irish Regiments in the Great*

War, 1914–18 (1992, p. 21).

Jourdain, H. F. N, *The Connaught Rangers Second Battalion, Formerly 94th Foot, Volume II* (1999, p412).

The Galway Express: 'Lieut-Col. The Hon. George Morris', 'A Brave and Brilliant Leader', '*How He Met His Fate*' (5-12-1914).

The Tuam Herald: 'The Connaught's Stand' (3-10-1914).

4. Documentary: The Battle of the Somme; the Bloodiest Battle of World War One.

Harris, H. E. D, *The Irish Regiments in the First World War* (1968, pp. 35, 36).

Hogg, I. V, *Dictionary of World War I* (1997, pp. 146, 156).

Johnson, T, *Orange, Green and Khaki, The Story of the Irish Regiments in the Great War, 1914–18* (1992, pp. 29, 35).

CHAPTER XII

1. Hogg, I. V, *Dictionary of World War I* (1997, p. 4).

Johnson, T, *Orange, Green and Khaki, The Story of the Irish Regiments in the Great War, 1914–18* (1992, pp. 37, 38).

Marshall, S, *The American Heritage History of World War I* (1964, pp. 73, 78, 239).

Sheffield, G, *Forgotten Victory The First World War: Myths and Realities* (2001, p. 90).

2. Hogg, I. V, *Dictionary of World War I* (1997, p. 4)

Jourdain, H. F. N, *The Connaught Rangers Second Battalion, Formerly 94th Foot, Volume II* (1999, p. 412).

Marshall, S, *The American Heritage History of World War I* (1964, p. 239).

3. Hogg, I. V, *Dictionary of World War I* (1997, pp. 4, 164).

Marshall, S, *The American Heritage History of World War I* (1964, pp. 278, 279, 280, 281, 282, 283).

CHAPTER XIII

1. Hogg, I. V, *Dictionary of World War I* (1997, p. 237)

Johnson, T, *Orange, Green and Khaki, The Story of the Irish Regiments in the Great War, 1914–18* (1992, pp. 52, 53, 54).

Keegan, J, *The First World War an Illustrated History* (2002, p. 116).

Marshall, S, *The American Heritage History of World War I* (1964, p. 76).

The Galway Express: 'Irish Nuns At Ypres' (9-1-1915).

2. Hogg, I. V, *Dictionary of World War I* (1997, p. 237).

Holt, Major & Mrs, *Battlefield Guide to the Ypres Salient* (2000, pp. 19, 20).

Johnson, T, *Orange, Green and Khaki, The Story of the Irish Regiments in the Great War, 1914-18* (1992, pp. 53, 54, 55).

Jourdain, H.F.N, *The Connaught Rangers Second Battalion, Formerly 94th Foot,* (Volume II, 1999, p. 433).

Marshall, S, *The American Heritage History of World War I* (1964, pp. 76, 77).

The Galway Express: 'Connaught Rangers Heavy Losses At Ypres – A Perfect Hell On Earth' (5-6-1915). 'The Splendid Action of the Connaught Rangers At Ypres' (29-5-1915).

The Irish Times: 'Destruction of Ypres – The Very Ruins in Flames' (10-11-1914).

3. Harris, H. E. D, *The Irish Regiments in the First World War* (1968, p. 38).

Hogg, I. V, *Dictionary of World War I* (1997, p. 237).

Johnson, T, *Orange, Green and Khaki, The Story of the Irish Regiments in the Great War, 1914-18* (1992, pp. 54, 55, 56).

Jourdain, H. F. N, *The Connaught Rangers Second Battalion, Formerly 94th Foot* (Volume II 1999, p. 439).

Marshall, S, *The American Heritage History of World War I* (1964, p. 77).

4. Fallon, O, *'The First Battle of Ypres', The New Ranger, No. 1* (Volume 1, July 2003, pp. 2, 3).

Hogg, I. V, *Dictionary of World War I* (1997, p. 237).

Ireland On Sunday: 'Memorial blocked for World War One's youngest casualty' (2-6-2002).

Marshall, S, *The American Heritage History of World War I* (1964, p. 107).

Sheffield, G, *Forgotten Victory The First World War: Myths and Realities* (2001, p. 103).

5 Hogg, I. V, *Dictionary of World War I* (1997, p. 237).

Johnson, T, *Orange, Green and Khaki, The Story of the Irish Regiments in the Great War, 1914-18* (1992, pp. 75, 76, 77, 79, 84, 85).

Jourdain, H. F. N, *The Connaught Rangers Second Battalion, Formerly 94th Foot, Volume II* (1999, pp. 460, 461, 462).

6 Hogg, I. V, *Dictionary of World War I* (1997), p. 238).

Marshall, S, *The American Heritage History of World War I* (1964, pp. 214, 215).

7 Bowman, T, *The Irish regiments in the Great War Discipline and morale* (2003, p. 332).

Hogg, I. V, *Dictionary of World War I* (1997, p. 238).

Holt, Major & Mrs, *Battlefield Guide to the Ypres Salient* (2000, p. 22).

Marshall, S, *The American Heritage History of World War I* (1964, p. 215).

Sheffield, G, *Forgotten Victory The First World War: Myths and Realities* (2001, pp. 174, 175, 176, 177, 178).

8. Hogg, I. V, *Dictionary of World War I* (1997, p. 238).

Marshall, S, *The American Heritage History of World War I* (1964, pp. 272, 273, 274).

CHAPTER XIV

1. Johnson, T, *Orange, Green and Khaki, The Story of the Irish Regiments in the Great War, 1914-18* (1992, p. 72).

Hogg, I. V, *Dictionary of World War I* (1997), p. 163).

Keegan, J, *The First World War an Illustrated History* (2002, pp. 172, 173).

Marshall, S, *The American Heritage History of World War I* (1964, p. 77).

'The Irish in the Great War'. (Tony Finnerty Archives).

2. Johnson, T, *Orange, Green and Khaki, The Story of the Irish Regiments in the Great War, 1914-18* (1992), p. 72).

Hogg, I. V, *Dictionary of World War I* (1997), p. 163).

Keegan, J, *The First World War an Illustrated History* (2002, pp. 174, 175).

Marshall, S, *The American Heritage History of World War I* (1964, p. 86, 87).

'The Irish in the Great War' (Tony Finnerty Archives).

The Galway Express: 'Most Sanguinary Fight Yet' (17-4-1915).

CHAPTER XV

1. Johnson, T, *Orange, Green and Khaki, The Story of the Irish Regiments in the Great War, 1914-18* (1992), p. 100).

Hogg, I. V, *Dictionary of World War I* (1997), pp. 45, 84, 86).

World Book Encyclopaedia, 'Dardanelles' (1986, pp. 28, 29).

2. Hogg, I. V, *Dictionary of World War I* (1997), pp. 84, 85, 95).

Keegan, J, *The First World War an Illustrated History* (2002, pp. 222, 225, 226, 227).

Marshall, S, *The American Heritage History of World War I, 1964, pp. 86, 87).*

The Galway Express: 'Thrilling Story of the Beach Fight' (28-8-1915).

'The Irish in the Great War' (Tony Finnerty Archives).

World Book Encyclopaedia:'Dardanelles' (1986, p. 372).

3. Hogg, I. V, *Dictionary of World War I* (1997, pp. 28, 84, 85).

Keegan, J, *The First World War an Illustrated History* (2002, pp. 225, 227, 229).

4. Johnson, T, *Orange, Green and Khaki, The Story of the Irish Regiments in the Great War, 1914-18* (1992, p. 125).

Keegan, J, *The First World War an Illustrated History* (2002, p. 229).

Marshall, S, *The American Heritage History of World War I* (1964, p. 118).

'The Irish in the Great War' (Tony Finnerty Archives).

5. Hogg, I. V, *Dictionary of World War I* (1997, p. 84, 85, 95).

    Keegan, J, *The First World War an Illustrated History* (2002, p. 234).

    Marshall, S, *The American Heritage History of World War I* (1964, p. 118).

    The Galway Express: 'Irish Valour' (4-9-1915).

    'The Irish in the Great War' (Tony Finnerty Archives).

CHAPTER XVI

1. Hogg, I. V, *Dictionary of World War I* (1997, pp. 118, 149, 150).

    Johnson, T, *Orange, Green and Khaki, The Story of the Irish Regiments in the Great War, 1914-18* (1992, p. 400).

    Keegan, J, *The First World War an Illustrated History* (2002, p. 251).

2. Hogg, I. V, *Dictionary of World War I* (1997, pp. 56, 87, 168, 196).

    Keegan, J, *The First World War an Illustrated History* (2002, p. 326).

3. Hogg, I. V, *Dictionary of World War I* (1997, pp. 190,191).

    Keegan, J, *The First World War an Illustrated History* (2002, pp. 235, 238, 239).

CHAPTER XVII

1. Hogg, I. V, *Dictionary of World War I* (1997, p. 130).

    Keegan, J, *The First World War an Illustrated History* (2002, pp. 181, 184).

    Marshall, S, *The American Heritage History of World War I* (1964, p. 135).

    'The Irish in the Great War' (Tony Finnerty Archives).

2. Hogg, I. V, *Dictionary of World War I* (1997, p. 130).

    Johnson, T, *Orange, Green and Khaki, The Story of the Irish Regiments in the Great War, 1914-18* (1992, pp. 156, 158).

    Keegan, J, *The First World War an Illustrated History* (2002, p. 267).

    Marshall, S, *The American Heritage History of World War I* (1964, p. 136).

    'The Irish in the Great War' (Tony Finnerty Archives).

CHAPTER XVIII

1. Hogg, I. V, *Dictionary of World War I* (1997, pp. 110, 185, 193).
    Keegan, J, *The First World War an Illustrated History* (2002, pp. 245, 246, 249).
    Marshall, S, *The American Heritage History of World War I* (1964, pp. 176, 177).
    Spector, R. H, *At War at Sea, Sailors and Naval Combat in the Twentieth Century* (2001, p. 92).
2. Hogg, I. V, *Dictionary of World War I* (1997, pp. 110, 185, 193).
    Keegan, J, *The First World War an Illustrated History* (2002, p. 249).
    Marshall, S, *The American Heritage History of World War I* (1964, p. 177).
    Spector, R. H, *At War at Sea, Sailors and Naval Combat in the Twentieth Century* (2001, pp. 83, 84, 92).
3. Hogg, I. V, *Dictionary of World War I* (1997, p. 111).
    Keegan, J, *The First World War an Illustrated History* (2002, p. 255).
    Marshall, S, *The American Heritage History of World War I* (1964, p. 177).
    Spector, R. H, *At War at Sea, Sailors and Naval Combat in the Twentieth Century* (2001, p. 93).

CHAPTER XIX

1. Documentary: The Battle of the Somme; the Bloodiest Battle of World War One.
    Hogg, I. V, *Dictionary of Battles* (1997, p. 152).
    Hogg, I. V, *Dictionary of World War I* (1997, pp. 203, 203).
    Johnson, T, *Orange, Green and Khaki, The Story of the Irish Regiments in the Great War, 1914-18* (1992, pp. 225, 226).
    Keegan, J, *The First World War an Illustrated History* (2002, p. 271).
    Marshall, S, *The American Heritage History of World War I* (1964, p. 180).
    'The Irish in the Great War' (Tony Finnerty Archives).
    Documentary: The Battle of the Somme; the Bloodiest Battle of World War One.
2. Documentary: The Battle of the Somme; the Bloodiest Battle of World War One.
    Hogg, I. V, *Dictionary of Battles* (1997, p. 152).
    Hogg, I. V, *Dictionary of World War I* (1997, pp. 202, 203).
    Johnson, T, *Orange, Green and Khaki, The Story of the Irish Regiments in the Great War, 1914-18* (1992, pp. 225, 226).
    Keegan, J, *The First World War an Illustrated History* (2002, p. 271).
    MacDonald, L, *Somme,* (1988, p. 55).

Marshall, S, *The American Heritage History of World War I* (1964, pp. 180, 181).

'The Irish in the Great War' (Tony Finnerty Archives).

3. Documentary: The Battle of the Somme; the Bloodiest Battle of World War One.

Hogg, I. V, *Dictionary of Battles* (1997, p. 152).

Hogg, I. V, *Dictionary of World War I* (1997, pp. 203, 203).

Johnson, T, *Orange, Green and Khaki, The Story of the Irish Regiments in the Great War, 1914-18* (1992, pp. 226, 227).

Keegan, J, *The First World War an Illustrated History* (2002, p. 271).

Marshall, S, *The American Heritage History of World War I* (1964, pp. 180, 181,196).

The Galway Express: 'Further Help for the Connaughts' (15-7-1916).

'The Irish in the Great War' (Tony Finnerty Archives).

4. Documentary: The Battle of the Somme; the Bloodiest Battle of World War One.

East Galway Democrat: 'Guillemont and Ginchy' (7-9-1918).

Hogg, I. V, *Dictionary of Battles* (1997, p. 152).

Hogg, I. V, *Dictionary of World War I* (1997, p. 202, 203).

Johnson, T, *Orange, Green and Khaki, The Story of the Irish Regiments in the Great War, 1914-18* (1992, p. 240).

Keegan, J, *The First World War an Illustrated History* (2002, p. 267).

Marshall, S, *The American Heritage History of World War I* (1964, p. 136).

Stedman, M, *Guillemont Somme Battleground Europe* (1998, p. 116).

'Gullemont And Ginchy', 'Anniversary of the Charge of the Irish Braigades' (7-9-1918).

'The Irish in the Great War' (Tony Finnerty Archives).

5. Hogg, I. V, *Dictionary of Battles* (1997, p. 152).

Hogg, I. V, *Dictionary of World War I* (1997, pp. 202, 203).

Interview: Val Raftery, 27-11-2004); Dennis Kearney, *5-2-2005)*.

Keegan, J, *The First World War an Illustrated History* (2002, p. 274).

The Connacht Tribune: 'Somme casualties' (7-10-1916).

6. Documentary: 'The Battle of the Somme; the Bloodiest Battle of World War One'.

Hogg, I. V, *Dictionary of Battles* (1997, p. 152).

Hogg, I. V, *Dictionary of World War I* (1997, pp. 202, 203).

Marshall, S, *The American Heritage History of World War I* (1964 pp. 267, 268, 270, 271).

CHAPTER XX

1. Hogg, I. V, *Dictionary of World War I* (1997, pp. 39, 100).

   Internet: Battle of Cambrai

   Johnson, T, *Orange, Green and Khaki, The Story of the Irish Regiments in the Great War, 1914–18* (1992, pp. 309, 311, 315).

   Keegan, J, *The First World War an Illustrated History* (2002, pp. 345, 348, 349).

   Marshall, S, *The American Heritage History of World War I* (1964, p. 220).

   Sheffield, G, *Forgotten Victory The First World War: Myths and Realities* (2001, p. 181).

2. Hogg, I. V, *Dictionary of World War I* (1997, p. 39).

   Internet: Battle of Cambrai

   Johnson, T, *Orange, Green and Khaki, The Story of the Irish Regiments in the Great War, 1914–18* (1992, pp. 413, 414, 415).

3. Bowman, T, *The Irish regiments in the Great War Discipline and morale* (2003, pp. 442, 443).

   Hogg, I. V, *Dictionary of World War I* (1997, pp. 39, 100).

   Johnson, T, *Orange, Green and Khaki, The Story of the Irish Regiments in the Great War, 1914–18* (1992, pp. 415, 424, 427).

   Keegan, J, *The First World War an Illustrated History* (2002, pp. 405, 407).

   Documentary: Two Civilisations; Days That Shook The World, RTÉ, *76883439, 6-5-2006).*

APPENDIX

1. Internet: The Princess Mary 1914 Christmas Gift.
2. Dennis, G, *'For Freedom and Honour'* (Tony Finnerty Archives).
3. Internet: The Gulliemont Ginchy Cross.
4. Internet: The Irish National War Memorial.
5. Internet: Remembrance – The History of the Cenotaph.
6. Internet: Remembrance – The Two Minutes Silence.
7. Internet: History of the Tomb.
8. *The Connacht Tribune*: 'Memory of the Dead' – 'Dedication of War Memorial at St. Nicholas' (21-2-1920).
9. Internet: 'The 36th (Ulster) Division, and the Battle of the Somme, *1915*'; *'The Ulster Tower'*.
10.   The Combined Irish Regiments Old Comrades Association Archives; Sheerin, N, *On Your Doorstep* (1977, p. 27).
11.   Holt, Major & Mrs, *Battlefield Guide to the Ypres Salient* (2000, pp. 28, 29, 30).
      'The Menin Gate', Journal of the Connaught Rangers Association: The New Ranger, (July 2003, pp. 2, 3).
12.   Internet: Thiepval Memorial; Thiepval, the Soome, *France*.
13. Loughnane, J, *Journal of the Connaught Rangers Association: The New Ranger* (July 2003, p. 6).
14.   Internet: The Island of Ireland Peacepark.

BIBLIOGRAPHY

Bartlett, T. (ed), *A Military History of Ireland* (Cambridge University Press, Cambridge, 1996).

Jeffery, K.

Bowman, T, *The Irish regiments in the Great War Discipline and morale* (Manchester University Press, Manchester, 2003).

Cassells, L, *The Archduke and the Assassin: Sarajevo, June 28th 1914* (Stein and Day, New York, 1985).

Castleden, R, *British History, A Chronological Dictionary of Dates* (Parragon Book Service Ltd., London, 1994).

Caulfield, M, *The Easter Rebellion* (Gill & Macmillan, Dublin, 1995)

Cooper, B, *The Tenth (Irish) Division in Gallipoli* (Irish Academic Press Ltd., Dublin, 1993).

Crealey, A. H, *An Irish Almanac* (Mercier Press Ltd., Cork, 1993).

Doherty, R, *Irish Winners of the Victoria Cross* (Four Courts Press, Dublin 2000).

Truesdale, D.

Dudley Edwards, R, *Patrick Pearse The Triumph of Failure* (Poolbeg Press, Dublin, 1990).

Ellis, B, *A Journey Of Remembrance – Walks in the Footsteps of Brandon Soldiers* (Brandon War Memorial Committee, Brandon, 2005).

Ferro, M, *The Great War 1914-1918* (Routledge, London, 2002).

Godsey, R, D, *Aristoctratic Redoubt: The Austro-Hungarian Foreign Office on the Eve of the Great War* (Perdue University Press, West Lafeyette, Ind, 1999).

Fitzpatrick, D, *Ireland and the First World War* (Trinity History Workshop, Dublin, 1986).

—— *The Two Irelands, 1912 – 1939* (Oxford University Press, Oxford 1998).

Forester, M, *Michael Collins, The Lost Leader* (Sphere Books, London, 1972).

Glover, M, *Warfare From Waterloo To Mons* (Book Club Associates London, 1980).

Hamilton, R. F, *The Origins of the Great War* (Cambridge University Press, Cambridge, 2003).

Hammerton, J. A, *The Great War, The Standard History of the All-Europe Conflict* (Volume II, The Wilson, H, W, Amalgamated Press Limited, London, 1914).

—— The Great War, The Standard History of the All-Europe Conflict, *Volume IV*

(The Wilson, H.W, Amalgamated Press Limited, London, 1915).

Hammerton, J.A, *The Great War, The Standard History of the All-Europe Conflict* (Volume VII, The Wilson, H, W, Amalgamated Press Limited, London, 1916).

Harris, H. E. D, *The Irish Regiments in the First World War* (The Mercier Press, Cork, 1968).

Henry, W, *The Shimmering Waste, The Life and Times of Robert O'Hara Burke* (William Henry, Galway, 1997).

—— St, Clerans, *The Tale of a Manor House* (Merv Griffin, 1999).

Henry, W, *Mervue 1955 – 2003* (Mervue Festival Committee, 2003).

—— *The Galway Arms Golfing Society, A History* (The Galway Arms Golfing Society, 2003).

Heringklee, S and Higgins, J, (Ed) *Monuments of St, Nicholas' Collegiate Church, Galway, A Historical Genealogical Archaeological Record* (Rock Crow's Press, Galway 1991)

Herwig, H. H, *The First World War Germany and Austria-Hungry 1914-1918* (Arnold, member of (Hodder Headline Group), London, 1997).

Hogg, I. V, *Dictionary of Battles* (Hutchinson, Brockhampton Press, London, 1997).

—— Dictionary of World War I (Hutchinson, Brockhampton Press, *London 1997).*

Holt, Major & Mrs, *Battlefield Guide to the Ypres Salient* (Leo Cooper, London, 2000).

Jeffery, K, *Ireland and the Great War* (Cambridge University Press, Cambridge, 2000).

Johnson, T, *Orange, Green and Khaki, The Story of the Irish Regiments in the Great War, 1914-18* (Gill and Macmillan Ltd, Dublin, 1992).

Joll, J, *The Origins of the First World War* (Longmans Publishing Group, Harlow, 2000).

Jourdain, H. F. N, *The Connaught Rangers First Battalion, Formerly 88th Foot* (Volume I, Schull Books, Fraser, E, Cork, 1999).

Jourdain, H. F. N, *The Connaught Rangers Second Battalion, Formerly 94th Foot* (Volume 2, Schull Books, Fraser, E, Cork, 1999).

Koch, W. H, *The Origins of the First World War: Great Power Rivalry and German War Aims* (Macmillan, London, 1984).

Keegan, J, *The First World War an Illustrated History* (Pimlico, London, 2002).

Keiger, J. V. F, *France and the Origins of the First World War* (Macmillan, London, 1983).

Kipling, R, *The Irish Guards In The Great War; Volume II The Second Battalion and Appendices* (MacMillan, London, 1923).

Lieven, D. C. B, *Russia and the Origins of the First World War* (Macmillan, London, 1983).

Loades, D, *Kings & Queens, An Essential A-Z Guide* (Starfire, London, 2001).

MacDonald, L, *Somme* (Papermac, London, 1988).

MacLochlainn, A, *Two Galway Schools, The Salthill Industrial School & The Claddagh Piscatory Regan, T, School* (Galway Labour History Group, Galway, 1993).

Marshall, S, *The American Heritage History of World War I* (American Heritage Publishing Company Inc., U.S.A, 1964).

Mombauer, A, *Helmuth von Moltke and the Origins of the First World War* (Cambridge University Press, Cambridge, 2001).

Mombauer, A, *The Origins of the First World War: Controversies and Consensus* (White Plains, New York, 2002).

O'Dowd, P, *Down By The Claddagh* (Kennys Bookshop and Art Galleries Ltd, 1993).

— *Galway City* (Galway Corporation (1998).

— *Galway In Old Photographs* (Gill & Macmillan, Dublin (2003).

— *Galway Lawn Tennis Club* – a History (Galway Lawn Tennis Club (2005)

O'Flaherty, M, *The Claddagh Boy* (Carlton Press, New York, 1963).

O'Hara, B, *Regional Technical College Galway, The First 21 Years* (The Research and Consultancy Unit, Regional Technical College Galway, 1993).

Sheerin, N, *On Your Doorstep* (Norbert Sheerin, 1977).

Sheffield, G, *Forgotten Victory The First World War: Myths and Realities* (Headline Book Publishing, 2001).

Spector, R. H, *At War at Sea Sailors and Naval Combat in the Twentieth Century* (Viking Penguin, member of (Penguin Putnam Inc.), 2001).

Stedman, M, *Gullemont Somme Battleground Europe* (Leo Cooper, South Yorkshire, 1998).

Steiner, Z. S, *Britain and the Origins of the First World War* (Macmillan, London, 1977).

Villiers-Tuthill, K, *Beyond The Twelve Bens* (Kathleen Villiers-Tuthill, 1990).

Williamson, S. R, *Austria-Hungary and the Origins of the First World War* (MacMillan, Basingstoke, 1991).

REFERENCES

Archives & Manuscripts:

American Army Records.

Army Service Records of World War I, Public Records Office, Kew, Surrey.

Ashe Family Archives.

Burgess Family Archives.

Campell Family Archives: Archives of the Naval Saving Bank, Portsmouth: Account Number 19688); Census of Ireland 1901 & 1911).

Commissioners of the Admiralty Document; Certificate for Wounds and Hurts Naval Service Document; Supplementary Prize Share Paid.

Commonwealth War Graves Commission Archives, United Kingdom.

Fahy Family Archives.

Finnerty, T, Archives: 'For Freedom and Honour', by Dennis G, Blair; 'The Irish in the Great War'; War Diary of the Second Battalion Connaught Rangers 1914).

Fahy Family Archives.

Furey Research Report, March (2005).

Flynn Family Archives: Pensions Appeal Tribunal Document; Ref.: 13 / MF / 2160).

Irish Guards Archives.

Jordan Family Archives.

Larkin Family Archives.

Loughrea Church Records.

Macken Family Archives.

McElroy Family Archives.

McNally, E, The Final Bell.

Noonan Family Archives.

O'Connor Family Archives.

O'Farrell Family Archives.

O'Flaherty Family Archives.

Renmore Barracks Museum Archives.

Soldiers Died in the Great War CD Rom by the Navy & Military Press Ltd.

State Records of Birth – District of Loughrea.

State Records of Marriage – District of Ballinasloe.

The Combined Irish Regiments Old Comrades Association Archives.

The Graphic Souvenir of the German Navy's Surrender, The Graphic Tallis House, London.

The History of the Irish Guards, Irish Guards Archives.

The National Library of Ireland Archives: Éamonn Ceannt, MS10883).

The Triumph of the Royal Navy, Hodder and Stoughton, London.

Tom Kenny Archives.

Ward Family Archives.

Booklets & Documentaries:

Documentary (Videotape) *The Battle of the Somme – The Bloodiest Battle of World War I.*

Documentary: *Two Civilisations; Days That Shook The World*, RTÉ, 76883439, 6-5-2006

Weldon's Practical Knitter, No, 171, Volume 15).

Internet Articles:

History of the Tomb.

Irish Regiments in World War I.

Regimental Mascots – Royal Munster Fusiliers.

Remembrance – The Two Minutes Silence.

Royal Munster Fusiliers.

South Irish Horse 'In Memory of the South Irish Horse 1914 – 1919'.

South Irish Horse 'The History'.

South of Ireland Yeomanry – South Irish Horse.

The 36th (Ulster) Division, and the Battle of the Somme, 1915).

The Gulliemont Ginchy Cross.

The Island of Ireland Peacepark.

The Irish National War Memorial.

The Long Long Trail – The South Irish Horse.

The Prince of Wales Leinster Regiment (Royal Canadians).

The Princess Mary 1914 Christmas Gift.

The Royal Dublin Fusiliers.

The Royal Irish Regiment.

The Ulster Tower.

Thiepval Memorial

Thiepval, the Soome, France.

Remembrance – The History of the Cenotaph.

Remembrance – The Two Minutes Silence.

Interviews:

John Jordan 12-11-2000); Jonie Fallon 13-11-2000); Elizabeth Hackett 13-11-2000); Mary Walsh 13-11-2000); Patsy O'Connor 15-11-2000); Sheila Jordan 28-6-2001); Annie Burke 27-8-2001); Frances Kenneen 19-9-2001); Johnny Flaherty 23-9-2001); Billy Lally 26-9-2001); Nora Cahill nee Hoare 8-10-2001); Carmel Colgan, 25-6-2003); Paddy O'Neill, 13-11-2003); Anne Everiss, 19-11-2003); Brian Fahy 5-3-2003; Michael Conneely, 28-11-2003; Mike Flynn, 28-11-2003; Anne Campbell, 29-11-2003; Billy Carr, 29-11-2003; Tommy Carr, 29-11-2003; Dickie Byrne, 29-11-2003; Noel Heaney, 8-8-2004); Michael Lynskey, 21-11-2004); Patrick Heaney, 23-11-2004); Val Raftery, 27-11-2004); Dennis Kearney, 5-2-2005); Frank Costello, 15-10-2005); Gerry Crane, 16-10-2005); Paddy Curran, 16-10-2005); Maureen Oliver, 16-10-2005); James Casserly, 18-11-2005); Paddy O'Neill, 25-11-2005); Martin Flaherty, 26-1-2006); Mary Lambe, 11-2-2006).

Journals:

English Historical Studies

Seligmann, M.S, '"A Barometer of National Confidence": A British Assessment of the Role of Insecurity in the formulation of German Military Policy Before the First World War', Volume 117 (2002).

Historical Journal

Ferguson, N, 'Germany and the Origins of the Great War: New perspectives', Volume 35 (1992).

Fitzpatrick, D, 'The Logic of the Collective Sacrifice: Ireland and the British Army, 1914 – 1918', Volume 38 1995).

Journal of Military History

Lyon, J.M.B, '"A Peasant Mob": The Serbian Army on the Eve of the Great War', Volume 61 (1997).

Journal of Modern History

Gordon, M. R, 'Domestic Conflict and the Origins of the First World War: The British and German Cases', Volume 46, 1974).

Kaiser, D. E, 'Germany and the Origins of the First World War', Volume 55, 1983).

Journal of the Connaught Rangers Association: The New Ranger

Loughnane, J, 'Connaught Ranger Memorial Window', No, 1, Volume 1, July 2003).

Fallon, O, 'The First Battle of Ypres', No, 1, Volume 1, July 2003).

'The Menin Gate', No, 1, Vol, 1, July 2003).

Journal of the Galway Archaeological and Historical Society

Blake, J, 'Field-Marshal Sir John French', Volume 8, No 4, 1913 – 1914).

Collins, T, 'The Helga/Muirchu: Her Contribution To Galway Maritime History', Volume 54 (2002).

Past & Present

Ferguson, N, 'Public Finance and National Security: The Domestic Origins of the First World War Revisited', Volume 142 (1994).

Lectures:

'Nora Barnacle', by Peadar O'Dowd, *14-6-2004*

McCarthy, M, 'Historico-Geographical Explorations of Ireland's heritages: Towards a Critical Understanding of the Nature of Memory and Identity', in M McCarthy (ed), Ireland's Heritages: Critical Perspectives on Memory and Identity, (Ashgate, Aldershot, 2005, pp, 3-54);

Morrissey, J, 'A Lost Heritage: The Connaught Rangers and Mutlivocal Irishness', in M McCarthy (ed), Ireland's Heritages: Critical Perspectives on Memory and Identity, (Ashgate, Aldershot, 2005, pp, 71-88).

Magazines:

Aide Memoire Ulster Military Historical Society.

'Remember John Condon, Age 14', *Issue 51, November 2001).*

Kylemore Abbey Information Leaflet

'The Neo-Gothic Church A Brief History.'

St, Patrick Parish Magazine: A series of articles by William Henry.

'Battlefield of the Somme, Part I' (2000).

'Battlefield of the Somme, Part II, *Angels of Mons'* (2001).

'Battlefield of the Somme, Part III, *Lost Youths of the Great War'* (2002).

'Battlefield of the Somme, Part VI' (2003).

'The Neptune Disaster' (2002).

Newspapers:

Daily Express:

'Honour at last for VC hero in pauper's grave' (18-1-1995).

East Galway Democrat:

'Ballinasloe War Needlework Guild' (3-3-1917).

'Guillemont and Ginchy' (7-9-1918).

'Ireland's Chance' (28-4-1917).

'Mr Devlin and Irish Conscription' (18-5-1918).

'New Rallying Song For Carson' (4-5-1918).

'Peace at Last' (16-11-1918).

Galway Advertiser:

'A Good Sport' (25-4-1999).

'Galway Diary' 'The Day the Germans almost got Monty' (3-6-2004 by Ronnie O'Gorman.

'Lady Gregory and The Fate of Coole Park' (26-1-1995, 'Galway Diary' by Ronnie O'Gorman.

'The Connaught Rangers go to war' (19-11-1998 by Tom Kenny.

'The Devil's Own' (28-9-2000 by Seathrun of Dubhros

'The King and I' (22-1-2004).

'The sinking of the LE Leinster, October 10 1918' (16-10-2003).

'The Shambles' (9-2-1995 by Tom Kenny.

'The sinking of the LE Leinster, October 10 1918' (16-10-2003, *'Galway Diary', by Ronnie O'Gorman.*

'The Woollen Mills' (7-5-1987 by Tom Kenny.

Ireland On Sunday:

'Memorial blocked for World War One's youngest casualty' (2-6-2002).

News of the World:

'Humble private who led an Irish revolt by the Devils' Own' (2-3-2003).

The City Tribune:

'Eighty years later and World War I grave discovered' (19-2-1999).

'The Devil's Own – Galway war heroes of another era' (7-2-1992).

The Connacht Tribune:

'4 Questions to the Women of Ireland' (20-2-1915).

'5 Reasons why Irishmen should join the Army' (20-3-1915).

'A Galway V.C.' (9-10-1915).

'Aggressive Politics' – 'Striking Pronouncement By Bishop of Clonfert' (15-6-1915).

'Alderman Michael O'Flaherty, P, C, *Death Of Former Mayor Of Galway*' (20-9-1959).

'Amongst The Fallen – Lieut, Alexander Young, *V.C., Killed*' (28-10-1916).

'A Mother's Woe' – 'Galway Officer's graphic tales of the Battlefield' – ' Interesting Letter from the Front' (6-3-1915).

'An Hitherto Unpublished Story of the Connaught Rangers' Gallantry' (1-6-1918).

'An Officer's Letter of Condolence' (7-10-1916).

'At Hill 70.' – Galway Student's Account of the Great Battle' (9-10-1915).

'A Soldier Journalist', October 1918).

'Bishop's Court, St, *Augustine St., Galway*' (21-9-1918).

'Blown to Atoms – Fate of Galway Trawler and Four Men' (29-12-1917).

'Capt, Alston Royal Air Force will Lecture' (28-9-1918).

'Catholic Chaplains' (2-9-1916).

'Catholic Chaplain's Story' (26-6-1915).

'City Paper Seized – "Galway Express" Offices taken by Military' (14-12-1918).

'Clifden Meeting' (3-7-1915).

'Co, Galway Farms Mapped Out In Berlin', *'What are you Going to do About It'*, *'Irishmen Have Something to Defend'*, *'Your Farm has Been "Mapped" by the Germans'*, *'What Would the Germans Do'* (8-4-1916).

'Come With Me' (3-8-1917).

'Compulsory Rationing' (10-11-1917).

'Connacht and the Fight for Freedom' (4-12-1915).

'Connacht Men Volunteer' (30-1-1915).

'Connaught Rangers' Colours' (24-5-1919).

'Conscription – How Ireland was saved from it by the Irish Party' (6-10-1917).

'Conscription Scare', 'Young Men Seek To Avoid Compulsory Service' (13-11-1916).

'Death And Desolation, Connaught Rangers Thrilling Story, *How Lieutenant Tulloch Died*' (20-2-1915).

'D.M.C, for Valour – The Gallant Connaughts' (10-4-1915).

'Enlistment of men in the stores sections of the Royal Engineers' (10-5-1919).

'Fighting Fishermen' (1-3-1919).

'Food Production in Ireland, 1917' – 'Farmers to the Rescue' (27-1-1917).

'Footwear for the Men at the Front' (23-1-1915).

'From Rostrum to Trench – Galway Technical Instructor's Experiences' (9-10-1915).

'From the Dardanelles – Interesting Letter from a Sergeant of the Connaughts' (9-10-1915).

'Gallant Connaught Ranger' (26-3-1918).

'Gallant Gentlemen' (20-6-1917).

'Galway as a Naval Base' (23-1-1915).

'Galway and Recruiting' (16-11-1918).

'Galway Civilians and the Sherwood Foresters' 8-7-1916); 22-5-1915).

'Galway Demobilized Service Men' (26-4-1919).

'Galway Electric Co., Limited – Notice' (21-9-1918).

'Galwaymen Fall' (14-7-1916).

'Galway Munition Factory' (8-7-1916).

'Galway Nurse Honoured' (27-10-1917).

'Galway Shell Factory' (14-7-1917).

'Galway Soldier's Story of Mons Battle' (10-10-1914).

'Germany's Desperate and Brutal Measures' (6-2-1915).

'God Bless Germany – Man who Declared that John Redmond would be Shot' (29-6-1916).

'Great Recruiting Demonstration at Clifden' (15-1-1916).

'Grammar School War Memorial' (14-6-1919).

'Gullemont And Ginchy' – 'Anniversary of the Charge of the Irish Braigades' (7-9-1918).

'Harbour Board – Excellent Work of Galway Munition Factory' (20-6-1917).

'Chaplain's Tribute – How a Brave Galway Soldier Died – An Example to the Regiment' (18-11-1916).

'How the Connaughts Held On' (1-6-1918).

'Important Proceedings at the Quarterly Meeting – Recruiting Question – The Chairman's Appeal For Men' (22-5-1915).

'In Connemara – Oughterard Discharged Soldiers' and Sailors' Society' (21-6-1919).

'In the Wake of War' (9-8-1919).

'In the West' (7-10-1916).

'Ireland And Conscription' (23-10-1915); 8-1-1916).

'Irish Aviation Station' (22-12-1917).

'Irish Bishops and the War' (11-3-1916).

'Irish Fishing Boats' (2-6-1917).

'Irish Girls – The Path to Danger' (24-5-1919).

'Irishmen in the United States Army' (10-8-1918).

'Irish Nationalists And Recruiting' (10-8-1918).

'Irish Sergeant's Story – It is Simply a Marvel that I am Alive' (29-5-1915).

'Irish War Hospital Depot' (28-10-1916).

'Is Ireland To Share Belgium's Fate' (25-2-1915).

'It is a Lie' (20-7-1918).

'Killed in Action – Portumna Families War Record – Brave Canadian's End' (30-12-1916).

'Letters from the Front' (22-5-1915).

'Left To Die' – 'Dying Sailor's Last Letters' (22-6-1918).

'Lieutenant Dudly Eyre Persse' (13-2-1915).

'Life On The Ocean Wave – Galway Recruits For The Navy – Stirring Address' (18-4-1916).

'List of Voluntary Recruits' – 'Royal Navy – Galway Area' – 'Army Galway Area' – 'Royal Air Force – Galway Area' (19-10-1919).

'Loughrea Priest in Exile – His part in the Great War' (18-7-1925).

'Lusitania Victims' (3-7-1915).

'Lusitania Victims – Brought Ashore at Galway' (22-5-1915).

'Memory of the Dead' – 'Dedication of War Memorial at St, Nicholas' (21-2-1920).

'Memorial Unveiling in Inverin' (19-6-1970).

'Men of Galway' (21-9-1918); 12-10-1918).

'Men Wanted – For Various Units of the Army' (5-7-1919).

'Midst Shot and Shell – Thrilling Stories from the Trenches – Former Galway Lad – On His Experiences in the Fateful Landing at Gallapoli – Chaplin's Story – Graphic Pictures of the Flanders Battlefield' (26-6-1915).

'Military Evicted' – 'Sixth Dragoon Guards Forced to Evacuate' (21-8-1920).

'More that half a Million Irish Catholics have Enlisted in U.S.A.' (13-7-1918).

'Munition Factory' (25-3-1916).

'Munition Factory – Interesting Interview with Captain Downie' (3-2-1917).

'Munition Making In Galway' (1-4-1916).

'Munitions Money And Men', – 'Loughrea And The War', *10-7-1915)*.

'Naval Recruiting' (21-11-1917).

'Neuve Chapelle, Old Connaughts Prominent Part in Fierce Battle' (1-5-1915).

'Notes & News – Wounded Soldiers for Galway' (29-5-1915).

'Off to the War' (25-3-1916).

'Peace Celebrations in Galway' (28-11-1918).

'Pier For Salthill' – 'Ministry of Reconstruction and Galway', 1919).

'Portumna Soldier's Death' (8-6-1918).

'Posthumous Award to Gallant Officer' (7-12-1918).

'Priests and People' (26-4-1919).

'Prisoners of War Entertainment' (19-1-1918).

'Prisoners of War – Galway Men's Appeal from Germany – For Cigarettes' (17-4-1915).

'Prisoner's Thanks' (12-6-1915).

'Ranger Officer a Prisoner – Interesting Letter' (24-10-1914).

'Recruiting Ceased' (16-11-1918).

'Recruiting Committee' (3-7-1915).

'Recruiting Council Appointment' (5-10-1918).

'Recruiting in Ireland' (19-8-1916).

'Recruiting Meeting at Loughrea' (10-7-1915).

'Recruiting Rally' (9-10-1915).

'Recruiting Returns' (28-9-1918); 5-10-1918); 12-10-1918).

'Recruiting – The Battalion for Commercial Men and Framers' (1-4-1916).

'Recruit Or – ?' (20-7-1918).

'Recruits Wanted' (30-8-1919).

'Released' – 'President Announces that the Connaught Rangers are Free' (6-1-1923).

'Remounts and Horse Transport – Army Service Corps Wants More Men' (21-9-1918).

'Renmore Tragedy' (10-4-1915).

'Republican Flags – Sunday Morning Decorations in Galway' (12-5-1917).

'Right Road – Home Rule within a Few Months' (6-4-1918).

'Roll of Honour' (8-2-1915).

'Seven Nations at War' (8-8-1914).

'Severe Sentences' (19-6-1915).

'Shell Factory' (6-1-1917).

'Sir Bryan Mahon and the Abbess' (27-9-1930).

'Somme Casualties' (7-10-1916).

'Soldiers and Sailors' Comforts' (6-4-1918).

'Still Mounting Up' (20-7-1918).

'Submarine off Galway' (20-3-1915).

'Submarine Victims' (22-6-1918).

'Surrounded By Fire' – 'Portumna Man's Terrible' – Dead and Dying in an Inferno' (13-11-1915).

'The Autumn Campaign' (28-9-1918).

'The Brand of Cain' (12-10-1918).

'The Carna Fund' (13-7-1918).

'The Connaught Rangers Mutiny' (4-11-1994).

'The Cry for Conscription' (15-12-1917).

'The Dardanelles' (29-5-1915).

'The Fighting Irish' – The Devil's Own' (5-10-1918).

'The Irish Party and Conscription' (15-1-1916).

'The Little Grey Home' – A Galway Sailor's Trilling Escape' (19-10-1918).

'The Mansion House "Leinster" Fund' (7-10-1918).

'The Memory of the Dead' (8-7-1916).

'The Military and the Town Hall' (14-6-1919).

'The Old Contemptibles' (16-3-1918).

'The Party and Military Service' (1-6-1918).

'The Rangers Band' (10-7-1915).

'The Rebuilding of the Claddagh' (9-8-1919).

'The Recruiting Campaign' (17-7-1915).

'The Retreat from Mons' (6-11-1915).

'The Two Policies' – 'The Practical and the Impracticable' (16-6-1917).

'The Unredeemed Sacrifice' (15-3-1919).

'The Volunteers' (1-5-1915).

'The War Game at Gallipoli' (30-10-1915). .

'Thirty-one Irish V, C.'s' (28-10-1916).

'Three Soldier Brothers – One Falls' (7-10-1916).

'To Command the Connaughts – Famous Irish V.C, for Galway' (30-10-1915).

'Troops of Western Command – Reviewed in Galway by Man who stopped first German Onrush' (21-7-1917).

'Two Ships Sunk' (17-3-1917).

'U, I, *League*' (15-1-1916).

'Uproar and Batons' (5-10-1918).

'Up the Kaiser' (3-2-1917).

'Victoria Cinema' (15-1-1916).

'Victory' (16-11-1918).

'Voluntary Aid Nursing Detachments' (30-10-1916).

'Voluntary Recruiting' (17-8-1917).

'War Fund'-'Annual Meeting of the Galway Assocation – Comforts for Soldiers and Prisoners' (3-6-1916).

'War Funds – Over £12, 000 Subscribed by Co, *Galway*' (29-6-1919).

'War Hospital Supply Depot' (3-3-1917).

'War Meetings' – 'Recruiting Gathering at Tuam And Clifden' (3-7-1915).

'War Rations' (10-3-1917).

'War Savings' – 'Executive Committee Formed For Co, Galway' (6-7-1918).

'War's Grim Trial' (5-10-1918).

'We are Still United' (27-7-1918).

'Where was Galway' (18-3-1916).

'Why Mr, Wm, *Redmond, M.P, joined the Army*' (27-3-1915).

'Will the War end this Year' (3-3-1917).

'Women and the War' (2-10-1915).

'Women's Recruiting League' (15-1-1916).

'Women's War' (2-6-1917).

The Galway Express:

'15 Per Cent – Thriving Condition of Galway Woollen Mills' (2-3-1918).

'8, 000 Germans In Clifden! How County Boys are Misled' (20-5-1916).

'A Gallant Galway Soldier – Trilling Story of Irish Bravery' (18-8-1917).

'An Iron Cross – Galway Soldier's Trophy' (17-7-1915).

'Another Galway Portest' (27-4-1918).

'Answering the Call – Claddagh's Magnificent Response' (24-4-1915).

'Anti-British Dog Sentenced to Death' (25-11-1917).

'At the Ocean's Mercy – Fate of Two Torpedoed Vessels' (17-3-1917).

'Austria and Serbia' (1-8-1914).

'A Victor Over The Germans – Galwayman's Fine Record' (10-10-1914).

'Belgian Refugees' (17-10-1914).

'Books for our Soldiers' (23-4-1916).

'Blackberries for Soldiers' (11-9-1915).

'Blown to Pieces – Tragedy of a Stray Mine' (23-6-1917).

'Brillant Bayonet Charge' (14-11-1914).

'British Battleship Blown Up – H.M.S, Bulwark Destroyed – The Cause of the Explosion – Galway Man on Board' (28-11-1914, *5-12-1914).*

'British Success – Enemy Repulsed with Heavy Losses' (24-4-1915).

'Canada's Clothing for Galway' (9-1-1915).

'Capt, Persse and the Volunteers' (19-9-1914).

'Christmas and the Connaught Rangers' (28-11-1914).

'Christmas Gifts from the United States' (12-12-1914).

'Cigaretts for the Connaught Rangers – Comforts in the Trenches' (28-11-1914).

'Claregalway Anti-Cobscription Fund' (22-3-1919).

'Co, Galway Motor Ambulance at the Front' (13-3-1915).

'Comforts for Connaught Rangers – Prisoners in Germany – Novel Entertainment in Galway' (24-4-1915).

'Comforts for our Fighters' (3-6-1917).

'Comforts for our Fighters – Concert and Operatic Performance in Galway' (12-12-1914).

'Conceived By Satan – Matured In Hell.' 15-5-1915).

'Concert at Soldiers and Sailors' Club' (12-2-1916).

'Connaught Rangers Comfort Fund' (12-9-1914).

'Connaught Rangers Fund' (13-3-1915).

'Connaught Rangers' Heavy Losses at Ypres – A Perfect Hell on Earth' (5-6-1915).

'Connaught Rangers Prisoner's Strong Appeal' (6-3-1915).

'Connaughts at Gallipoli – Record of Success' (24-3-1917).

'Connaughts to the Rescue' (26-12-1914).

'Connaught Rangers to the Rescue' (20-2-1915).

'Connaught Rangers Heavy Losses At Ypres – A Perfect Hell on Earth' (5-6-1915).

'Cross-Country – Inter-Regimental Team Race' (18-3-1916).

'Departure of the Sherwood Foresters' (3-12-1916).

'Distinction for Nurse Daly' (6-1-1917).

'Dreadful Suicide at Renmore' (10-4-1915).

'England's Hypocrisy' (10-8-1918).

'Field Marshal French – Visits Galway' (21-7-1917).

'Foullest Crime on Record – Lusitania Torpedoed off Irish Coast – Notable Irish Victim' (15-5-1915).

'For Belgian Soldiers' Comforts' (27-2-1915).

'For the Front – Galway RIC Volunteers' (2-1-1915).

'From Anzac to Salonika' (15-1-1916).

'Further Help for the Connaughts' (15-7-1916).

'Galway Bay Mine Disaster Fund' (2-3-1918).

'Galway Children Entertained' (24-4-1915).

'Galway Harbour Board – Raid on English Towns' (26-12-1914).

'Galway Lady Lost in Lusitania' (15-5-1915).

'Galway Man Killed at the Dardanelles' (11-9-1915).

'Galway Naval Basis – Definite Arrangements – Repairing Dock Proposed' (23-1-1915).

'Galway Port Project and the Lusitania Tragedy' (15-5-1915).

'Galway Prisoners of War Fund – Appeal for a Co, Galway War Plate' (4-9-1915).

'Galway R.A.M.C, Man a Prisoner of War' (31-10-1914).

'Galway Ranger Writes to the "Express"' (5-12-1914).

'Galway Sailors Rescued in North Sea' (1-4-1916).

'Galway Soldiers' and Sailors' Club' (13-3-1915).

'Galway Sergeant's Story – Terrible Scenes in the Dardanelles' (29-5-1915).

'Galway Soldier at Mons – Instance of Savagery' (3-10-1914).

'Galway Soldier – Describes Fighting at Suvia Bay' (25-9-1915).

'Galway Soldier's Experience at Mons' (12-9-1914).

'Galway to the Fore – Remarkable Recruiting' (12-12-1914).

'Galway's Town Clerk – A Noble Example' (7-11-1914).

'Galway Volunteers – "Manifesto" by The Sinn Feiners' (24-10-1914).

'Galway Women's Recruiting League' (15-1-1916).

'Galway Women to the Rescue' (21-7-1917).

'Galway Woollen Industry' (20-2-1915).

'German Huns in Galway' (10-10-1914).

'German Submarines on the West Coast – Murder on the High Seas – Steamship Fulgent Sunk – Portion of Crew Landed at Galway' (8-5-1915).

'God Save Ireland and the Devil's Own' (12-6-1915).

'Government Pounce' (25-5-1918).

'Great Galway Carnival' (29-7-1916).

'Great Recruiting Meeting at Oughterard' (22-1-1916).

'Gwynn, Lynch and Sullivan in Galway' (3-8-1918).

'Help Our Wounded' (5-12-1914).

'Heavy Gun Firing Heard Near Galway' 7-11-1914).

'Hoping On – Hon, Colonel George Morris' (31-10-1914).

'How the Connaughts Saved the Situation' (19-12-1914).

'How they Fought at the Aisne – Galway Soldier's Interesting Letter – Simple Narrative of Heroism' (14-11-1914).

'In Aid of Wounded Soldiers at Renmore Hospital', Jan 1916).

'Ireland's Appeal to America' (3-7-1918).

'Ireland's Manpower – Remarkable Official Figures – 161, 000 Men Still Available' (18-11-1916).

'Irish At Loos – Galway Officer's Narrative' (13-5-1916).

'Irish Guards Visit' (24-4-1915).

'Irish Guards Visit – Galway's Enthusiastic Reception of the Band – Public Meetings and Speeches – Good Response to the Call – Sunday's Proceedings' (1-5-1915).

'Irish Nuns at Ypres' (9-1-1915).

'Irish Valour' (4-9-1915).

'King's Congratulations to Galway Woman – Five Sons at the Front' (31-10-1914).

'Lady Clancarty's Concert' (30-1-1915).

'Lady Clancarty's Concert – A Huge Success' (23-1-1915).

'Lieut-Col, The Hon, *George Morris*', '*A Brave And Brilliant Leader*', '*How He Met His Fate*' (5-12-1914).

'Lieutenant R, A, *Persse Killed*' (9-1-1915).

'Lieutenant Robert de Stacpoole' (3-10-1914).

'Lieut, Fisher Killed' (15-7-1916).

'Local Items of War' (15-8-1914).

'Local War Items: Lieut.–Col, The Hon, *George Morris'; Mr, Woods, D.I., for the Front'*
(17-10-1914); 29-8-1914); 17-10-1914); 6-2-1915); 19-12-1914); 28-11-1914);
12-12-1914); 26-12-1914); 6-3-1915); 13-2-1915); 9-1-1915); 16-1-1915); 30-
1-1915); 10-10-1914); 23-12-1915); 27-2-1915); 19-9-1914); 28-10-1916).

'Looking After Our Fighters – Reading Room for Soldiers and Sailors Opened in
Galway' (27-2-1915).

'Mesopotamia Day' (14-4-1917).

'Most Sanguinary Fight Yet' (17-4-1915).

'Motor Ambulance' (28-11-1914).

'Mrs, O'Sullivan and Recruiting' (15-1-1916).

'Nationalists and the Army – Meeting of Volunteers at Tuam – Mr, John Redmond's
Interesting Figures and Deducations – Home Rule and the War – Letter from
The Right Rev, *Dr Plunkett, Bishop of Tuam'* (12-12-1914).

'National Society for the Prevention of Cruelty to Children', April 1915).

'New Irish Regiment for South Africa' (23-1-1915).

'No German Toys' (5-12-1914).

'N.S.P, C.C, – *Children's Day in Galway'* (8-5-1915).

'Order for Galway Woollen Factory' (19-9-1914).

'Oughterard Soldier's Experience – Sharp Conflict with the Germans – A Narrow
Escape and a "Run For It", 5-12-1914).

'Our London Letter – Duration Of The War' (9-1-1915).

'Our Oldest Lieutenant: Past M.F.H., Galway' (17-10-1914).

'Over the Top – Galway Officer's Narrative' (2-6-1917).

'Presentation at Seamen's Home, Galway' (19-2-1916).

'Presents for Soldiers Friends' (21-11-1914).

'Princess Mary and *The Galway Express'* (8-5-1915).

'Ranger Officer a Prisoner – Interesting letter' (24-10-1914).

'Reading and Recreation Room in Galway for Sailors and Soldiers' (30-1-1915).

'Red Cross Day in Galway' (28-11-1914).

'Red Cross Flag Day in Galway' (5-12-1914).

'Renmore Fete – In Aid of Prisoners of War Fund – Successful Function' (11-9-
1915).

'Riot Sequel – The Carter Appeal Case – Fighting ib Galway Streets Described
– Soldiers' Stories of Assault with Wooden Guns – Decision of Magistrates
Altered' (30-1-1915).

'Sarsfield and other Heroes' (26-12-1914).

'Second Lieutenant Roderick De Sackpoole, R.F.A., *29-5-1915)*.

'Soldiers' and Sailors' Families Association' (5-9-1914).

'Soldiers' and Sailors' Reading Room' (27-2-1915).

'Soldiers' Wives – Public Houses and Wage Earners' (26-12-1914).

'Some Not Wanted In Galway' (15-5-1915).

'Spreading False Reports – Galway Postman Charged – Under Defence of the Realm Act – Alleged Sinking of British Ships – A Large Fine' (13-2-1915).

'Stephen Gwynn' (25-5-1918).

'Stories From The Front – Connaught Rangers' Breezy Letter' (17-10-1914).

'Submarine – Enemy's Craft off Galway Coast' (13-3-1915).

'Submarines – Off the West Coast – Pirate Craft's Second Visit – Mines Laid in the Bay' (3-4-1915).

'The Connaughts'-'How They Fought at the Aisne'-'Galway Soldier's Interesting Letter'-'Simple Narrative Of Heroism' (14-11-1914).

'The Connaught Rangers' (28-10-1916).

'The Connaught Rangers – (1793 – 1916) – The Recent Recognition of Irish Valour' (30-9-1916).

'The Connaught Rangers – An Appeal' (15-8-1914).

'The Connaught Rangers – Romantic Record of a Great Irish Regiment' (26-12-1914).

'The Firing Line – At Home' (17-10-1914).

'The Heroic Connaughts' (16-10-1915).

'The Kaiser Ruminating' (17-10-1914).

'The Late Captain Kinkead' (7-11-1914).

'The Late Capt, Kinkead, *R.A.M.C, – A Soldier's Tribute*' (7-11-1914).

'The Late Major Sarsfield' (17-10-1914).

'The Late Lieut, R.P, *D, Nolan*' (21-11-1914).

'The New Leader and the Old Policy' (23-3-1918).

'The N.S.P, C.C, *and the War – Remarkable Record in Army and Navy Rank*', 1915).

'The Position of the National Volunteers' (13-3-1915).

'The Push On The Somme' (10-3-1917).

'The Submarine "Blockade"' (10-4-1915).

'The Voice of Connaught – Great Recruiting Conference in Galway' (5-2-1916).

'The Women of Galway – A Deserved Tribute' (28-11-1914).

'Tobacco And Cigarettes For The Connaught Rangers' (5-9-1914).

'Tommy's Thanks', 'Cigarettes for the Connaught Rangers', *'Comforts in the Trenches'*

(28-11-1914

'To the Friends of the Rangers' (21-11-1914).

'Trench Warfare – Described by a Galway Soldier' (28-8-1915).

'Trilling Story of the Beach Fight' (28-8-1915).

'Under Shell Fire At Mons' – 'Trilling Experience of a Galway Soldier' (19-9-1914).

'Voluntary Enlistment – Appeal For More Recruits' (3-4-1915).

'War and Child Neglect' (29-5-1915).

'War – Battle In The Streets Of Galway – Extraordinary Scenes in the City – Sinn Feiners with Rifles and Bayonets – Run From Unarmed Crowd – Window Breaking after the Fight' (17-10-1914).

'War Fund', 'What Renmore Fete Achieved For The Connaughts', *Result Of The Competitions'* (18-9-1915).

'What General Sir Horace Smith-Dorrien Says' (12-12-1914).

'What the Soldier's Wife Will Get' (19-9-1914).

'When the Volunteers Come Home' (6-2-1915).

'Women Take a Hand – To Further Recruiting in Galway' (8-1-1916).

'Xmas Puddings For The Forces' (21-11-1914).

'Young Galway Lady's Exciting Adventures In Germany' (15-8-1914).

'Young Galway Soldier Receives the D.M.C.' (15-5-1915).

'Zeppelin Raid on London – Ninty Bombs Drooped' (5-6-1915).

The Irish Independent: 'A Battle In Mexico' (15-4-1916).

The Irish Times: 'Destruction of Ypres – The Very Ruins In Flames' (10-11-1914).

The Tuam Herald:

'A Brave Galway Family – A Loughrea Batch of Heroes' (28-8-1915).

'A Connaught Ranger On The German Savages' (21-11-1914).

'A Fiendish Crime – U-Boat Crew's Inhumanity To Galway Fishermen' (15-6-1918).

'An Ambulance For Galway' (17-7-1815).

'Books for Soldiers' (29-4-1916).

'Brevities' (22-4-1916).

'County Galway Red Cross Flag Week' (2-1-1915).

'Death of a Young Tuam Man at the Front' (5-6-1915).

'Defence of the Realm (Consolidation) Regulations', 1914, *16-10-1915)*.

'From Our Own Correspondent' (28-4-1917).

'Galway Notes' (27-3-1915); 17-2-1917).

'Galway to the Front Again – Why Not Galway Bay' (16-12-1916).

'Galway War Fund Association' (5-8-1916).

'Ireland and Conscription' (8-1-1916).

'Ireland and the Navy' (11-3-1916).

'Local War Items' (27-3-1915); 8-4-1916).

'Private Stephen O'Shaughnessy' (17-4-1915).

'Recruiting at Williamstown' (4-9-1915).

'Sir Edward Carson' (7-4-1917).

'The County of Galway Naval and Military War Fund' (4-9-1915).

'The Connaught Rangers' (29-5-1915).

'The Connaught Rangers – (1793 – 1916) – At Guillemont and Ginchy' (14-10-1916).

'The Connaught's Stand' (3-10-1914).

'The Irish Brigade – Recruiting Meeting In Tuam' (15-5-1915).

'The Role Of Honour – Second Lieutenant Gabriel P, Costello, *R.E.'* (28-8-1915).

'The Splendid Action of the Connaught Rangers At Ypres' (29-5-1915).

'Tuam Girl on the Ill-Fated Lusitania' (15-5-1915).

'War Notes' (30-6-1917).

Personal Letters:

P, J Summerly (2002); Richard Conneely, *9-12-2003); Michael Joseph Gardiner, 26-11-2003);*

Mary Jane Carter (2002); Michael Coughlan (2002); Leo Larkin (2002); Francis Kearney (2002);

Francis Keaney (2002); Seán Malone, 14-3-2003; John Lawless (2003); Vivienne O'Connor, *November* (2002);

Corporal G, Gill, *8-12-1918).*

Profiles:

James (Jim) Comber by Gerald Comber (2002).

John Joe Leonard, by Val Raftery, *27-11-2004).*

World Book Encyclopaedia:

'Dardanelles', 'Jutland, *Battle of'*, *'World War I'*.

INDEX

G

H

M

Q

R

S

T

U